Sunbelt | Frostbelt

JAMES A. JOHNSON METRO SERIES

JAMES A. JOHNSON
METRO SERIES

The Metropolitan Policy Program at the Brookings Institution is integrating research and practical experience into a policy agenda for cities and metropolitan areas. By bringing fresh analyses and policy ideas to the public debate, the program hopes to inform key decisionmakers and civic leaders in ways that will spur meaningful change in our nation's communities.

As part of this effort, the James A. Johnson Metro Series aims to introduce new perspectives and policy thinking on current issues and attempt to lay the foundation for longer-term policy reforms. The series examines traditional urban issues, such as neighborhood assets and central city competitiveness, as well as larger metropolitan concerns, such as regional growth, development, and employment patterns. The James A. Johnson Metro Series consists of concise studies and collections of essays designed to appeal to a broad audience. While these studies are formally reviewed, some will not be verified like other research publications. As with all publications, the judgments, conclusions, and recommendations presented in the studies are solely those of the authors and should not be attributed to the trustees, officers, or other staff members of the Institution.

Also available in this series:

Edgeless Cities: Exploring the Elusive Metropolis
Robert E. Lang

Evaluating Gun Policy: Effects on Crime and Violence
Jens Ludwig and Philip J. Cook, editors

Growth and Convergence in Metropolitan America
Janet Rothenberg Pack

Growth Management and Affordable Housing
Anthony Downs, editor

Laws of the Landscape:
How Policies Shape Cities in Europe and America
Pietro S. Nivola

Low-Income Homeownership: Examining the Unexamined Goal
Nicolas P. Retsinas and Eric S. Belsky, editors

Redefining Urban and Suburban America:
Evidence from Census 2000, Volume One
Bruce Katz and Robert E. Lang, editors

Redefining Urban and Suburban America:
Evidence from Census 2000, Volume Two
Alan Berube, Bruce Katz, and Robert E. Lang, editors

Reflections on Regionalism
Bruce Katz, editor

Savings for the Poor: The Hidden Benefits of Electronic Banking
Michael A. Stegman

Still Stuck in Traffic: Coping with Peak-Hour Traffic Congestion
Anthony Downs

Taking the High Road: A Metropolitan Agenda for Transportation Reform
Bruce Katz and Robert Puentes, editors

Sunbelt | Frostbelt

PUBLIC POLICIES AND MARKET FORCES
IN METROPOLITAN DEVELOPMENT

Janet Rothenberg Pack
Editor

Brookings Institution Press
Washington, D.C.

Library of Congress Cataloging-in-Publication data
Sunbelt/frostbelt : public policies and market forces in metropolitan development /
    Janet Rothenberg Pack, editor.
        p.   cm. — (James A. Johnson metro series)
    Summary: "The product of a multiyear project looking at how government policies
shape growth patterns in five metropolitan areas—Los Angeles, Phoenix, Pittsburgh,
Chicago, and Philadelphia—this book examines how these sunbelt and frostbelt
metro areas have tried to use policy reform to address their individual development
challenges"—Provided by publisher.
    Includes bibliographical references and index.
    ISBN-13: 978-0-8157-6810-4 (pbk. : alk. paper)
    ISBN-10: 0-8157-6810-9
    1. Metropolitan areas—United States. 2. Metropolitan areas—Government policy—
United States. 3. Regional planning—United States. 4. Cities and towns—
United States—Growth. I. Pack, Janet Rothenberg. II. Title. III. Series.
    HT334.U5S86 2005
    307.76'4'0973—dc22   2005001163

9 8 7 6 5 4 3 2 1
The paper used in this publication meets minimum requirements of the American
National Standard for Information Sciences—Permanence of Paper for Printed
Library Materials: ANSI Z39.48-1992.

Typeset in Sabon and Myriad

Composition by OSP
Arlington, Virginia

Printed by The Sheridan Press
Hanover, Pennsylvania

Contents

Foreword

How are America's major cities faring? And what of the regions surrounding them? Do federal, state, and local policies work in tandem with market forces or against reasonable development? Those are among the core questions that the Brookings Metropolitan Policy Program addresses all the time—and that this book goes a long way toward answering.

Sunbelt/Frostbelt profiles five metropolitan areas across the country. It is timely, relevant, and particularly valuable because it provides a practical view of how different regions of the country pursue dissimilar solutions to try and grapple with each unique challenge. In that regard, these cases clearly show that there is no one-size-fits-all picture or approach to metropolitan growth issues. Edited by Janet Rothenberg Pack, who has studied urban and regional development extensively, the portraits offered here comprise a careful, clear, well-organized and objective depiction of metropolitan growth and development patterns and how public policies facilitate that growth by continuing to underwrite the expansion of new suburbs and the decline of cities and older places.

The book results from a multiyear project led by Janet and a team of university scholars from the five regions. Its genesis was a project undertaken several years ago by what we call at Brookings our "Metro" program (which was then known as the Center on Urban and Metropolitan

Policy). That project was designed to examine whether and to what extent major national and local policies and expenditures are undermining older core economies. To the extent they are, the volume includes a set of recommendations that policymakers and stakeholders can use to pursue more balanced growth in their respective cities and regions.

Beyond the well-known programs that have fueled suburbanization (for example, those created by the Interstate Highway Act and Federal Housing Administration mortgage financing), specific public policies highlighted in this volume include the mortgage interest tax deduction that subsidizes the construction of large lot homes on the suburban fringe, regulations that make the redevelopment of some urban land almost prohibitively expensive, and infrastructure spending that facilitates outward expansion.

Because it illuminates this broad set of public policies that support metropolitan decentralization, this volume is an important contribution to the urban and metropolitan literature. It is intended to provide students, scholars, and practitioners a useful one-stop resource to review and compare recent trends, consequences, and policy approaches to metropolitan decentralization in places as diverse as Phoenix and Los Angeles in the sunbelt and Chicago, Philadelphia, and Pittsburgh in the rustbelt.

I join the Metro program's director, Bruce Katz, in thanking the Fannie Mae Foundation for general financial support to the Metro program, and the Ford Foundation, the George Gund Foundation, the Joyce Foundation, the John D. and Catherine T. MacArthur Foundation, and the Charles Stewart Mott Foundation for their support of the program's work on metropolitan growth and urban reinvestment trends. We also acknowledge with gratitude the generous support of local philanthropic groups who helped fund the work in the metropolitan areas profiled in this book.

Strobe Talbott
President

Washington, D.C.
January 2005

Acknowledgments

This volume began with a series of meetings involving urban research teams from several metropolitan areas, including the five represented in the volume. The meetings were organized by the Brookings Metropolitan Policy Program (then called the Center on Urban and Metropolitan Policy), directed by Bruce Katz. Amy Liu and Robert Puentes played major roles in structuring the early meetings. Stephan Rodiger, former senior research analyst, was an important assistant in this process. As a result of these meetings, at which the metropolitan research teams made presentations, the outline for the volume evolved.

Throughout this process, Robert Puentes provided helpful comments on individual chapters, particularly in the integration of two separate contributions to the Pittsburgh chapter. He was also the liaison for administrative details with each of the research groups.

At Brookings Institution Press, Janet Walker, managing editor, oversaw the organization of the many parts of the manuscript to produce the book. Janet Mowery was our capable, cooperative, and patient copy editor. Larry Converse, production manager, directed the typesetting and printing, and Susan Woollen coordinated the cover design.

The volume owes most to the research teams, to the responsiveness of the team leaders to my numerous rounds of comments and questions, and to their ultimate willingness to keep at it.

CHAPTER 1

Metropolitan Development: Patterns, Problems, Causes, Policy Proposals

Janet Rothenberg Pack

The literature on urban development of the past decade (since about the mid-1990s) has been characterized by the introduction of two concepts: "the New Metropolitanism" and "the New Urbanism." A recent essay refers to the new metropolitanism as a "paradigm shift."[1] Although the term takes on many different meanings, its principal components are "urban sprawl" as the problem and "smart growth" as the solution. Moreover, there are many variations on the definitions of the two components in the scholarly literature, in the increasing outpouring of government studies, in general-interest articles on the subject, and, as will be seen, in the chapters in this volume. Despite the differences, there is, nonetheless, broad agreement on the major themes, however defined— sprawl and smart growth.

The New Urbanism is largely about urban design. The organization Congress for the New Urbanism, founded by a group of architects and town planners (http://user.gru.net/domz/charter.htm), emphasizes the design features of new communities. In their introduction to a forum on the New Urbanism, Sohmer and Lang refer to it as "architecture's answer to our rediscovered urban heritage. New Urbanism models its developments on an eclectic combination of traditional urban neighborhoods. . . . Neotraditional building styles and mixed-use, mixed-income, and pedestrian-oriented development are New Urbanism's defining

1. Katz (2002).

characteristics."[2] The tie between the two—New Metropolitanism and New Urbanism—may be seen in a description by Burchell and his coauthors of smart growth as "an effort, through the use of public and private subsidies, to create a supportive environment for refocusing a share of regional growth within central cities and inner suburbs. At the same time, a share of growth is taken away from the rural and undeveloped portions of the metropolitan area."[3]

The rapidity with which these issues have reached the policy agenda is attested to by the numerous ballot issues related to its themes. The ubiquity of the discussion is also evident in the rapidly growing number of professional books and articles on the subject by economists, urban planners, sociologists, and health professionals (to list only a few), and the numerous popular articles—ranging from the *National Geographic* to the *New York Times Magazine*.[4] Not all "urbanists" subscribe to either of the new views of urban development, but no discussion of urban policy can ignore them.[5]

Case Studies of Urban Development

The studies in this volume have been designed to improve our understanding of the patterns of metropolitan development over the past few decades. Studying several metropolitan areas intensively—using case studies rather than a broad cross-sectional analysis—permits a deeper understanding of the common factors affecting development, in historical and specific institutional and political contexts. Some of the common factors are federal tax laws that apply to housing and funding for transportation infrastructure. Other important influences may be unique to particular places: historical factors, local culture, state policies, topography. The limitation of case studies, given the unique characteristics of each area, is the difficulty of generalization.

With these advantages and limitations in mind, the study was designed to include both older urban areas, developed before the automobile age, during the years when manufacturing dominated economic activity (including Philadelphia, Pittsburgh, and Chicago) and newer, rapidly growing, automobile-age metropolitan areas (Phoenix and Los

2. Sohmer and Lang (2000, p. 751).

3. Burchell, Lisotkin, and Galley, p. 823.

4. See Myers and Puentes (2001); Brueckner (2001); *National Geographic*, January 7, 2001; and Michael Janofsky, "Phoenix Counts Its Many Challenges," *New York Times Magazine*, April 11, 2001.

5. See papers by Gordon and Richardson (2000, 1998a, and 1998b) for critiques.

Angeles). The older areas are generally assumed to face formidable challenges; the more recently developed metropolitan areas are viewed as having (limitless) opportunities.

What is surprising in these studies are the specific ways in which the older and more recently developed metropolitan areas, both slow and rapidly growing areas, appear to identify similar problems and propose similar remedies, as well as the ways in which they differ on these issues.[6]

History of the Project

The project that led to this book was begun in the late 1990s and the case studies were completed before the 2000 Census data were available, although all of them incorporated local and other data sources extending well into the 1990s. It is clear from the 2000 Census data and numerous other sources that the patterns identified earlier, the issues raised, and the policy discussion are no less pertinent now than they were then; if anything, the urban policy agenda appears to have become even more focused on these issues.

Various participants in the project were concerned with the role played in urban development patterns—spatial patterns—by public policies, in particular highway versus transit investments, the federal mortgage interest deduction, and intergovernmental aid. The discussion considered the possible distorting effects of those policies and explored proposals for changes in existing policies and new policies at the federal, state, and local levels that might have a more positive influence on development patterns.

The result of numerous discussions and preliminary presentations by the participants was a template for the studies. The broad outline guiding each case study included the following four topics. The full template is in the appendix at the end of this chapter.

—Metropolitan growth and development patterns: activity, land use, and infrastructure

—Government spending and regulatory activity

—Problems and positive implications of development and policy

—Policy recommendations

The case studies vary in the extent to which they incorporate or emphasize all of the elements of the template, and some include other issues as well. This is to be expected from five such diverse metropolitan

6. Different areas, however, may define issues differently.

Table 1-1. Population Growth, 1960–2000

Percent

Metropolitan area	Metropolitan population growth		Central city population growth		Suburban population growth	
	1960–90	1990–2000	1960–90	1990–2000	1960–90	1990–2000
Chicago	9.8	7.8	−21.6	4.5	66.2	10.8
Philadelphia	11.8	3.7	−20.8	−4.3	39.8	7.6
Pittsburgh	−13.1	−2.6	−38.8	−8.5	−4.3	−1.27
Los Angeles	46.8		40.6	5.9	51.1	8.4
Los Angeles–Long Beach		7.4				
Oxnard–Ventura		12.6				
Riverside–San Bernardino		25.7				
Phoenix	219.8	44.8	123.9	33.6	407.6	54.5

Source: Computations by the author from U.S. Censuses of Population, 1960, 1980, 1990, and 2000.

areas and is one of the major virtues of case studies: the ability to see how the characteristics cited earlier, historical circumstances, state and local interactions, and differing natural environments affect what is viewed as a problem and the policy agenda.

The Continuity and Correspondence of Socioeconomic Patterns

Population change and its specific demographic characteristics will have major impacts on the course of metropolitan development. Whether population is gained as a result of natural growth, immigration, migration for economic benefit, or retirement will influence the nature of change and the links between population growth and economic development. Not only are different parts of the country subject to different underlying sources of population growth and decline, they may experience these discontinuously, with periods of rapid or slow growth or decline.

Population Change

Population growth appears to be a major determinant of urban development patterns. The differences among these metropolitan areas and the continuity over time may be seen in table 1-1, where the population growth between 1960 and 1990 is compared with that in the most recent decade for which full census data are available, the 1990s.

As expected, population in the older metropolitan areas has grown very slowly or, in the case of Pittsburgh, declined. However, with the exception of Pittsburgh their suburbs have grown but their central cities have all lost substantial parts of their population. In contrast, in the Los Angeles and Phoenix metropolitan areas, the rates of metropolitan population growth are far greater, and *both* the cities and their suburbs have grown substantially. The very large percentage growth for Phoenix reflects its very small 1960 population base. The continuity of these patterns is evident in the data for the 1990s. Pittsburgh was still the only declining metropolitan area, Phoenix was still growing most rapidly, and the other metropolitan areas continued to increase in population.

These differences in the growth of the metropolitan area populations mirror the changes experienced by their respective states and by the larger regions of which they are a part. Between 1990 and 2000 the population of the United States increased by 13.2 percent. In twelve states—eight in the West and four in the South—the population increased by more than 20 percent. Of the nineteen states whose populations increased by less than 9 percent, eight were in the Northeast, an additional eight were in the Midwest; only two were in the South, and one was in the West. The growth rates in the five metropolitan areas in this study are consistent with their state rankings. The most rapidly growing of the five metropolitan areas, Phoenix, is in the second fastest growing state, Arizona, with a population increase over the decade of 40 percent.[7] California ranks eighteenth among the states, with population growth of nearly 14 percent. Illinois and Pennsylvania, with the three older metropolitan areas, ranked thirty-fourth (growth in population 8.6 percent) and forty-eighth (growth of 3.4 percent), respectively.

Employment Growth and Economic Dynamism

The correspondence or correlation of economic changes with these population changes may be seen in the comparison of the population growth rates with job growth figures. The component of the Forbes/Milken index "Best Places to Do Business and Advance a Career," which ranks 294 metropolitan areas, includes a component that ranks relative job growth in 2000 indexed to 1995 (see table 1-2).

---

7. A major factor in the growth of Arizona and Phoenix is immigration. The immigrants have been attracted by the growth in the state and they have "helped sustain the state's buoyant economy." "From 1990 to 2000, the Hispanic population [of Maricopa County—Phoenix] swelled by 108 percent, a rate fueled by a rising flow of illegal immigration as well as higher-than-average birth rates and migration from other states. . . . Of the four states bordering Mexico, Arizona had the greatest [percentage increase in Hispanic population], 76.7 percent, compared with an increase of 33.4 percent of California" (Janofsky, "Phoenix Counts Its Many Challenges").

Table 1-2. Job Growth

Metropolitan area	Relative job growth, 2000[a]
Los Angeles	184
Orange County	31
Ventura County	72
Riverside–San Bernardino	7
Phoenix–Mesa	4
Chicago	207
Philadelphia	192
Pittsburgh	231

Source: Forbes/Milken Institute, "Best Places to Do Business and Advance a Career" (rankings for 2002 and 2001) (www.forbes.com/bestplaces).

a. Indexed to 1995, rank among 294 metro areas.

As for population, so too for employment growth. Phoenix is the high-growth standout, with the outer counties of the Los Angeles metropolitan area not far behind, and Pittsburgh is generally the low-growth pole (see table 1-3).

The full Forbes/Milken Institute measure of urban vitality for 2002 and 2001 again compares these five metropolitan areas with one another and with the 294 metropolitan areas included in the index. This ranking takes into account wage and salary growth, job growth, and high-tech output growth and once again indicates the relationship of the various measures of urban vitality—population and employment growth and economic development potential.

The Los Angeles and Phoenix metropolitan areas, where population growth has been rapid, are found at the top of the rankings. In Los Angeles, the outer counties account for the high rating, consistent with the population growth figures in table 1-1. Not surprisingly, the older metropolitan areas are further down in the rankings, although they are mid-ranked locations, far from the bottom of the nearly 300 places included.

There is yet another important indicator of major determinants of urban development patterns and of the relationship of the case study metropolitan areas to one another and to the larger universe, the Milken Institute's "State Science and Technology Index." In this index, five technology-related factors are included for states: Research & Development Inputs, Risk Capital and Entrepreneurial Infrastructure, Human Capital Investment, Technology and Science Workforce, and Technology Concentration and Dynamism.[8] In this index, all four of the states in which

8. DeVol and others (2002, Executive Summary, p. 1).

Table 1-3. Forbes/Milken Best Places to Do Business and Advance a Career, 2001 and 2002

Metropolitan area	Forbes/Milken rank, 2002	Forbes/Milken rank, 2001
Los Angeles–L.A. County	100	118
Ventura County	4	18
Orange County	10	12
Riverside County	11	27
Phoenix	17	9
Philadelphia	116	122
Pittsburgh	132	113
Chicago	141	100

Source: www.forbes.com/bestplaces.

the case study metropolitan areas are located rank in the top twenty of the fifty states on a weighted average of these factors: California ranks third, Pennsylvania sixteenth, Arizona eighteenth, and Illinois nineteenth.

Summarizing the Case Studies

Against this background of enormous differences in population and employment growth, the analyses and conclusions of the case studies are remarkably similar.

The Problems

—extensive decentralization, often referred to as urban sprawl, which is associated with increased road congestion (paradoxically associated with excessive suburban road construction), pollution; loss of open space; lack of space for new development;

—spatial inequality—that is, income and racial segregation;

—wide fiscal differences among jurisdictions within the metropolitan area—between central city and suburbs and among older (inner) and newer (outer) suburbs (the exception here appears to be Phoenix);

—a spatial mismatch between the location of growing employment opportunities and the residences of the urban poor.

In several of the studies, these problems are attributed to, or believed to be exacerbated by, public policies that favor suburban locations over central cities. Among the causal public policies are:

—the federal mortgage interest deductions for homeownership;

—federal and state transportation subsidies that favor highway construction over mass transit maintenance and construction;

—federal and state subsidies for new water and sewer systems;

—state policies that cede control over land use to local governments, resulting in large lot zoning and fiscal zoning.

The Policy Recommendations

An important impetus for these studies was the growing evidence that urban development patterns were influenced in important ways—many of them negatively—by public policies. The studies identify the ways in which policies have had distorting effects and recommend numerous policies for remedy; policies that would remove the distortions, as well as others that would be more likely to bring about desired changed n the patterns of urban development. These include:

—correcting the "distorting" public policies;

—greater regional policy coordination;[9]

—coordinated land-use policy and a variety of measures to control growth;

—regional sharing of the fiscal base; greater fiscal equalization by state governments.

Comparisons

Although there is remarkable similarity among the case studies' identification of problems and policies, often the definitions of problems and specific policies are somewhat different. In most cases the differences may be attributed to local circumstances. For example, the case studies use somewhat different definitions of urban decentralization or sprawl, and these differences affect their analysis of the problem, its causes, and potential policy interventions.

The Philadelphia analysis emphasizes the influence of public policies on excessive land use: "Not only do intergovernmental aid flows not function to level the fiscal playing field between fiscal capacities and public service needs—but public capital spending and federal tax policy related to owner-occupied housing also tend to favor the better-off suburban areas. Consequently, the location decisions of some firms and

---

9. Current data are available for four of the five case study metropolitan areas: Chicago leads the four with 567 local governments, followed by Philadelphia with 442, Pittsburgh with 418, and Phoenix with only 34. However, the decentralization takes on a different meaning when local governments are related to population—that is, local governments per 100,000 residents. For the latter, Pittsburgh stands out with 17.7, with Philadelphia and Chicago well behind with only 7.4 and 6.6, respectively, and Phoenix even less decentralized with only 1.2 local governments per 100,000 residents. See Puentes and Orfield (2002, p. 13).

middle-class (and above) households are distorted, leading to unbalanced and inefficiently allocated growth and development throughout the region."

The authors of the Chicago study refer often to Chicago as a sprawled region, and the definition of sprawl appears to be an increase in developed land area that exceeds the growth of population: "Between 1970 and 1990, the population of the metropolitan area increased by only 4 percent, but the urbanized or developed land area increased by more than 47 percent. In other words, in only a twenty-year period, roughly the same number of people came to be spread out over almost half again as much land."

In Los Angeles and Phoenix, where metropolitan areas have been experiencing rapid population growth and an expanding economy, we find yet another definition of sprawl. In the Los Angeles study, the authors consider sprawl a major problem despite the fact that population growth exceeded the growth in developed land (contrast Chicago): "Between 1982 and 1992, regional population grew by almost 25 percent, while urbanized land increased only about 20 percent. . . . [Thus] despite relatively high densities, the sheer size of the region and its rapid population growth meant that more than 400,000 acres of land were urbanized between 1982 and 1997, leading to a shortage of developable land in the region. Significant portions of undeveloped land are either too steep or ecologically sensitive, or are farmlands, state and national forests, or lands protected by conservation efforts through the Endangered Species Act." Here the problem appears to be rapid development of land due to growth, resulting in a shortage of developable land, not low density or population growth outstripping growth in undeveloped land, or lack of open space.

The situation in Phoenix with respect to sprawl is similar to that in Los Angeles. Population is growing and density is increasing, but population growth is so great that even at increased densities: "Between 1993 and 1998, the urban edge advanced nearly one-half mile per year. In the southeast, the fringe pushed out an average of three-fourths of a mile each year. . . . Calculations from aerial photographs show that between 1975 and 1995 some 40 percent of all agricultural land and 32 percent of all undeveloped desert land was lost to urbanization." Thus, here too the concern stems from growth and the additional development of formerly undeveloped land, albeit at high densities, and this is defined as sprawl.

Pittsburgh provides yet another contrast: "Policy choices regarding new development in the Pittsburgh region are not rooted in the context of growth-induced sprawl creating a multi-centered dispersed metro region, but rather sprawl in the context of minimal or negative growth pressure. Growth in Pittsburgh after World War II did not transform the prewar pattern of development until the 1990s. Instead, growth was accommodated within an earlier decentralized pinwheel pattern, one that was established to accommodate the economic and social needs of heavy manufacturing between 1880 and 1920." As will be clear in the Pittsburgh chapter, the implicit definition of sprawl there is recent growth outside of traditional areas.

In sum, our case studies offer four different definitions of sprawl: (1) inequitable and inefficient policy-distorted location by households and firms, favoring suburbs over central city (Philadelphia); (2) greater percentage increases in developed land than in population (Chicago); (3) development outside of traditional areas (Pittsburgh): and (4) large increases in developed land to accommodate rapidly growing population (Los Angeles and Phoenix).

There are also important differences in the extent of the problems and emphasis on particular policies in the five case studies. There is no bright line between these distinctions. Although they are useful ways of characterizing the emphases in the studies, the distinctions are not black and white; there is overlap but there are substantial gray areas. Thus this summary is an attempt to highlight the relative emphases. The differences can be characterized as follows:

—Saving/revitalizing central cities: This appears to be the major reason for concern with sprawl or decentralization in Philadelphia and Chicago. Given the relatively low rates of metropolitan population growth, growth per se cannot be an important cause of sprawl. The Chicago study emphasizes the much larger percentage increase in developed land than in population. This may be due to the increased demand for land per household, as incomes increase, or per firm, as technology changes and more land is needed for parking in suburban shopping and commercial centers, which have largely replaced or absorbed the growth that might have been expected to occur in the walking downtown shopping and commercial areas of central cities and older suburbs. Although Pittsburgh too has been concerned with preserving the core of the region, its major preoccupation is with overall metropolitan decline.

—Accommodating future growth and protecting open space: These appear to be the major concerns in Los Angeles and Phoenix, not surprisingly, given their past and anticipated growth in population and economic activity.

Table 1-4. Poverty Rates in Cities, Suburbs, and Metropolitan Areas, 1990 and 2000

Metro area	1990			2000		
	City	Suburbs	Metro area	City	Suburbs	Metro area
Chicago	21.6	5.1	11.3	19.6	5.5	11.7
Philadelphia	20.3	5.7	10.4	22.9	6.1	11.2
Pittsburgh	21.4	10.5	12.1	20.3	9.3	11.1
Los Angeles	18.9	12.6	15.1	22.1	15.2	17.9
Phoenix	14.2	11.9	12.9	15.8	8.7	11.7

Source: Computations by the author from U.S. Censuses of Population, 1990 and 2000.

— More equitable development: Not only are these studies and much of the literature on urban development concerned with achieving more efficient development, an equal concern is more equitable development, given the substantial income disparities between central cities and suburbs (see table 1-4).[10]

There are several notable contrasts to be seen in these data, both across metropolitan areas and over the decade of the 1990s. Phoenix had a relatively minor difference in the spatial incidence of poverty in 1990; however, it was the only one of the five metropolitan areas in which the difference in poverty rates between city and suburbs widened substantially over the decade. At least in this dimension, in the 1990s the fear of the authors of the Phoenix case study that Phoenix might begin to experience problems similar to older metro areas was being realized.[11] There is no simple discernible pattern in comparisons of the metropolitan areas over time. Some metropolitan areas had an increase in poverty rates; others did not, and the difference is not between older and newer metropolitan areas. In Pittsburgh and Phoenix the overall poverty rate declined somewhat, but in the other metropolitan areas it increased. In Chicago and Pittsburgh the city poverty rate fell, but in the others it rose. Poverty rates also rose in the suburbs of Chicago and Philadelphia (slightly) and Los Angeles, but fell in Pittsburgh and Phoenix. The most straightforward conclusion is that there is a persistent and substantial difference between city and suburban poverty rates:

—The concentration of the poor in central cities, the problems of the

10. These figures do not take into account the substantial differences among older and newer suburbs, which would make interjurisdictional income and tax-base disparities even more substantial.

11. The city of Phoenix is much more like a metropolitan area. As a result of extensive annexation, much of the city consists of what in most other areas would be suburbs.

poor, and the further problems engendered by their concentration are major concerns in Philadelphia and Chicago.

—But the Los Angeles study has the most detailed set of policy recommendations for dealing with the problems of the poor. The concern in Los Angeles appears to have less to do with the relationship between the poor and urban development patterns than with an intrinsic interest in reducing poverty and relieving the problems of a poor population.

—In Phoenix there are fewer major economic differences between city and suburbs, although there are differences in the socioeconomic characteristics of large swaths of neighborhoods.

—In Pittsburgh socioeconomic disparities are seen as reflecting a need to strengthen the links between places of employment and residence.

Most major local public services are financed by local governments. Achieving greater tax base equalization—more precisely, greater parity between public revenues and public needs—is a major issue since it is widely held that that many or most local public expenditures, including education, public safety, and sanitation, should not be a function of income. However, many studies, including those here, find that federal and state aid do not offset the differences between the tax base and necessary expenditures among jurisdictions.

These contrasts illustrate the ways in which problems are viewed. On the policy side, there are also some major differences in emphasis. These differences have less to do with the contrasting identification of problems than with basic approaches to policy interventions.

—In Philadelphia, the principal approach to policy is to correct the inefficiencies of existing policies that distort location decisions.

—In Los Angeles, policy proposals seek to prevent inefficient location decisions but also enumerate a broad range of additional policies that are cited as responsible for the problems.

—Chicago's policy agenda contains elements of both the narrower Philadelphia approach and the broad Los Angeles agenda.

—Phoenix is more tentative about policy proposals since it is trying to anticipate and therefore avoid problems that do not yet demand solution—although it is concerned about the loss of open space to development in recent years.

—In Pittsburgh the policy discussion is focused on how to make the entire metropolitan area more attractive for new development, with a major emphasis on regional coordination. Here too, the aim is to promote development where it already exists, both in and outside of the city.

The Metro Case Studies: Problems, Causes, and Policy

With these contrasts in mind, the following is a broad summary of the studies in which the discussion of problems, causes, and policy proposals are woven together to facilitate comparisons among them.

Philadelphia

In Philadelphia, the major concern appears to be the economic inefficiency associated with excessive decentralization of the metropolitan area, in particular the negative implications for the central city. The authors attribute this excessive decentralization to location-distorting federal public policies—in particular, federal policies that subsidize suburban locations, a major example being the mortgage tax deduction on federal income taxes. They find that the benefits of the mortgage tax deduction go largely to the suburban communities: the benefits to the entire Philadelphia Primary Metropolitan Statistical Area (PMSA) were $2.7 billion in 1989, with 84 percent, about $2.3 billion, going to suburban homeowners.

The problems associated with this excessive decentralization include substantial differences between economic and social conditions in the city of Philadelphia and its suburbs. The concentration of poverty in the city results in lower fiscal capacity and higher tax burdens borne by city residents and firms. This makes the city less attractive and the suburbs a more attractive location for both residents and firms. The relocation of firms and households reinforces the initial impetus for movement, causing additional firms and residents to leave the city and still greater concentrations of poverty in the city, which in turn provides additional incentive for the exodus of city residents and firms.

Moreover, intergovernmental aid flows do not level the fiscal playing field across localities; to level the disparities between fiscal capacities and public service needs would further distort the location decisions of some firms and households, "leading to unbalanced and inefficiently allocated growth and development throughout the region." Among these unequal flows is assistance for capital spending that can and does affect local economic activity. The authors "believe that the playing field is tilted in favor of the suburbs in the Philadelphia metropolitan area, with population and employment growth higher in suburban areas because of spatially biased roadway investments in particular."

Chicago

The Chicago case study too emphasizes the substantial spatial decentralization of the metropolitan area and the problems associated with the metropolitan area's fragmentation into many separate jurisdictions. As in Philadelphia, the many jurisdictions in the Chicago metropolitan area have disparate tax bases. Moreover, between 1980 and 1993 the inequalities in local governments' fiscal capacities widened substantially. As in Philadelphia, in Chicago too the decline of the central city and expansion of the suburbs is associated with large socioeconomic disparities between the two: a concentration of racial minority groups, lower incomes, and greater poverty rates characterize the city. Unemployment rates of Chicago residents are substantially higher than in the suburbs. The Chicago study also emphasizes the loss of open space as a result of development in the suburbs and on the periphery of the metropolitan area.

Persky, Kurban, and Lester estimate the per capita distribution of federal funds in the Chicago metropolitan area. They find that the income tax subsidy for housing (the mortgage interest deduction) is the largest of the spatially related categories of federal expenditures by far.[12] Consistent with the Philadelphia findings, they find that this tax subsidy overwhelmingly favors suburbs over the central city, with the city of Chicago receiving about $125 per capita and the suburbs more than $500 per capita in both periods, 1989–92 and 1993–96.[13] Thus the conclusion is that the subsidy has both a purely spatial impact and an unequal equity impact, with the subsidy going to more higher-income suburban residents than to lower-income, non-homeowning, non-deduction-itemizing poorer households concentrated in the central city.

In Chicago, it is noted that "the city . . . would not have developed into the metropolis that it is today had it not been for large amounts of federal, state, and private money spent building up the city's infrastructure (in addition to the significant funds invested by the city itself). . . .

12. Persky, Kurban, and Lester (2000). The other spatially related categories of federal aid are funding for highways and related items, public transit, other infrastructure, environment, and disaster and crime. They also calculate the spatial distribution of other federal expenditures, the largest of which are nonspatial redistribution programs and retirement benefits; the latter are found to flow disproportionately to cities and older suburbs.

13. Here too the authors recognize the importance of assumptions about the elasticity of supply of land; they too assume that in the suburbs land is abundant and that the subsidies reduce the real costs of land, whereas in the city, where land is largely developed, subsidies will be capitalized in housing prices and benefits will be modest at best.

[In the postwar period] the expressway system in particular laid the grid for suburban expansion."

Given the emphasis on problems associated with regional government decentralization, it is not surprising that greater regional coordination in order to bring about changes in the trajectory of urban development is a major priority. The Chicago authors believe that Illinois can learn from the state of Maryland, where the state provides incentives for municipalities to "grow smart" but does not restrict land use by local governments. As long as they do not use state funds, they may choose where in the county to spend their development money. Although Illinois counties do not have as much control over land-use issues as those in Maryland, Illinois could institute a program "that would require municipalities and counties to make development plans, and then channeled state infrastructure funding only to designated growth areas seems likely to reduce land consumption."

Los Angeles

The Los Angeles metropolitan area experienced rapid population growth, with most of the fastest-growing cities on the region's fringe. Despite the rapid expansion of the economy and a concentration of this expansion in the suburbs, Los Angeles County, unlike the older metropolitan areas, still contains the majority of the region's jobs. Nonetheless, the Los Angeles–Long Beach Primary Metropolitan Statistical Area had one of the nation's most decentralized employment patterns by the late 1990s. This seeming contradiction is related to the jurisdictional boundaries, namely the fact that Los Angeles County is large. Although only 7 percent of all jobs in the metro area are within a three-mile radius of the downtown, the city (Los Angeles County) still contains a majority of the jobs in the metropolitan area.

Like the older metropolitan areas, Chicago and Philadelphia, the Los Angeles area is also characterized by high concentrations of poverty, substantial spatial mismatch between the location of employment and the location of job seekers, particularly for low-income central city residents, and growing income inequality. A major associated result is a severe housing affordability problem.

Contrary to its image as a sprawling metropolis, population densities are high. This is due to the fact that much of the land is physically undevelopable, because of the presence of desert and mountains, so the populated parts of the outlying counties are quite dense. Again, contrary to popular impression, and in contrast to both the older Philadelphia and

Chicago metropolitan areas, in southern California the percentage growth in population exceeded that in urbanized land areas. Despite the high density and the fact that much open space is not suitable for development, rapid population growth in the region resulted in more than 400,000 acres of land becoming urbanized between 1982 and 1997. Thus the need to accommodate growth, not the decline of the central city, appears to be the major reason for the concern about urban decentralization in Los Angeles.

The investment in highways also looms large in the explanation of urban decentralization. However, some large investments in transit have not succeeded in slowing automobile use: Between 1982 and 1999 VMT (vehicle miles traveled) increased by more than twice the increase in population; hours of delay increased substantially. Both of these were accompanied by associated negative externalities—increased air pollution and wasted fuel. According to the authors, "At the same time, total public transit trips declined . . . during the 1990s. And the *share* of transit users fell . . . despite heavy investment in transit in L.A. County. By century's end, 93 percent of all regional commuters were still using cars." The study attributes the continued dominance of the car in L.A. to the city's radial design focused on the downtown core; a design that "[cannot] adequately serve a polycentric metropolis burdened by severe jobs/housing imbalances; many bus systems are overcrowded, outdated, and perceived as unsafe; and segregation of land uses in relatively low-density suburbs makes driving unavoidable." The downtown-oriented design might have been intended to strengthen the downtown core by making location along the transit way more attractive. A polycentric design might have induced more people to ride public transit but might also have facilitated development outside the core—further suburbanization and sprawl—by improving travel from one suburb to another. It may be difficult to achieve two goals—reducing automobile use and stemming suburban sprawl—with one policy instrument, public transit.

With respect to stemming suburban sprawl the authors note that in Los Angeles "differences between southern California and other metro areas . . . mean that current nationwide calls for 'smart growth' policies may need some alteration to effectively moderate inequities, slow sprawl, and promote more livable communities in the southern California region." They call for a new framework and specific policy approaches, including equitable housing and transportation goals that will accommodate the region's future geographic scale: "The region must begin tracking land supply, setting large-scale goals, integrating land-use and transportation planning, and linking natural resources and protection efforts." Southern California might also emulate Maryland's policy of "earmarking state funds to encourage smart-growth planning and development, to provide incentives for urban land recycling and infill development, and to create high-density, transportation-oriented developments. . . . [And] organizations representing low- and moderate-income people . . . must be included in the planning process."

Phoenix

Development in Phoenix is more like that in Los Angeles than in the older metropolitan areas—in both expected and unexpected dimensions. Contrary to general perception, but like Los Angeles, density is increasing. Also like Los Angeles, but unlike central cities in the older metropolitan areas, employment remains concentrated in the metropolitan Phoenix core, and both population and employment rose in the heart of the metropolitan area in the 1990s, although the rate of expansion was slower than in other parts of the region. Despite the increasing density and relative concentration in the core, Phoenix, like the other metropolitan areas, is increasingly concerned about the decentralization of the metropolitan area. But as in Los Angeles, the increased use of land is attributable to a growing population and economy.[14]

A major difference, however, between the Phoenix metropolitan area and the others is the absence of glaring disparities in housing values, jobs, and retail activity between the city of Phoenix and the next largest cities in the metropolitan area. However, like other regions, there are other regional disparities—racial, economic, and neighborhood. The areas north and northeast of downtown Phoenix, including Scottsdale, are affluent. In contrast, poor whites and low-income minorities are concentrated in the central and southern portions of the city.

The Phoenix metropolitan area is also far less fragmented than the other metropolitan areas: there are only twenty-four cities and towns in the Phoenix region. Eighty-two percent of the region's population lives in either the city of Phoenix or one of its five large suburbs. In contrast, each of the other metropolitan regions includes several hundred separate jurisdictions. Thus fiscal disparities are far less of a problem, and less

---

14. Although rapid growth means much of the population is new to the area, a recent survey indicated that 80 percent of residents were "concerned" or "very concerned" about the region's growth, with nearly half of the respondents indicating that they would leave Phoenix tomorrow if they could.

likely to be a motivating force for firms and households to leave the central city.

The picture with respect to highway investment has been quite different from that in the other metropolitan areas. In Phoenix, it is argued, too little investment in highways has caused problems without deterring decentralization: "In early 2000 it completed a freeway system that was begun in 1957 but expanded little between 1970 and 1985, and over the next twelve years limited-access lane miles tripled from 290 to 870. [Nonetheless] metropolitan Phoenix makes do with a less-extensive limited-access road network than most regions its size. . . . As a result, while traffic is increasing, its negative impacts have not yet become unmanageable. . . . [and there is] less congestion in the city of Phoenix than in comparable cities. Daily vehicle miles traveled per capita increased in the early 1990s, but have remained on par with the rate of population growth."

As elsewhere, another concern is that a small public transit system limits the access of lower-income citizens to employment and other activities. Voters in Mesa, Tempe, and Phoenix, however, have recently approved tax assessments to pay for more bus service and the start of a light-rail project in the central employment areas.

Pittsburgh

Despite being bracketed with Philadelphia and Chicago as one of the older, pre-auto-age, manufacturing-based metropolitan areas, Pittsburgh's development has been different. The metropolitan area as a whole is losing population and economic activity rather than simply experiencing slow growth. Between 1970 and 1996 the Pittsburgh metropolitan area—a region of concentrated heavy industry—lost nearly 57 percent of its manufacturing jobs. In addition, Pittsburgh had one of the slowest-growing service sectors. These two factors resulted in employment growth of less than 16 percent between 1970 and 1996. This may be compared with the U.S. national average growth in employment of 64 percent.

After failing to revive the downtown, the Allegheny County government turned its attention to the undeveloped suburban corridor. Airport capacity was expanded and more than 16 million square feet of new office space was added in the 1980s in the downtown and along the airport corridor. Between 1990 and 1996, however, new office space construction was only about one-fourth the rate in the previous decade, and vacancy rates rose as corporate downsizing continued. Also unsuccessful were the efforts to establish a suburban job corridor near the airport. As table 1-1 shows, the Pittsburgh region is one of only a handful of metropolitan areas that is experiencing overall population loss, and its rate of job growth is only about one-third of the national average. Thus the challenges facing the Pittsburgh metropolitan area are population loss, sluggish job growth, and fragile tax bases.

In Pittsburgh, local transportation and downtown-oriented planning were widely supported. However, "federal legislation has broadened the input of interests from outside Allegheny County, thereby stimulating more interest in decentralized transportation infrastructure. The voting structure of the Metropolitan Planning Organization (MPO), which also serves the Economic Development District, ensures that each county receives equal votes regardless of population. Outlying counties are eager to appropriate 'their share' of federal funding, but in a no-growth environment, that occurs at a cost to the region's core." Thus in Pittsburgh, federal highway investment is viewed as a threat to the region's still centralized form.

The emphasis in the Pittsburgh metropolitan area study is on stanching the loss of population and employment sources. The policies emphasize the need for greater regional coordination and growth management. The study's authors say, "Without a unifying regional strategy, the pinwheel development pattern will continue to dissolve as growth spills over the fringes. The urban core already faces the prospect of bankruptcy." With respect to growth management, they say that office construction in the airport corridor also threatens the downtown: "The old [development] coalition itself needs to resolve the contradictions between the goal of airport corridor growth and the goal of reinforcing downtown. . . . Retail and office development has competed for a shrinking pool of consumers and workers. . . . Development that grows the market, rather than shifting it, should receive priority."

The Proposals: Simultaneity, Costs and Benefits, the Politics of Policy Enactment

Most of the case studies recommend the enactment of several policies simultaneously—for example, greater regional coordination of land-use and fiscal policy, elimination or modification of distorting federal policies like the mortgage tax deductions, and greater funding for transit compared with highways. A major difficulty in considering such changes is that their joint impacts are largely unknown. The political process usually enacts and implements policy without much thought to coordination with other policies. This may be due to divided responsibilities among public agencies and independent jurisdictions, or the result of federal and state programs being available at particular times. It is not surprising that the academic literature reflects this piecemeal process in its policy evaluations. Studies of transit systems and of highways abound; proposals and evaluations of fiscal integration are numerous. What is missing is a simulation model that can analyze the enactment of several policy interventions simultaneously. For example, what could be expected if prices were corrected to account for negative (or positive externalities) associated with automobile travel, at the same time that regional land-use planning and perhaps fiscal integration were adopted? Such a literature is nonexistent.

Given the emphasis in these studies on excessive decentralization and sprawl and the explicit and implicit policy recommendations to control further decentralization and sprawl in favor of more compact development, it would be important to carefully compare the costs and benefits of maintaining current land-use developments with those of more compact development. Indeed, a prior step would be to develop a simulation model to predict the outcomes of the recommended policies. In particular, would they result in welfare-improving, more compact development? Given the vast changes that have occurred in a great many factors associated with density, it is not surprising to see far lower-density development in the second half of the twentieth century than in earlier decades. The issue raised here and in much of the literature is whether this development has been efficient and equitable, whether, despite the obvious factors resulting in demands for more extensive land development, the extent of land development has been excessive, and in particular, whether the forces behind these increased demands have been exaggerated by government policies.

Income increases, population growth, technological changes such as the widespread increase in reliance on automobiles for personal transportation and trucking for the shipment of goods, the development of air conditioning and airplanes, changes in industrial processes, the decline of manufacturing and increase in the service sectors—all directly or indirectly result in a demand for less-dense land development, the growth of suburbs and airport corridors, and the relocation of population from the Northeast and Midwest to the South and West. Facilitating this increased demand for land is the enormous increase in agricultural productivity, making much urban fringe land more valuable for residential, industrial, or office uses than for agriculture.

Demographic changes—the increased total population, relocation, and thus rapid growth in many parts of the South and West and in suburbs rather than central cities—required additional space, or substantial increases in density, for housing and relocating economic activities. On this count alone, a careful enumeration of the benefits to the persons and firms choosing these locations and the costs to them and others would be appropriate. The decrease in densities was for a long time considered beneficial. The literature on optimum-sized cities was concerned with excessive city density, traffic congestion, and air pollution (which still characterizes major cities). The suburbs offered less congestion, open space, and greater ability to become a homeowner. Higher incomes reinforced and increased the demand for homeownership and larger homes on larger lots.

The process may, however, have been excessive as a result of the many policy distortions and the inattention to negative externalities that accompanied the post–World War II decentralization. Fragmented metropolitan areas do provide the possibility for improved welfare when multiple jurisdictions supply public goods appropriate for households and firms with different tastes. However, as these studies emphasize, such differences also reinforce interjurisdictional inequalities.

In sum, in evaluating whether something is a problem and in assessing the likelihood that the problem can be ameliorated by particular public policy interventions—either new or modified policies—both costs and benefits must be considered. Assessing both the problems and the proposed solutions cited in these five case studies and the broader literature requires careful cost-benefit analysis, taking into account both tangible and intangible benefits and costs, and considering all who bear costs and realize benefits.

It seems clear that major changes in the use and development of land through greater emphasis on transit relative to roads will take several decades. As the case studies emphasize in their policy recommendations, substantial change would require major *coordinated* changes in public policy. Infrastructure and land use in place could be modified only slowly, and incentives for behavioral change would have to be substantial. The ultimate question is whether such changes would be welfare-improving: would the policy changes increase efficiency and equity? That is, would benefits outweigh costs, or would their costs, both direct and indirect, outweigh their benefits?

A final, nontrivial issue is whether and where such proposals are likely to be politically acceptable. There are many examples of different outcomes, places where anti-sprawl, growth-control measures have been adopted and places where they have been opposed, or adopted and subverted. Regional political coalitions are not based on *net* costs and benefits but rather on who benefits and who bears the costs and how political influence is associated with winners and losers. It is easy to find examples of all of these combinations.

Conclusion

The analyses in these studies, the problems they identify, the causes to which the problems are attributed, and the proposed policy interventions to remedy the problems directly or reduce or remove their causes are representative, in a broad sense, of the current urban policy discussion in the nation. These issues will undoubtedly be the backbone of the urban development and policy discussion in the early twenty-first century. The problems have been building at least since the post–World War II period; the distorting public policies, or lack of appropriate public policies, have been part of the story for at least as long.

The demographics of baby-boom population growth, a major factor in post–World War II suburbanization, has now and for the future resulted in the aging of the population. There are indications that this favors more dense, less automobile-dependent development. The arrival of a younger population of immigrants and their rapid rate of suburbanization works in the opposite direction. A major unknown for the future is the nature and impact of technological change. The automobile, the increased use of trucking for goods transport, and the changes from vertical to horizontal manufacturing processes all reinforced decentralization over the past few decades. Many believe that recent technological changes have facilitated further decentralization (such as communications developments that reduce the need for face-to-face contact and allow individuals to work together at long distances). However, other factors may increase concentration. Perhaps most important are the changes in the employment base of the United States toward even more intensive concentration in the service sector. This may increase the importance of agglomeration—despite the communications developments and outsourcing—and thus result in more concentrated employment locations, albeit not necessarily in the established metropolitan centers.

However these factors interact, the policies proposed in these studies and their ability to turn urban development away from its current trajectory will require the policy community to enact major policy changes *simultaneously*, rather than piecemeal. A major emphasis in these studies is the need for *coordinated* policy changes. A final set of issues, requiring further analysis with simulation models that are capable of considering simultaneous changes, concerns whether the public—households and firms—will respond to the incentives of such policy changes in the anticipated directions.[15]

Appendix. Chapter Outline for the Case Studies

Section 1: Metropolitan Growth and Development Patterns: Activity, Land Use, and Infrastructure

a. What did the spatial distribution of activity (employment/firms, population/housing units, vacant land) look like in the base period—for example, 1960?

b. What did the spatial distribution of infrastructure (roads, public transit, airports, water and sewer systems) look like in the base period?

c. How did each of these change through 199x?

d. What special factors in the history, political economy, topography . . . of the region influenced the development and policy described in a, b, and c?

e. What problems (efficiency—environmental deterioration, increased congestion, segregation, land consumption—or equity) arise from these spatial patterns? Why/how do these regulatory policies affect the spatial distribution of activity? Do they cause (reinforce) problems, solve (assist in the solution of) problems?

f. What are the positive implications (efficiency—increased consumer satisfaction, productivity improvement, decreased congestion, improved environmental quality, Tiebout type increased public goods choices—and equity) of these spatial patterns?

Section 2: Government Spending and Regulatory Activity

a. What are the major flows of federal funds to the area? To which places, for what functions?

b. State flows of funds? For what functions?

c. Local spending patterns and revenue sources; tax burdens.

---

15. Brueckner (2001) has used such a model to investigate the implications of policies to control urban sprawl.

d. Describe federal, state, and local regulatory and administrative policies with implications for spatial distribution of activity.

Section 3: Problems and Positive Implications of Development and Policy

a. Can the problems identified in Section 1 be attributed to/are they caused by or reinforced by the patterns/timing of infrastructure investment? Alternatively, is the infrastructure investment a response to the problems? (Is inference based upon historical patterns or analytic model? Describe.)

b. Can the positive implications identified in Section 1 be attributed to/are they caused by or reinforced by the patterns/timing of infrastructure investment? Alternatively, is the infrastructure investment a response to the problems? (Is inference based upon historical patterns or analytic model? Describe.)

c. Why/how do the intergovernmental flows of funds, local spending and revenue patterns, or regulatory policies affect the problems or positive implications identified in Section 1? Do they cause (reinforce) problems, solve (assist in the solution of) problems?

Section 4: Policy Recommendations

a. What policy recommendations—for federal, state, and local governments—follow from the identification of problems and positive outcomes and their sources identified in Sections 2 and 3?

b. Do these recommendations deal with efficiency/equity issues?

c. What are the major unknowns with respect to appropriate policy interventions? Problem clear, policy unclear; policy not likely to be politically acceptable; policy difficult to implement?

References

Brooks, David G. 2004. "Our Sprawling Supersize Utopia." *New York Times Magazine* (April 4).

Brueckner, Jan K. 2001. "Urban Sprawl: Lessons from Urban Economics." In William G. Gale and Janet Rothenberg Pack, eds., *Brookings-Wharton Papers on Urban Affairs 2001*, pp. 65–89. Brookings.

Burchell, Robert W., David Lisotkin, and Catherine C. Galley. 2000. "Smart Growth: More than a Ghost of Urban Policy Past, Less than a Bold New Horizon." *Housing Policy Debate* (Fannie Mae Foundation) 11, no. 4: 821–79.

DeVol, Ross C., Rob Koepp, and Frank Fogelbach. 2002. "State Technology and Science Index: Comparing and Contrasting California." Santa Monica, Calif.: Milken Institute.

Glaeser, Edward, and Matthew Kahn. 2001. "Decentralized Employment and the Transformation of the American City." In *Brookings-Wharton Papers on Urban Affairs*, edited by William G. Gale and Janet Rothenberg Pack, pp. 1–64.

Gordon, Peter, and Harry W. Richardson. 1998a. "A Critique of New Urbanism." Paper presented at the annual meeting of the American Collegiate Schools of Planning, Pasadena, Calif.

———. 1998b. "Prove It: The Costs and Benefits of Sprawl." *Brookings Review* (Fall): 23–25.

———. 2000. "Defending Suburban Sprawl." *Public Interest* (Spring): 65–71.

Katz, Bruce C. 2002. "Smart Growth: The Future of the American Metropolis?" CASE Paper. London School of Economics, Centre for Analysis of Social Exclusion.

Mitchell, John G. 2001. "Urban Sprawl." *National Geographic* (January).

Myers, Phyllis, and Robert Puentes. 2001. "Growth at the Ballot Box: Electing the Shape of Communities in November 2000." Brookings Institution, Center for Urban and Metropolitan Policy (February 2001).

Persky, Joseph, Haydar Kurban, and Thomas W. Lester. 2000. "The Impact of Federal and State Expenditures on Residential Land Absorption: A Quantitative Case Study—Chicago." Paper prepared for Chicago Metropolitan Case Study. Great Cities Institute, Chicago.

Puentes, Robert, and Myron Orfield. 2002. "Valuing America's First Suburbs: A Policy Agenda for Older Suburbs in the Midwest." Brookings, Center for Urban and Metropolitan Policy.

Sohmer, Rebecca R, and Robert E. Lang. 2000. "Editors' Introduction: From Seaside to Southside: New Urbanism's Quest to Save the Inner City." *Housing Policy Debate* (Fannie Mae Foundation) 11, no. 4: 751–60.

CHAPTER **2**

Chicago:

Metropolitan Decentralization

Wim Wiewel, Joseph Persky, and Kimberly Schaffer

Large enough to intensely manifest big-city problems, but not so different as to suggest a lack of generalizability, Chicago is the urban laboratory par excellence. A focus on this Midwest giant makes particularly good sense in a consideration of sprawl.

Given its rising per capita incomes, flat geography, and long-standing racial tensions, Chicago provides a likely setting for sprawl. And the Chicago region has sprawled. Despite slow population growth, the Chicago urbanized area has spread out. Over the past twenty to thirty years, this process has been encouraged by a preexisting highway system, continuing federal subsidies for housing, permissive local governments, and politically weak regional planning agencies. Chicago provides a classic case study of how a relatively dense city can develop into a sprawled region, not so much at the instigation of the public sector, but with its general assistance.

This project was supported by funding from the John D. and Catherine T. MacArthur Foundation to the Brookings Institution. This chapter on Chicago is based on working papers written by faculty and researchers at the Great Cities Institute of the University of Illinois at Chicago. The papers have been published in *Suburban Sprawl: Private Decisions and Public Policy*, edited by Wim Wiewel and Joseph Persky (Armonk, N.Y.: M. E. Sharpe, 2002). We acknowledge the contributions of the participants in this project: Joseph DiJohn, Richard Dye, Daniel Felsenstein, Haydar Kurban, Thomas Lester, Bonnie Lindstrom, John McDonald, Daniel McMillen, Therese McGuire, Charles Orlebeke, Jean Templeton, Piyushimita Thakuriah, Y. Q. Wang, and Tingwei Zhang.

The Main Trends, 1970–2000

Major changes have occurred in the Chicago metropolitan area since the 1970s. Between 1970 and 1990, the population of the metropolitan area increased by only 4 percent, but the urbanized or developed land area increased by more than 47 percent. In other words, in only a twenty-year period, roughly the same number of people came to be spread out over almost half again as much land.[1]

Urban Land, Population, and Density

The changes in land-use patterns, as measured in 1972, 1985, and 1997, are dramatic (see color plates, map 2-1). Urban buildup in the six-county area increased over the twenty-five-year period, at the expense of agricultural and natural land area. Moreover, the loss of open space increased during this time. Nearly 275,000 acres became urbanized in the region between 1972 and 1997—increasing 14.5 percent between 1972 and 1985 and 30 percent between 1985 and 1997. There was a 21 percent loss of natural area and a 37 percent loss of agricultural land in the Chicago region during the same twenty-five-year period. The greatest proportion of urbanized land growth and natural and farmland conversion took place on the fringes of the Chicago metropolitan area, thirty to sixty-five kilometers (and beyond) from the city of Chicago. These land-use changes described above are related to shifting populations and development at lower densities.

As elsewhere, over the past half-century there has been a huge population shift from city to suburbs. The population of the city of Chicago peaked at 3.6 million in 1950, constituting 70 percent of metropolitan area residents. By 2000, 2.9 million Chicagoans made up only 36 percent of the region's population. Despite a much heralded turnaround in the 2000 Census, Chicago's population in that year was 14 percent less than it had been in 1970 and 20 percent less than the 1950 peak.

Chicago's suburbs may be divided into three groups—those urbanized by 1950, the original 1950 inner-ring suburbs;[2] the middle ring, joining the urbanized area in the 1960 or 1970 Census; and the post-1970 suburbs forming a third ring that includes several of the older satellite cities and the new distant suburbs beyond them. In the Chicago

1. Moskovits and Shopland (1999).
2. Roughly speaking, the U.S. Bureau of the Census defined the Chicago urbanized area as those contiguous municipalities and nonincorporated lands with 1,000 persons per square mile.

metropolitan area, geographic rings are shaped like concentric half-circles, since the region is bordered on one side by Lake Michigan.

The suburbs are characterized by far lower densities than the city. As the suburban population share has grown, this growth has taken the form of new suburbs with low densities. In 1990 the city had approximately 12,300 people per square mile, compared with 4,300 people per square mile in the oldest suburbs and only 1,600 people per square mile in the most recently developed suburbs. These new suburbs, with 14 percent of the land in the urbanized area, accounted for less than 5 percent of the Chicago region's population.

At the beginning of the 2000s, new growth is beginning to occur beyond the boundaries of the urbanized area as it has long been defined. The built-up area in the Chicago region has traditionally been bounded by a ring of older industrial cities spanning from Waukegan on the north, through Elgin and Aurora on the west, to Joliet on the south. These cities formed a circumferential arc and served as the terminal points for the region's commuter railroads into the city. For the past 100 years, growth has consisted largely of in-fill within this arc. Until 1950 much of that growth was dominated by increasing densities along the commuter rail lines. In the last half of the twentieth century, an automobile-led development made use of cheaper lands between the older rail spokes. Now, however, growth is spilling beyond the "boundary" of satellite cities, into the rural areas of Kane, McHenry, and Will Counties. With no natural limits to constrain it, growth seems poised to continue consuming farmland and other open space. If past development is a guide, as growth moves outward from this arc, distances across the region will grow geometrically.

However, forecasts of the pace of conversion of the region's open space to urbanized land in the near future are complicated by demographic forecasts. The Northeastern Illinois Planning Commission (NIPC) has predicted faster population growth for the Chicago region over the next two decades: 25 percent, or about 1.8 million people between 1990 and 2020, compared with only 4 percent between 1970 and 1990.[3] However, partially offsetting this acceleration in population growth, the NIPC projections suggest that the growth rate in the number of households in the metropolitan area will decline somewhat, from 22 percent over the two decades 1970 to 1990, to 29 percent for the thirty years 1990–2020. Nonetheless, land absorption is likely to continue at about the same rate.

3. Northeast Illinois Planning Commission (2000).

In Chicago, as in other metropolitan areas of the East Coast and Midwest, densities fall steeply from the core to the suburban fringe. This pattern of sprawl contrasts sharply with that of Los Angeles. Contrary to the southern California myth, for example, L.A.'s suburbs are nearly twice as dense as Chicago's. Even Sunbelt metropolitan areas such as Miami, New Orleans, and Denver have higher suburban population densities than the Chicago region.[4]

The Demographics of Sprawl

The dramatic suburban population growth in the Chicago region can be further described in terms of its race and class composition. While numerous factors have stimulated Chicago suburbanization, as in many other U.S. metropolitan areas, that process can be characterized as "white flight." By 2000, 37 percent of the city residents were black and 26 percent were Latino or Hispanic.[5] Only 31 percent of the city's population was non-Hispanic white. The rest of Cook County, which includes an inner ring of poor black suburbs and several more affluent black communities, was still only 14 percent black or African American. Even more dramatically, four of the five "collar" counties were less than 10 percent black or African American (see table 2-1). The only exception was Will County, at 11 percent. Will County has a long-standing black population, located primarily in Joliet, an older, industrial satellite city.

Differences in the racial composition of Chicago and its suburbs are associated with socioeconomic inequality. Since 1970 a huge income gap has opened between the city and the suburban counties. Average per capita personal income in the city of Chicago in 1969 was 98 percent of that in the metropolitan area. However, between 1969 and 1997, metropolitan per capita income in real terms grew more than 50 percent, while per capita incomes in the city grew by only 16 percent. For the decade of the 1980s, per capita city incomes were virtually flat (see table 2-2).

Official poverty rates also confirm high levels of inequality between Chicago and its suburbs. Twenty-two percent of city residents lived below the federal poverty line in 1990.[6] Between 1970 and 1990, the poverty rate for blacks living in Chicago increased by 7.5 percent—from 25.1 to 32.6 percent. In the ten neighborhoods that make up Chicago's Black Belt, the official poverty rate increased from 32.5 percent to 50.4

4. Urban Transportation Center (1998).
5. U.S. Bureau of the Census (2000).
6. Northeastern Illinois Planning Commission (1999a).

Table 2-1. Minority Populations in Metropolitan Counties, 2000
Percent

County	Black	Latino
Cook (including Chicago)	27	16
DuPage	3	9
Kane	6	24
Lake	8	14
McHenry	1	8
Will	11	9

Source: U.S. Census Bureau (2000).

Table 2-2. Real per Capita Personal Income in the Chicago Region, 1969–97
1997 dollars unless otherwise indicated

Area	1969	1979	1989	1997
City	20,407	22,275	22,492	23,611
Metro area (six counties)	20,861	24,421	28,054	31,715
Ratio of city to metro area (percent)	97.8	91.2	80.2	74.4

Sources: Bureau of Economic Analysis and Chicago Model produced by Regional Economic Models, Inc. (REMI).

percent between 1970 and 1990.[7] Suburban populations had much lower poverty rates than Cook County (see figure 2-1).

In the last few years of the twentieth century, the city of Chicago experienced a real estate renaissance. Gentrification in a number of working-class and low-income neighborhoods resulted in modest increases in the city's population. Such countertendencies can be expected to slow the widening of income differentials between city and suburbs, but a reversal remains quite unlikely.

In sum, the post–World War II suburbanization of the Chicago population has followed a classic pattern. The still-dense central city has been left smaller; poverty is highly concentrated in the city and some of its inner suburbs; and the new suburbs of the urban periphery are overwhelmingly white.

Employment

Jobs in the Chicago region have suburbanized even faster than population. The city of Chicago lost approximately 350,000 jobs between 1972 and 1995, but all of its suburban counties posted substantial employment gains. As a result, the city's share of total metropolitan area

7. Wilson (1996, pp. 15–16).

Figure 2-1. Estimated Poverty in the Chicago Region by County, 1995

Percent of poor population

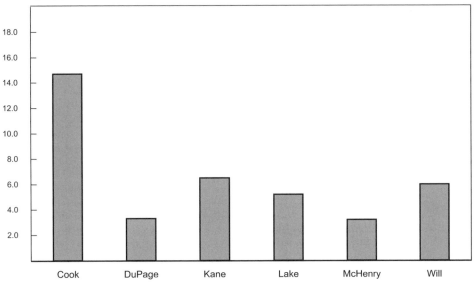

Source: Northeast Illinois Planning Commission.

employment fell from 56 percent to 34 percent between 1972 and 1995 (see table 2-3).

Employment growth (or decline) between 1970 and 1990 in the six-county Chicago region was very unequal. Almost all of the job loss occurred in the city of Chicago, and the largest job gains were concentrated in DuPage County and northern Cook County.

Table 2-3. Private Employment in the Chicago Region, 1972 and 1995

City or county	1972		1995	
	Employment (1,000s)	Percent	Employment (1,000s)	Percent
Chicago	1,347	56	1,097	34
Suburban Cook	698	29	1,131	35
DuPage	117	5	460	14
Lake	91	4	219	7
Kane	78	3	134	4
Will	54	2	95	3
McHenry	27	1	64	2
Total	2,412	100	3,200	100

Source: Illinois Department of Employment Security (2000).

Between 1973 and 1997, employment in the Chicago Central Business District (CBD) held steady, but jobs in Chicago outside of the CBD declined consistently. Meanwhile, suburban job growth was significant over the entire twenty-five-year period.[8] It is clear that some kinds of suburbs have profited more than others from recent employment growth. Between 1980 and 1990, "old industrial suburbs" and "post–World War II industrial suburbs" tended to lose employment (with a few exceptions, most notably in the area immediately surrounding O'Hare International Airport); "old satellite cities" and "service and retail centers" have tended to retain jobs but have had little employment growth. The "new industrial/retail suburbs" and "edge cities" (farthest from the metropolitan core) have seen dramatic increases in employment.[9]

The development of high-tech industry has also contributed to the suburbanization and deconcentration of jobs in the Chicago region. Widmayer and Greenberg estimate that more than 340,000 employees are working in technology-based companies in metropolitan Chicago, producing about 11.5 percent of the gross state product of Illinois.[10] Seventy-five percent of these companies are located in the six-county metropolitan area outside the city of Chicago.

The deconcentration of employment in the Chicago region slowed in the boom of the 1990s. But even that most robust national expansion increased the city's employment only modestly. Between 1994 and 1997, employment in the metropolitan area grew 6.9 percent, but the city of Chicago lagged far behind, with a growth rate of only 2.5 percent.[11]

Another way to compare the effects of the deconcentration of jobs on the city and the suburbs is to look at unemployment rates. Between 1990 and 1998 the city rate paralleled the suburban rate but was significantly higher. By 1998, in the midst of the national economic boom and a purported urban renaissance in Chicago, the city unemployment rate stood at 5.7 percent, while the rate was 4.7 percent in Cook County (including the city), 2.7 percent in DuPage, 3.7 percent in Lake, 3.9 percent in Kane, 3.5 percent in McHenry, and 4.2 percent in Will Counties.[12] These differences reflect not only differences in employment

8. Testa (1999).

9. U.S. Census Bureau, "Journey to Work Data for 1980 and 1990," provided to the Chicago Metropolitan Case Study by the Northwestern Illinois Planning Commission.

10. Widmayer and Greenberg (1998).

11. Putnam and others (2000).

12. Northeastern Illinois Planning Commission (1999a).

growth, but also the considerable share of central-city jobs held by suburban commuters.

Overall, compared with other large metropolitan areas in the United
States, how has the deconcentration of employment in the Chicago
region affected the central city? For the ninety-two largest metropolitan
areas, Brennan and Hill compare the competitiveness of central cities
and their suburbs in attracting and maintaining employers and employment.[13] During the period 1993–96, twenty-three central cities lost private employment. Seventeen central cities actually gained jobs at a faster
rate than their suburbs. Fifty-two central cities gained jobs, but at a
slower rate than their surrounding metropolitan areas; in this category
Chicago ranked near the bottom. Between 1993 and 1996, Chicago had
0.4 percent employment growth while the metropolitan area beyond the
city experienced 9 percent job growth. Chicago's "central city employment competitiveness" ranked seventy-seventh among the ninety-two
regions studied.

Finally, the deconcentration of employment is not unrelated to the
deconcentration of population or residence. Industrial development and
commercial development create jobs. In the Chicago region, industrial
development is taking place primarily close to O'Hare International Airport and outside of Cook County. Commercial development is taking
place in many locations, but is concentrated around highway inter-
changes and suburban employment centers. Residential development,
however, continues to be scattered throughout the metropolitan area,
not adhering to places of industrial or commercial employment.[14] Both
employment and population have become less concentrated, but not in
the same direction: people are likely to live in one place, work in
another, and shop in yet another—at ever increasing distances. This pattern of decentralization of jobs and housing reinforces the spatial mismatch between jobs and housing referred to earlier.

Tax Base

Regional solutions to problems of urban sprawl are extremely difficult to achieve. The Chicago metropolitan area is fragmented into some
270 municipalities. Since these municipalities are, for the most part,
dependent on local property taxes for their revenue, the population and
employment shifts resulting from deconcentration and sprawl affect the
fiscal capacity of these local governments. In 1993 the average property

13. Brennan and Hill (1999).
14. McDonald and McMillen (1999).

tax base per household in the Chicago region was $121,007.[15] In the city of Chicago the average tax base per household was $83,884 in 1993. Fifty-nine suburbs, mostly inner-ring suburbs, predominately black suburbs, and older satellite cities, had a tax base lower than Chicago. Robbins, a poor and black south suburb, had an average property tax base per household of only $23,616 in 1993. On the other end, forty-eight suburbs had more than twice the regional average tax base per household, and twenty-four had more than three times the metropolitan area tax base. These are primarily newer northern and western suburbs.

Across the board, in the Chicago region, sprawl appears to have produced more fiscal "losers" than "winners." In 1993 the total population of the 106 municipalities with a below-average property tax base per household was 4,568,300; 68 percent of the metropolitan area's total population. Fiscal winners are able to attract and retain the industrial, commercial, and residential property tax base that will allow them to provide even more and higher-quality services—including schools—or lower property tax rates (or both), thereby making them even more attractive places for development. But fiscal losers have the opposite experience.

Inequalities in local governments' fiscal capacity have widened as the Chicago region has decentralized. Between 1980 and 1993, twenty-six suburbs lost tax base, some by as much as 36 percent. Almost all of these municipalities were predominately black, inner-ring southern suburbs. During the same period, the property tax base increased by more than 48 percent in seventy-seven suburbs. These municipalities, strong to begin with, were predominately white and affluent northern and western suburbs.

Chicago Sprawl—Its Impact on Social Welfare

As noted earlier, Chicago's sprawl follows a classic pattern. The dense, monocentric, central city has given way to a multi-centered, much lower-density, metropolitan agglomeration. O'Hare Airport, once close to the periphery of the area, is now the statistical center of regional population and employment. City-based minority populations have been

15. All of the property tax data in this section are from 1980 and 1993 municipal taxation reports of the County Clerks' Offices of Cook, DuPage, Kane, Lake, McHenry, and Will counties and the U.S. Census Bureau's 1980 and 1990 Censuses of Population and Housing.

left far from suburban employment growth nodes, and poverty has become ever more concentrated. Some inner suburbs have experienced substantial poverty rates, and a number of blue-collar suburbs have struggled to meet their public service needs, but the income gap between the city and the more affluent suburbs has grown steadily. The city has lost population and employment; increasingly distant suburbs have gained both.

Has Chicago's classic sprawl been good or bad for the region? How has the most important regional trend—the trend in overall well-being—been affected by sprawl? This remains a contentious question in the region, as in the nation as a whole. The Urban Transportation Center of the University of Illinois at Chicago emphasized sprawl's positive role, pointing to a fundamental connection between low density and more affordable housing prices.[16] In addition, the report documented the cost advantages of outer suburban locations for a wide range of businesses.

There can be little doubt that sprawl generates a range of privately appropriated benefits. Households and businesses make their location decisions voluntarily, and in these decisions they attempt to improve their welfare and profits. But private gains do not tell the entire story. Numerous claims have been made about the costs of sprawl. A recent survey presents extensive annotation of key studies in this area.[17] Considerable disagreement still exists over the magnitude of these costs.

Recent studies of the Chicago region have weighed private benefits against the externalities and public costs engendered by outer suburban development of land for residential and business uses.[18] Their findings suggest that the social costs of sprawl just about equal the private benefits. For example, in comparing the consequences of siting a manufacturing plant of 1,000 workers in a greenfield location in the outer suburbs with doing so in a central city location, they find the significant private benefits more than offset by external and public sector costs. Land costs are lower in the outer suburbs. Wages are lower too. But Persky and Wiewel's studies find that these gains, at least for Chicago, are heavily subsidized by public dollars and unpaid social costs, so much so that employment decentralization generates no net efficiency gains. When net efficiency gains are nonexistent, attention naturally shifts to questions of distribution. At least from the Persky and Wiewel studies it

16. Urban Transportation Center (1998).
17. Burchell and others (1998).
18. Persky and Wiewel (1999, 2000).

Table 2-4. Annual Costs and Benefits of Choosing a Greenfield Plant Site
1995 thousands of dollars

Type	(Cost)	Income group	Benefit
Externalities	(1,121)	Low	(636)
Public sector impact	(1,548)	Medium	(970)
Private benefits	2,597	High	1,534
Net benefit or cost	(72)	Net benefit or cost	(72)

Source: Persky and Wiewel (2000).

Notes: Each entry reflects the difference between a greenfield and central-city location for a manufacturing plant with 1,000 workers. Low-income households are defined as those with annual income of less than $30,000; medium with income between $30,000 and $75,000; high with income above $75,000.

would seem that employment decentralization in Chicago favors high-income households (see table 2-4).

Sprawl generates both real benefits and costs. It generates significant redistribution. The full reckoning of net benefits is yet to be completed. Under the circumstances, prudence would seem the most reasonable course for public policy. And prudence suggests a careful review of federal and state policies to determine which policies have encouraged or limited sprawl.

Federal and State Policies That Have Affected Sprawl

Location decisions are highly decentralized. Millions of individuals and thousands of businesses make individual choices. In most cases, these choices are realized through the agency of real estate developers, who themselves form a competitive and decentralized industry. In some immediate sense, it has been these developer-suppliers, in combination with the private customers to whom they cater, that have led the private sector in turning Illinois greenfields into sites for suburban homes and businesses.[19]

But market forces have been supported and facilitated by public policies—policies that have influenced demand and shaped supply. Although the public sector has never declared itself in favor of or opposed to sprawl, its actions have consistently encouraged the decentralization of private residences and businesses. This is true at all levels of government.

19. Urban Transportation Center (1998); Zhang and Zhu (1999).

In this section, we examine some of the public policies that helped determine growth patterns in the Chicago region, with an emphasis on those that have most often been mentioned as encouraging sprawl.

Land Use

As in many other places, Illinois gives strong authority over land-use decisions to individual municipalities. This includes the authority to determine zoning and establish minimum lot sizes and maximum densities. Combined with a system of education funding that relies primarily on local property taxes, this has encouraged municipalities to oppose the development of low- or moderate-income housing in favor of "high-end" low-density residential and commercial development.

But state policies have in many ways framed local land-use decisions. In particular, the early proliferation of local governments across the Chicago region and the highly permissive, subsequent attitude toward low-density annexations have been the direct products of state-level policies. Thus efforts to promote land-use planning at a regional level have resulted in only limited public coordination.

A PROLIFERATION OF MUNICIPALITIES AND SPECIAL-PURPOSE DISTRICTS. The Chicago metropolitan region today has more than 1,200 units of local government, including municipalities, townships, counties, special-purpose districts, and public authorities. This proliferation occurred in part as a result of older state policies: it used to be easier to incorporate a new municipality than it was to annex population into the central city. In addition, municipalities were limited in their powers to tax or incur debt, so numerous special districts were created that had the powers to bond and tax to provide additional services.[20]

Undoubtedly, coordination and regional planning will be more difficult in an area with a large number of municipalities. But having more municipalities may affect land-use patterns more directly. Dye and McGuire's analysis of more than 100 metropolitan areas showed that a greater number of municipalities in a region was significantly related to a higher share of the population in the collar counties.[21] However, there is no clear evidence of a relationship between the number of municipalities and the annual growth in total urbanized land area.

Annexation policies. Many rapidly growing suburban municipalities have been able to annex large amounts of land, often well in advance of

20. Lindstrom (1999b).
21. Dye and McGuire (1999, p. 8).

actual development. In 1990 the village of Huntley was two square miles. Through annexation of vacant land that surrounded it, the village was eleven square miles by the end of the decade. Its acquisitions were done quickly, without referendums or court approval, and entirely legally. In the thirty years from 1960 to 1990, the satellite cities of Elgin, Joliet, and Waukegan had all doubled in physical size, and Aurora tripled its land mass. There is really no reason for a municipality *not* to annex as much adjoining land as possible. Because developers are usually eager to have their new developments incorporated (for the fire, police, and other services the municipality then provides its buyers), they often make substantial payments to the municipality.[22] Municipalities are usually also eager to incorporate new growth, especially if it is commercial, so they can reap the tax revenue benefits.[23] More generally, municipalities want to be able to exert some control over new development, which they can do only if it is within their borders. In addition, annexation provides municipalities with an easy way to increase their importance regionally. These benefits of annexation accrue only to municipalities that are surrounded by vacant land—those on the urban fringe.

Of course, the annexation itself is not the problem, since fewer large municipalities may be more desirable than many small and newly incorporated ones. However, as currently formulated, these permissive annexation policies do nothing to restrict development in outlying unincorporated areas. Given that developers see a benefit from having their developments in incorporated areas, if municipalities were given incentives not to annex additional land, growth could be steered into existing municipalities.

LIMITED REGIONAL PLANNING. The separation and uneven funding of the Northeastern Illinois Planning Commission and the Chicago Area Transportation Study reflect the region's decentralized political realities. Planning agencies must rely on consensus among a large number of government entities. They face funding difficulties and have limited statutory ability to enforce or implement plans.

22. Templeton (1999).

23. As noted above, a growing literature suggests that outer suburban development will not usually pay large dividends or even cover its cost if any reasonably comprehensive measures are applied. See Persky and Wiewel (1999, 2000) and Altshuler and Gómez-Ibáñez (1993). While an individual municipality may gain, its neighbors will often suffer significant losses.

The Chicago Area Transportation Study (CATS, the region's metropolitan transportation planning organization) and the Northeastern Illinois Planning Commission (NIPC) have each created plans that could have been important to the region. But NIPC's plans are not enforceable and, since it is dependent on the donations of local governments for its funding, its actions are subject to local approval. Since CATS is officially a part of the Illinois Department of Transportation, its plans are influenced significantly by that state agency.[24]

Local land-use policies in the Chicago region have been built on a framework supplied by the State of Illinois. It has provided little defense against sprawl, and it has failed to empower regional bodies to plan effectively. Although the state's framework did not require the substantial absorption of open land, it disarmed a possible public control on such growth.

The Intrametropolitan Distribution of Federal and State Spending

Throughout the country, central cities receive a higher share of state and federal per capita spending than their suburban neighbors. Such spending in the form of intergovernmental transfers, payroll, purchasing, and especially transfer payments has been interpreted as a "stealth urban policy."[25] Relative to its suburbs, Chicago has experienced a considerably higher level of federal spending per capita. Federal per capita expenditures decrease more or less smoothly from the central city out toward the newest suburbs. The Chicago central city figure of about $5,300 annually contrasts particularly sharply with federal spending in the newest cohort of outer suburbs, about $2,750 per capita. These suburbs are first included in the urbanized area in the 1980 or 1990 Census. A large portion of this difference is accounted for by transfer payments for the aged and the poor, who historically have been more concentrated in the central city and older suburbs.

Putting aside the specific programmatic purposes of the federal government, it is tempting to speculate that these intrametropolitan differences in per capita expenditures would have a substantial centralizing effect on the region's economy. Just spending all that money in the city relative to the suburbs should presumably work to limit the spread of the metropolitan area. But federal spending in Chicago has done little to stem the outward flow of population and jobs. An extensive simulation

24. Lindstrom (1999b).
25. Parker (1995, 1997).

of the Chicago region suggests the centripetal impact of federal spending streams is small. Had federal spending been equalized across suburban rings, only about 2,000 acres of outer suburban residential land would have been saved. As a share of all the residential land in the collar counties this amounts to only 0.6 percent.[26] A similar simulation of state-level programs shows even smaller overall effects.

A benchmark for judging these effects can be gleaned from the case of high-technology development in Chicago's outer suburban regions. That development has led to the absorption of 24,000 acres of land, 18,000 acres more than would have been developed if these industries and many of their workers had located in the city instead.[27] Thus the modest impact of federal and state general spending is far overshadowed by the larger forces pushing new industries to the periphery.

But if the overall spatial distribution of federal and state spending has done little to stem Chicago sprawl, specific federal and state programs are strongly implicated in the classic outward movement of the region. Chief among these are housing, transportation, and school funding.

Housing Policies

Federal housing policies have helped to shape Chicago-area residential patterns over the past forty years. For example, the construction of high-rise inner-city public housing units has contributed directly to the residential landscape and may have contributed to white flight.

Despite the multiplicity of programs, the central focus of federal housing policy has long been home ownership. Today the most significant tool for encouraging home ownership is the federal income tax code. These provisions heavily subsidize home ownership. From the perspective of sprawl, tax expenditures encourage the conversion of open space into peripheral suburban development. Persky and Kurban find that federal tax subsidies of housing have prompted Chicago households in new suburbs to consume larger houses on larger lots.[28] If the tax subsidies were removed, these Chicago households would have consumed significantly less land, reducing residential land absorption in the younger suburbs (areas that became urbanized in 1970 and 1990) by as much as 20 percent.

The tax subsidies for housing may not have brought households to the suburbs, but these subsidies have encouraged those households, once

26. Persky and Kurban (1999).
27. Felsenstein (1999).
28. Persky and Kurban (1999).

located in the suburbs, to consume considerably more land than they would have otherwise.

Transportation and Infrastructure Policies

The city of Chicago would not have developed into the metropolis that it is today had it not been for large amounts of federal, state, and private money spent building up the city's infrastructure (in addition to the significant funds invested by the city itself).[29] From the building of the Illinois and Michigan Canal and the railroads in the 1840s to the Interstate Highway system and the tunnel and reservoir system of the postwar period, the city's form has been shaped by external funding. The expressway system, in particular, laid the grid for suburban expansion.

In the Chicago region, from 1973 to 1993 vehicle miles traveled increased by 57.6 percent, but transit ridership fell by 18.5 percent.[30] Economic prosperity has certainly allowed more individuals to purchase and maintain a personal automobile, but federal and state policies have also played a role in the increased use of automobiles. From 1965 to the mid-1990s, the federal government spent hundreds of billions of dollars on highway aid. In roughly the same time period, the federal government spent only about one-seventh the amount in federal aid to public bus and subway systems.[31] Although the federal highway system was not constructed to promote suburban development and these expenditures do not account for the differences in numbers of automobile and transit users, the transit system would likely have had more riders if it had received greater funding. The federal government did not begin to finance mass transit until 1961, when it provided funds in the Housing and Urban Development Act. Similarly, it was not until the 1970 constitutional convention that Illinois designated transit as a legitimate public purpose on which state funds could be spent.[32] Until then, all transit was provided by private companies, and the state supported only roads.

Before 1956, revenues from motor fuel taxes went directly into the federal government's general fund. The Highway Revenue Act of 1956 created the Highway Trust Fund as a way to guarantee funding for the construction of the new Interstate Highway System. Today, even though the highway system is largely completed, all federal fuel tax funds

29. Lindstrom (1999).
30. DiJohn (1999).
31. Rusk (1999).
32. DiJohn (1999).

(excluding a 4.3 cent tax per gallon that is sent to the general fund for deficit reduction) and other user taxes are channeled directly into the trust fund, where they must be spent exclusively on transportation projects. In fiscal year 1996, the Highway Trust Fund received $24.7 billion in tax revenues: 89 percent ($22.0 billion) was allocated to the highway account and 10.5 percent to transit. Only since 1983 was any part of the Highway Trust Fund spent on transit.[33] Thus the Highway Trust Fund has skewed federal priorities by creating a dedicated funding source for transportation projects.[34]

Of course, not all road funding allocations encourage sprawl, and it could also be argued that extending transit systems in outlying areas does almost as much to draw new businesses and residents to exurban communities as a new road does. Indeed, Warner's classic *Streetcar Suburbs* makes just that point in regard to the development of Boston.[35] In the Chicago area, most of the older suburbs were developed along the rail lines that entrepreneurial companies put in.

Much of the Chicago region's decrease in transit ridership came during a financial crisis of the early 1980s, when funding shortfalls caused the regional transit agencies to raise fares and cut service. In turn, riders abandoned the system rather than pay more for less, causing even greater deficits. During just one two-year period, 1981 to 1983 (which also coincided with a recession), the system lost 113 million riders.[36] Although ridership took a slight upswing in 1998, it was not enough to offset the losses of the previous twenty years. For transit to be viable, it needs to be funded proactively, and alternatives to fixed route systems need to be considered seriously.

It appears that some of these past trends are changing. During the period 1989–96, federal spending on infrastructure and transportation programs has not been large enough, or sufficiently concentrated, to play a major decentralizing role.[37] While substantial absolute amounts of federal dollars were devoted to highways and roads used by outer suburban residents, the per capita expenditures were not large, amounting to less than $100 per year. Moreover, these expenditures were more than offset on a per capita basis by federal public transit funds and other infrastructure grants received by the city. Per capita expenditures

33. Federal Highway Administration (1999).
34. Nivola (1999).
35. Warner (1969).
36. DiJohn (1999).
37. Persky and Kurban (1999).

Table 2-5. Federal and State Expenditures in the Chicago Urbanized Area, 1989–96
Average dollars per capita

Annual expenditures, highways, public transit, and other infrastructure	City	Urbanized by 1950	Urbanized by 1970	Urbanized by 1990
Federal				
Highways and related	24	52	62	86
Public transit	72	37	24	21
Other infrastructure	23	4	1	0
Total	119	93	87	107
State				
Highways and related	45	76	101	128
Public transit	74	42	28	21
Other infrastructure	2	2	0.5	0.5
Total	122	120	129	149

Source: Persky and Wiewel (2000).

on these same program areas at the state level show a spatial distribution similar to the federal expenditures. This is perhaps not surprising, since federal dollars for infrastructure and transportation must often be leveraged with state or local money, or both. The differences, although not large, favor the newer suburbs of the outer rings (see table 2-5).

Between 1989 and 1996 highway investments in the Chicago region took the form largely of rebuilding and maintenance rather than expansion. While more aggressive highway investments in the past laid a foundation for sprawling land-use patterns in the region, recent history suggests a more cautious approach by both the federal and state government, offset by some investments in public transit. Thus the sprawl-inducing effects of earlier transportation funding may slowly be mitigated.

School Funding and Property Taxes

On the one hand, policies to equalize school funding and provide more state aid could lower the level of sprawl in a region. If inner-city schools are underfunded and suburban schools are well funded, in the absence of other alternatives, families with children will move to the outer areas. On the other hand, as state aid becomes more equalizing, more families with school-age children might choose to stay in the region's core, resulting in a lower share of the region's population in the collar counties. Dye and McGuire find that, between 1970 and 1990, sprawl may have been lower in regions whose states contributed a larger share of school district revenues and had policies that equalized the distribution of these revenues.[38] A higher degree of equalization in the state aid formula, for example, "has a negative effect . . . on the share of total population residing in the collar counties and on the growth of the urbanized land area, but a positive effect on the share of the total land categorized as urbanized."[39]

Compared with most other metropolitan areas observed, the Chicago region is losing ground in state equalization policies. In Illinois, the main source of school funding is the local property tax, but each district also receives aid from the state, in the form of formula grants and categorical grants.[40] Between 1980 and 1990, the state of Illinois decreased its share of school district revenues, although in the late 1990s the state share once again began to increase.[41] The degree of equalization in the distribution of state revenues also decreased dramatically in the 1980s. By 1990 the amount of variation in state funding of Illinois school districts was two times that of Wisconsin and Indiana, and three and one-half times that of Michigan. In fact, in a study of state education expenditures in 1989–90, only Alaska had more variation. For example, Chicago, despite having a poverty rate of nearly twice the statewide average, received only about 70 percent of the mean downstate level of formula aid.[42] This is because the state uses assessed value in its allocation formula, without including a more direct measure of poverty.

The insufficiency of state equalization leaves Illinois school districts heavily dependent on local property taxes. The lowest quartile of municipalities, those with property tax rates ranging from 3.3 to 6.8 percent, are clustered in DuPage County and scattered throughout the five other collar counties. The highest quartile, with rates ranging from 9.8 to 17.4 percent, is almost exclusively in suburban Cook County.[43] In addition, a preliminary study of the Chicago region suggests that higher property tax rates may discourage economic activity.[44] After

38. Dye and McGuire (1999).

39. Ibid., p. 8.

40. Formula aid is the state's equalizing grant and targets low-wealth, low-income districts. It constitutes about two-thirds of all state aid and averages $1,453 per elementary student. Categorical aid makes up the remainder of state aid and is allocated to districts for specific programs (McGuire and Merriman, 1997).

41. Goldstein and Njus (1999).

42. McGuire and Merriman (1997).

43. Dye and McGuire (1999).

44. Dye, McGuire, and Merriman (1999).

adjusting for several relevant variables, a Cook County location remains a statistically significant deterrent to industry.[45] While Cook County has a number of characteristics that might account for this observation, it remains true that the county assesses industrial and commercial properties at high rates relative to its neighbors. Because Cook County is the core county, its higher rates push some commercial and industrial development to seek locations in outer counties. All of these factors combine to make outer suburban locations more attractive for households with school-age children.

Thus federal and state policies have played a considerable role in facilitating Chicago sprawl. Although designed for purposes only incidentally concerned with population density and land use, these policies have generally reinforced other factors driving decentralization.

Slowing Sprawl in the Chicago Region

The Chicago Metropolitan Case Study demonstrates that a range of federal and state policies have reinforced the other factors behind decentralization in the region. If, as suggested by Persky and Wiewel, the region's decentralized urban pattern provides little net gain on efficiency grounds, serious attention should be paid to changing policies to reduce subsidies and enhance equity.[46]

Chicago's sprawl will not be reversed by new federal and state policies; however, it can be slowed by a conscious shift away from current federal and state policies.

A Regional Agenda

We propose a five-point agenda for the Chicago region. The proposals underscore the priorities suggested by the research. The items have been chosen to emphasize policies that "do no harm," that is, those that can be strongly justified even if their impact on sprawl proves to be modest.

I. IMPOSE HIGHER IMPACT FEES AT A REGIONAL LEVEL. For better or worse, the federal government's income tax code encourages excessive land absorption. The most direct way for the state to counter such subsidies is through promoting or even mandating higher and more realistic impact fees on new development.

45. McDonald and McMillen (1999).
46. Persky and Wiewel (2000).

Although there are many types of impact fees, the term usually describes fees paid to municipalities by developers to offset the marginal costs associated with new development—requirements for new infrastructure or additional demands on schools. Because such fees attempt to make new development "pay for itself" and reduce the fiscal impact of new growth on current residents, impact fees are popular in many states.

Illinois municipalities have the right to impose impact fees, but their ability to do so is more strictly regulated than in many other states.[47] While many Illinois municipalities do impose some type of impact fee on developers, many forgo monetary fees and are content to receive dedications for park and school land, which may be worth less than the public costs they are meant to offset. This is unfortunate, since impact fees are an effective—and largely equitable—tool to control sprawl. By raising the cost of building new homes, impact fees reduce demand for larger homes on larger lots (and by extension new homes in general). Although impact fees do raise the costs of development, it seems fair and reasonable to impose the costs of new development on the beneficiaries. Moreover, impact fees, like property taxes, can be made proportional to the value and size of new developments, thus lessening their regressivity. They can also be dampened through density bonuses for employer-assisted housing and other developments that include affordable housing.

While research in this area is just beginning, Skidmore and Peddle conclude that imposing impact fees does decrease residential development.[48] Analyzing a sample of municipalities in DuPage County, a Chicago-region collar county, they found that the presence of fees led to a net reduction in development by 25 percent. However, they caution that several questions remain to be answered, including whether developers then tend to locate in municipalities that do not have impact fees, thereby increasing the rate of development elsewhere. For these reasons, we advocate better state legislation to allow for the collection of impact fees on a regional (or at least county) basis.

2. DIRECTLY PRESERVE OPEN SPACE THROUGH THE PURCHASE OR TRANSFER OF DEVELOPMENT RIGHTS. Open space and farmland preservation efforts are among the most popular growth control measures nationwide. In the Chicago region, residents in four of the collar counties supported more than $200 million in bond issues in

47. Templeton (1999).
48. Skidmore and Peddle (1998).

1999 to preserve farmland and open space.[49] In addition, the state of Illinois is beginning to take more interest in open-space preservation. As part of the Illinois Open Land Trust initiative, passed unanimously by the House of Representatives, the state will provide $160 million over four years (2000–2004) for the state and local governments to acquire land for conservation or recreation.[50]

There are two main ways a region can preserve open space—either through the transfer of development rights, or through the outright purchase of those rights (also known as conservation easements). In the latter program, farmers permanently give up the right to develop their land in exchange for a cash payment. Farmers are compensated for the difference between what the farm would sell for in agriculture use, and what it would sell for if developed. In Pennsylvania's program, payments average about $2,000 per acre.[51] The farmer may sell the land at any time, but the easement remains with the property permanently.

A transfer of development rights program is usually more complex to administer and may take more forms. Usually, however, the local government designates areas within its boundaries as "sending areas" and other areas as "receiving areas." Such programs may be voluntary (developers may get density bonuses by buying the rights) or mandatory (owners are not permitted to build in sending areas), and developers may not build in receiving areas without purchasing rights.

3. EQUALIZE SCHOOL FUNDING. The first major step in this direction must be to equalize school funding at the state level. We find evidence that school funding policies affect the level of sprawl in a metropolitan area. These findings, although preliminary, suggest a need for a larger state role in education funding and in the equalization of that funding as a possible deterrent to residents moving out of the central city and increasing land consumption. Regardless of their effect on land-use patterns, however, these fiscal disparities also need to be addressed because of the equity issues they raise within the region. As we noted above, sprawl has significant equity consequences. Therefore, we recommend that the state of Illinois shift education funding from local property taxes to state income taxes.

49. Casey Bukro, "Illinois a Leader in Land Preservation," *Chicago Tribune*, October 12, 1999 (www.chicagotribune.com).

50. The Governor's Open Land Trust proposal was approved by the Illinois General Assembly in 1999 (press release, Springfield, May 5, 1999).

51. Freese (1995).

4. DISCOURAGE MAJOR INFRASTRUCTURE INVESTMENTS IN OUTER PARTS OF THE REGION. Several states have enacted programs to ensure that the central cores remain the focus of the state's infrastructure funding. Most notable is Maryland's Smart Growth Initiatives, enacted by the state legislature in 1997. The program contains five components, the centerpiece of which is the creation of Priority Funding Areas (the other components are a Rural Legacies program, a brownfields program, Job Creation Tax Credits, and Live Near Your Work). Since October 1998, state funds for projects such as roads, water, and sewer, and state facilities have been directed to the state's priority funding areas, which include every municipality, areas inside the Baltimore and Washington beltways, and designated enterprise zones. Since the program is new, its effects are still uncertain.[52]

The Maryland Priority Funding Areas program holds important lessons for the State of Illinois. While it provides incentives for municipalities to "grow smart," it does not put direct land-use restrictions on local governments. They remain free to encourage development wherever in the county they choose, so long as no state funds are involved. Implementing a similar program in the Chicago region would no doubt be much more difficult. Illinois counties do not have as much control over land-use issues as counties in Maryland do. However, a program here that would require municipalities and counties to make development plans and then channeled state infrastructure funding only to designated growth areas seems likely to reduce land consumption.

5. INCREASE INCENTIVES FOR EMPLOYERS TO LOCATE IN THE CENTRAL CITY. Employment deconcentration has provided new fuel to residential sprawl. For city business locations to compete with cheap peripheral sites, infrastructure and other public support have often been necessary. When carefully pursued these are not corporate welfare, but serious investments.

Chicago has one of the most successful brownfields redevelopment programs in the country. These programs should certainly be continued and even strengthened. At the state level, Illinois is moving toward proportionate share liability as law in dealing with brownfields, which is meant to help ensure that investors not responsible for the environmental condition of the land are not held liable for its condition.[53] As they continue, the effects of these programs should be monitored and adapted as necessary.

52. Maryland Office of Planning (1999); Gurwitt (1999).
53. City of Chicago Department of Environment (1998).

Other widely used policies employed by regional, state, and federal agencies that can help to redirect industrial development to the inner city include tax increment financing districts, site assembly, workforce training programs, and property tax abatements and subsidies to retain and expand the employment base, as well as to create a mix of housing options. There is no doubt that these incentives have occasionally been abused. The danger remains of simplistically interpreting any industrial investment as economic development, or of identifying residential gentrification with a general improvement in housing standards. However, when intelligently designed and well administered, they can provide critical tools for the rebuilding of the employment base of the central city.[54]

Toward Effective Implementation

A regional effort to consciously limit sprawl requires a regional planning authority with effective political power. In order to become more useful to area residents, planning in the Chicago region must be more comprehensive and effective. First, the functions of CATS (the regional metropolitan planning organization) and NIPC (the regional planning commission) should be merged and a new agency created that is responsible for both land use and transportation planning. Second, the new agency needs to be provided with a guaranteed funding stream to remove any question of local political influence.

The new body should draw on the experience of the Portland (Oregon) Metro. There the regional planning agency was approved by the state legislature and voters and formed in 1970, at which time it lacked a steady revenue stream and was responsible only for solid waste planning for the region and, later, the Portland Zoo. Today, Metro has home rule and is responsible for drawing and overseeing changes to Portland's urban growth boundaries; for coordinating plans of the three counties, twenty-four cities, sixty special districts and other state and regional agencies; and for developing the region's 2040 plan.[55]

The Chicago region should push for authority from the state to create such a regional planning body. To create a body with home rule, however, would require a three-fifths majority vote in the legislature to change the state constitution—something unlikely to happen in the near future. Concern over lack of an effective regional planning agency is echoed in the Chicago Metropolis 2020 report, which advocates creating a regional coordinating mechanism that would take responsibility

54. See Bingham and Mier (1997); Blair and Reese (1999).
55. Porter (1996).

for regional efforts in housing, transportation, fiscal policies, and general regional planning efforts, among other tasks. Because the report acknowledges that structuring and funding such a body could take several years, it advocates in the meantime consolidating CATS, NIPC, and the planning function of the Regional Transportation Authority (RTA).

As the Portland Metro example shows, the body would also need a permanent funding stream to be successful. Other lessons include the importance of planning through consensus building, not mandates. If such a body were developed in the Chicago region, it could coordinate with other agencies to implement many of the programs described here, including regional impact fees, regional affordable housing programs, a tax base sharing program, and general planning responsibilities.

Which of the five policy initiatives should have priority is largely a matter of political realities—what coalitions can be formed and which areas provide opportunities for intervention. We remind our readers what Foster has pointed out: in many cases, it is not so much the policies a region has, but how the region takes advantage of the policies, that makes the difference.[56] This makes our recommendation to develop a regional planning body with legislated powers all the more important. In this way, regional leaders can build the authority to develop and implement regional programs that can best take advantage of current policies, as they work to bring about other reforms that benefit the region.

References

Altshuler, Alan, and José Gómez-Ibáñez. 1994. *Regulation for Revenue*. Washington: Brookings and Lincoln Institute for Land Policy.

Bingham, Richard, and Robert Mier, eds. 1997. *Dilemmas of Urban Economic Development: Issues in Theory and Practice*. Thousand Oaks, Calif.: Sage.

Blair, John P., and Laura A. Reese. 1999. *Approaches to Economic Development*. Thousand Oaks, Calif.: Sage.

Brennan, John, and Edward W. Hill. 1999. "Identifying Large Central Cities That Are Competitive Employment Locations: The Index of Competitive Central Cities." Paper presented to the annual meeting of the Association of Collegiate Schools of Planning. Chicago, October 21–24.

Burchell, Robert, and others. 1998. "Costs of Sprawl Revisited: The Evidence of Sprawl's Negative and Positive Impacts." Washington: Transportation Research Board.

56. Foster (2000).

City of Chicago, Department of Environment. 1998. *Chicago Brownfields Report* 3. (Spring) (www.cityofchicago.org/Environment/Brownfields/ Newsletter.97.08.html).

Cox, Wendell. 1999. "U.S. Urbanized Areas 1950–1990: Urbanized Area Data." Belleville, Ill.: Wendell Cox Consultancy and the Public Purpose (www.publicpurpose.com/dm-uad.htm).

DiJohn, Joseph. 1999. "Transportation in the Chicago Metropolitan Region since 1970." Working Paper. Great Cities Institute, University of Illinois at Chicago.

Dye, Richard F., and Therese J. McGuire. 1999. "Property Taxes, Schools, and Sprawl." Working Paper. Great Cities Institute, University of Illinois at Chicago.

Dye, Richard F., Therese J. McGuire, and David F. Merriman. 1999. "The Impact of Property Taxes and Property Tax Classification on Business Locations: Evidence from the Chicago Metropolitan Area." University of Illinois at Chicago.

Fannie Mae. 1999. "Products for Untapped Markets: Employer-Assisted Housing Plans (EAH)" (www.fanniemae.com/neighborhoods/products/housing/ employer_assisted_housing.html).

Federal Highway Administration. 1999. "Highway Trust Fund Primer: A Summary" (http://fhwa.dot.gov/pubstats.html [October 2, 1999]).

Federal Highway Administration. 2000. "TEA-21: Moving Americans into the 21st Century" (www.fhwa.dot.gov/tea21/index.htm).

Felsenstein, Daniel. 1999. "The Impact of High-Technology Employment Concentration on Urban Sprawl in the Chicago Metropolitan Area." Working Paper. Great Cities Institute, University of Illinois at Chicago.

Foster, Kathryn. 2000. "Regional Capital." In *Urban-Suburban Interdependencies*, edited by Wim Wiewel and Rosalind Greenstein, pp. 83–118. Cambridge, Mass.: Lincoln Institute for Land Policy.

Freese, Betty. 1995. *Saving the Farm. Successful Farming* (Iowa ed.) 93 (August): 30–31.

Goldstein, Scott, and Jonathan Njus. 1999. *Back to School: The State's Expanding Role in Funding Public Education*. Chicago: Metropolitan Planning Council.

Gordon, Peter, and Harry W. Richardson. 1997. "Are Compact Cities a Desirable Planning Goal?" *Journal of the American Planning Association* 63 (Winter): 95–106.

Gurwitt, Rob. 1999. "The State vs. Sprawl." *Governing* 12 (January): 18–23.

Hughes, Mark Alan, and Julie E. Sternberg. 1992. *The New Metropolitan Reality: Where the Rubber Meets the Road in Antipoverty Policy*. Washington, D.C.: Urban Institute.

Illinois Department of Employment Security. 2000. "Where Workers Work in the Chicago Metro Area. Summary Report: 1972–1997" (http:// lmi.ides.state.il.us/wwwork/intro.htm).

Johnson, Elmer W. 1999. *Chicago Metropolis 2020: Preparing Metropolitan Chicago for the 21st Century*. Commercial Club of Chicago.

Lindstrom, Bonnie. 1999a. "Public Works and Land Use Policies: The Importance of Public Infrastructure in Chicago's Metropolitan Development, 1830–1970." Working Paper. Great Cities Institute, University of Illinois at Chicago.

———. 1999b. "The Role of Regional Planning Agencies in Suburban Deconcentration." Working Paper. Great Cities Institute, University of Illinois at Chicago.

Maryland Office of Planning. 1999. "Maryland's Smart Growth Initiatives 1997" (www.op.state.md.us/smartgrowth/initiatv.html).

Maryland State Government Geographic Coordinating Committee. 1999. "The Technology Toolbox from the Environmental Agenda of Governor Parris N. Glendening" (www.fgdc.gov/obp/mdtool.html).

Maynard, Lehigh J., John C. Becker, Timothy W. Kelsey, and Stanford M. Lembeck. 1998. "Early Experience with Pennsylvania's Agricultural Conservation Easement Program." *Journal of Soil and Water Conservation* 53, no. 2: 106–12.

McDonald, John F., and Daniel P. McMillen. 1999. "Employment Subcenters and Subsequent Real Estate Development in Suburban Chicago." Working Paper. Great Cities Institute, University of Illinois at Chicago.

McGuire, Therese J., and David F. Merriman. 1997. "Disparities among Illinois' School Districts." Institute of Government and Public Affairs, University of Illinois at Chicago.

MetroLinks. 1999. *HUD Awards Rental Assistance Vouchers to MetroLinks: First Ever Tri-County Coordination of Housing Services*. Chicago: MetroLinks.

Metropolitan Planning Council. 1995. *Creating a Regional Community: The Case for Metropolitan Cooperation*. Chicago: Metropolitan Planning Council.

Montgomery County, Maryland, Division of Housing and Code Enforcement. "The Moderately Priced Dwelling Unit Program: Montgomery County, Maryland's, Inclusionary Zoning Ordinance. Program Summary and Background" (www.co.mo.md.us//services/hca/Housing/MPDU/summary.htm [February 20, 2000]).

Moskovits, Debra, and Jennifer Shopland. 1999. *Satellites Work for Nature in the Metropolis*. Chicago: Chicago Wilderness.

Nivola, Pietro S. 1999. *Laws of the Landscape: How Policies Shape Cities in Europe and America*. Brookings.

Northeastern Illinois Planning Commission (NIPC). 1999a. "Census Bureau Releases Updated Income and Poverty Estimates for Illinois and Northeastern Illinois Counties (2/12/99)." Chicago (www.nipc.cog.il.us/pov95nei.htm).

———. 1999b. "Unemployment Rates by County in Northeastern Illinois, 1990–99 Annual Averages." Chicago (www.nipc.cog.il.us/lausdata.htm).

———. 1997. "Final Forecast Results." Chicago (www.nipc.cog.il.us/2020-sum.htm).

———. 2000. "Population, Household and Employment Forecasts for Counties and Municipalities in Northeastern Illinois." Chicago (www.nipc.cog.il.us/fore2020.htm).

Orfield, Myron. 1997. *Metropolitics: A Regional Agenda for Community and Stability.* Washington: Brookings and Lincoln Institute for Land Policy.

Orlebeke, Charles J. 1999. "Housing Policy and Urban Sprawl in the Chicago Metropolitan Region." Working Paper. Great Cities Institute, University of Illinois at Chicago.

Parker, R. Andrew. 1995. "Patterns of Federal Urban Spending: Central Cities and Their Suburbs, 1983–1992." *Urban Affairs Review* 31, no. 2: 184–205.

———. 1997. "A Stealth Urban Policy in the U.S.? Federal Spending in Five Large Metropolitan Regions, 1984–1993." *Urban Studies* 34, no. 11: 1831–50.

Pennsylvania Department of Community and Economic Development. 1999. "Shared Municipal Services" (www.dced.state.pa.us/PA_Exec/DCED/government/shared.htm).

Persky, Joseph, and Haydar Kurban. 1999. "Federal and Residential Land Absorption: A Quantitative Case Study—Chicago." Working Paper. Great Cities Institute, University of Illinois at Chicago.

Persky, Joseph, and Thomas W. Lester. 2000. "Expenditures by the State of Illinois and Residential Land Absorption in Chicago." Working Paper. Great Cities Institute, University of Illinois at Chicago.

Persky, Joseph, and Wim Wiewel. 1999. "Economic Development and Metropolitan Sprawl: Changing Who Pays and Who Benefits." In *The End of Welfare? Consequences of Federal Devolution for the Nation*, edited by Max Sawicky, pp. 127–56. Armonk, N.Y.: M. E. Sharpe.

Persky, Joseph and Wim Wiewel. 2000. *When Corporations Leave Town: The Costs and Benefits of Metropolitan Job Sprawl.* Detroit: Wayne State University Press.

Porter, Douglas R., and others. 1996. *Profiles in Growth Management: An Assessment of Current Programs and Guidelines for Effective Management.* Washington: Urban Land Institute.

Putnam, George, and others. 2000. "Restructuring, Decentralizing, and Stabilizing: Chicago Area Employment during the Boom." University of Illinois at Chicago. Mimeo.

Rusk, David. 1999. *Inside Game/Outside Game: Winning Strategies for Saving Urban America.* Washington: Brookings.

Silicon Valley Manufacturing Group. 1999a. "Annual Report—Housing" (www.svmg.org/htm/annual_housing.htm).

———. 1999b. "Silicon Valley Employers Meet County's Challenge, Provide $1 Million in 'Seed Funds' to Housing Trust Fund" (www.svmg.org/htm/new_housing_fund.htm).

Skidmore, Mark, and Michael Peddle. 1998. "Do Development Impact Fees Reduce the Rate of Residential Development?" *Growth and Change* 29, no. 4: 383–400.

State of Illinois. 2000. 91st General Assembly Legislation: Status of HB4074 (www.legis.state.il.us).

Templeton, Jean M. 1999. "Land-Use Planning Tools in Illinois: Preventing or Promoting Sprawl?" Working Paper. Great Cities Institute, University of Illinois at Chicago.

Testa, William. 1999. "Cities in the Midwest: Are They Coming Back?" Presented at the Great Cities Winter Forum. University of Illinois at Chicago, December.

Thakuriah, Piyushimita. 1999. "Commercial Motor Carrier Operations in the Northeast Illinois Region: Impacts on Land-Use Trends since 1970." Working Paper. Great Cities Institute, University of Illinois at Chicago.

U.S. Bureau of the Census. 1992. *Census of Population and Housing, 1990: Public Use Microdata Sample U.S. Technical Documentation.*

———. *Census of Population and Housing, 2000.*

U.S. Department of Housing and Urban Development. 1999. "Community Development Block Grant (CDBG) Entitlement Communities Program" (www.hud.gov/progdesc/cdbgent.html).

University of Illinois at Chicago. 1999. "For Rent . . . Housing Options in the Chicago Region." A regional rental market analysis summary report prepared for the Metropolitan Planning Council by the University of Illinois at Chicago.

Urban Transportation Center. 1998. *Highways and Urban Decentralization.* University of Illinois, Chicago.

Wang, Y. Q. 1999. "A Regional Pattern of Urban Land Cover Change in Northeastern Illinois: A Landsat View from 1972 to 1997." Working Paper. Great Cities Institute, University of Illinois at Chicago.

Warner, Sam Bass. 1969. *Streetcar Suburbs: The Process of Growth in Boston, 1900–1970.* New York: Athenaeum.

Widmayer, Patricia, and Gary Greenberg. 1998. "Putting Our Minds Together: The Digital Network Infrastructure and Metropolitan Chicago." Chicago: Metropolitan Planning Council (http://www.metroplanning.org).

Wiewel, Wim, and Kimberly Schaffer. 2000. "New Federal and State Policies for Metropolitan Equity." Working Paper. Great Cities Institute, University of Illinois at Chicago.

Wilson, William J. 1996. *When Work Disappears: The World of the New Urban Poor.* New York: Alfred A. Knopf.

Zhang, Tingwei, and Jihong Zhu. 1999. "Community Features and Urban Sprawl: The Case of the Chicago Metropolitan Region." Working Paper. Great Cities Institute, University of Illinois at Chicago.

Map 2-1. Land Cover Change of the Chicago Metropolitan Region, 1972–97

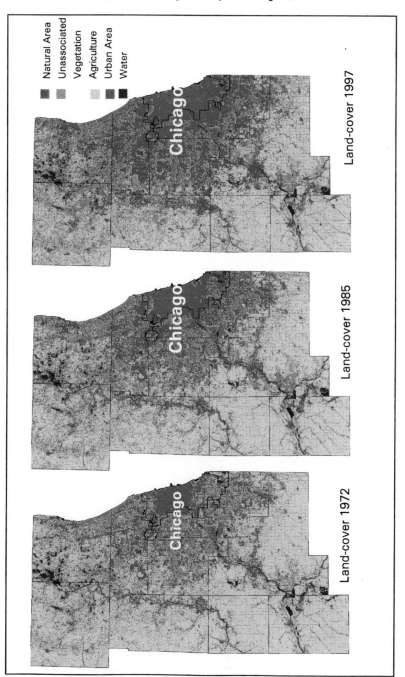

Source: Calculated from aerial snapshots by the Landsat satellite that passes over Chicago once every sixteen days. Project funded by the National Aeronautics and Space Administration (Wang 1999).

Map 4-1. Percentage Change in Population, 1990–1996: MCDs in Pennsylvania Counties of the Philadelphia MSA

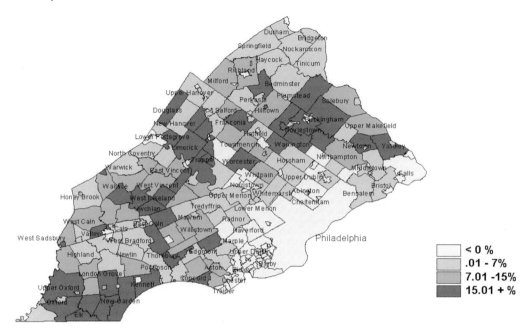

< 0 %
.01 - 7%
7.01 -15%
15.01 + %

Map 4-2. Percentage in Poverty, 1990: MCDs in Pennsylvania Counties of the Philadelphia MSA

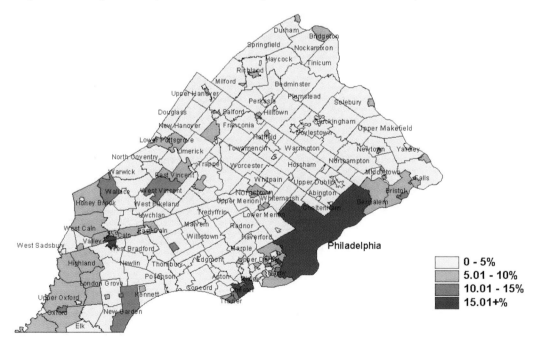

0 - 5%
5.01 - 10%
10.01 - 15%
15.01+%

Map 4-3. Average Household Income by Tract: Philadelphia and Pennsylvania Portion of the Philadelphia MSA, 1989

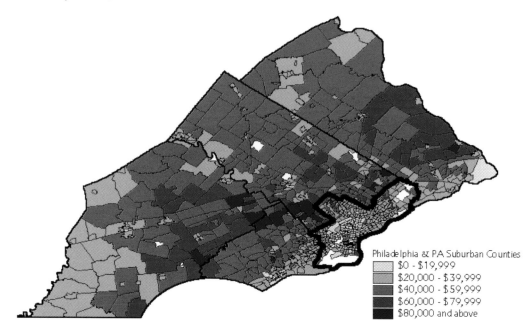

Philadelphia & PA Suburban Counties
- $0 - $19,999
- $20,000 - $39,999
- $40,000 - $59,999
- $60,000 - $79,999
- $80,000 and above

Map 4-4. Median House Value by Tract: Philadelphia and Pennsylvania Portion of the Philadelphia MSA, 1989

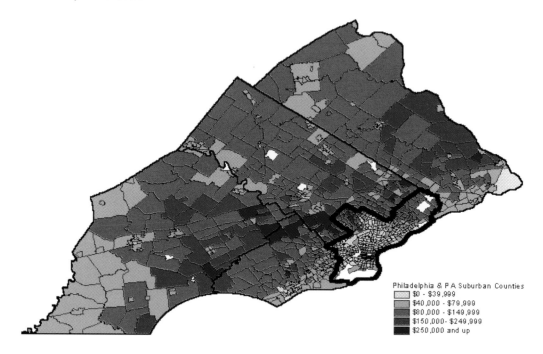

Philadelphia & PA Suburban Counties
- $0 - $39,999
- $40,000 - $79,999
- $80,000 - $149,999
- $150,000 - $249,999
- $250,000 and up

Map 4-5. Value of Aggregate Tax Benefit per Owner-Occupied Household: Philadelphia and Pennsylvania Portion of the Philadelphia MSA, 1989

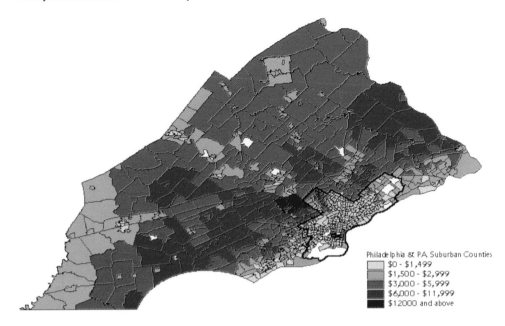

Philadelphia & PA Suburban Counties
- $0 - $1,499
- $1,500 - $2,999
- $3,000 - $5,999
- $6,000 - $11,999
- $12000 and above

Map 4-6. Value of Aggregate Tax Benefits: Philadelphia and Pennsylvania Portion of the Philadelphia MSA, 1989

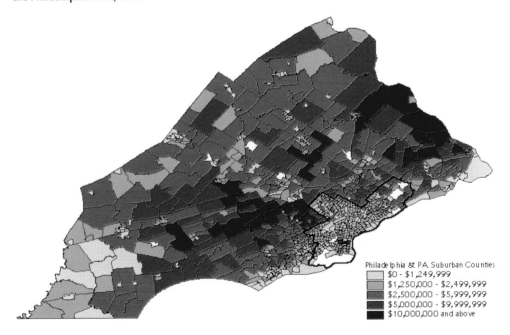

Philadelphia & PA Suburban Counties
- $0 - $1,249,999
- $1,250,000 - $2,499,999
- $2,500,000 - $5,999,999
- $5,000,000 - $9,999,999
- $10,000,000 and above

Map 5-1. Jurisdictional Boundaries of Metropolitan Phoenix, 1997

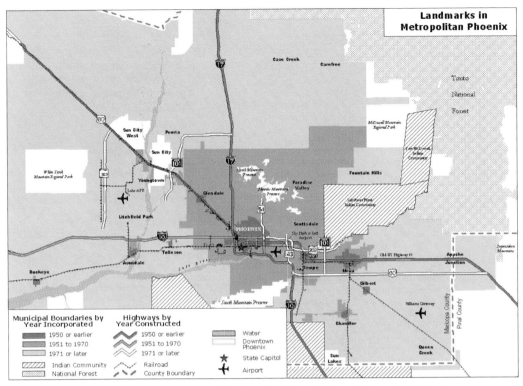

Source: 1999 U.S. Census Bureau. Map prepared by the Arizona State University, IT Research Support Lab - GIS Services.

Map 5-2. Guide to Official Descriptions of Metropolitan Phoenix

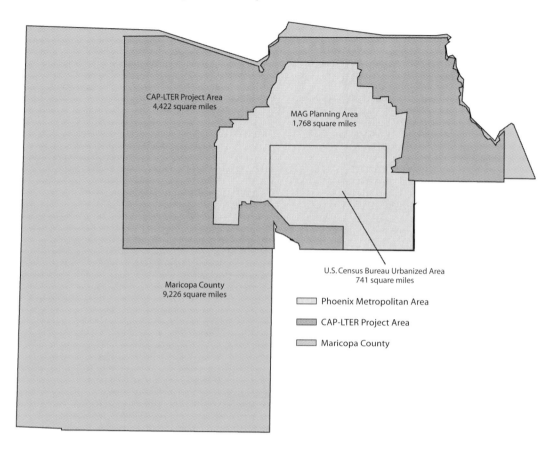

CAP-LTER Project Area
4,422 square miles

MAG Planning Area
1,768 square miles

U.S. Census Bureau Urbanized Area
741 square miles

Maricopa County
9,226 square miles

Phoenix Metropolitan Area

CAP-LTER Project Area

Maricopa County

Map 5-3. Metropolitan Phoenix Freeways

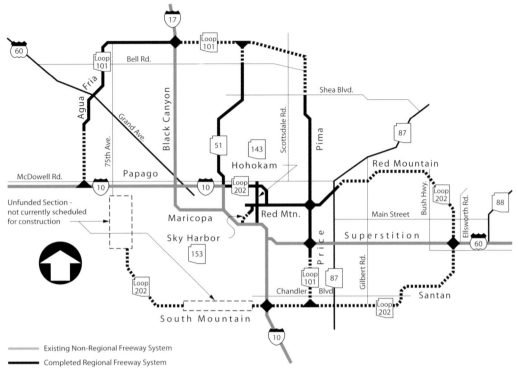

Unfunded Section - not currently scheduled for construction

Legend:
- Existing Non-Regional Freeway System
- Completed Regional Freeway System
- Under Construction or Planned for Construction by 2007

Map 5-4. Percent of Hispanic Population in Metropolitan Phoenix, 2000 (percent)

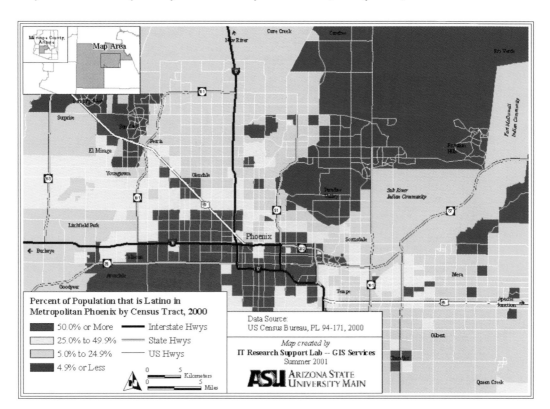

Map 5-5. Employment Concentration in Metropolitan Phoenix

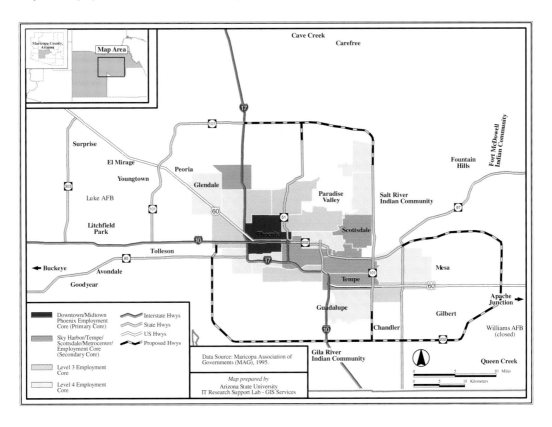

Map 5-6. Land Use Change in Metropolitan Phoenix , 1975–95

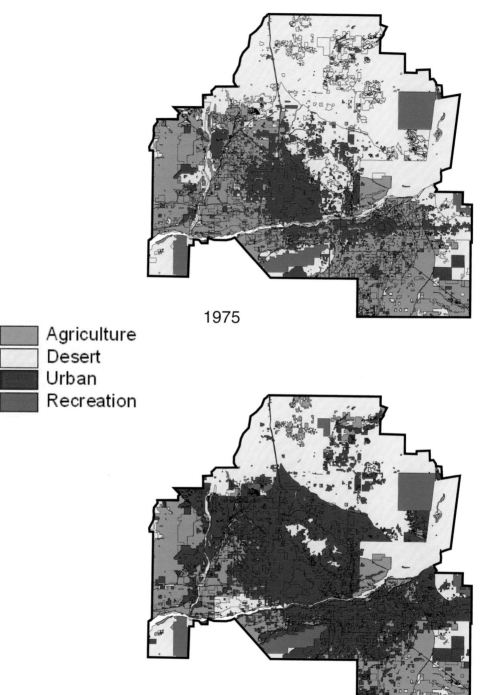

1975

Agriculture
Desert
Urban
Recreation

1995

Map 5-7. School Test Results by District in Metropolitan Phoenix

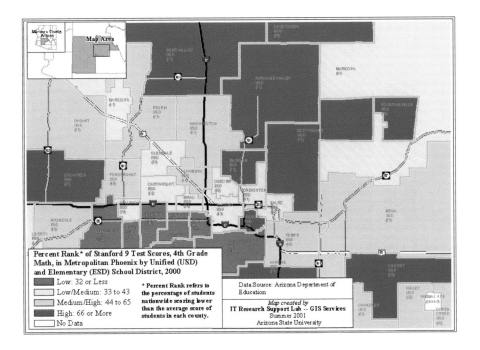

Percent Rank* of Stanford 9 Test Scores, 4th Grade
Math, in Metropolitan Phoenix by Unified (USD)
and Elementary (ESD) School District, 2000

Low: 32 or Less
Low/Medium: 33 to 43
Medium/High: 44 to 65
High: 66 or More
No Data

* Percent Rank refers to
the percentage of students
nationwide scoring lower
than the average score of
students in each county.

Data Source: Arizona Department of
Education

Map created by
IT Research Support Lab -- GIS Services
Summer 2001
Arizona State University

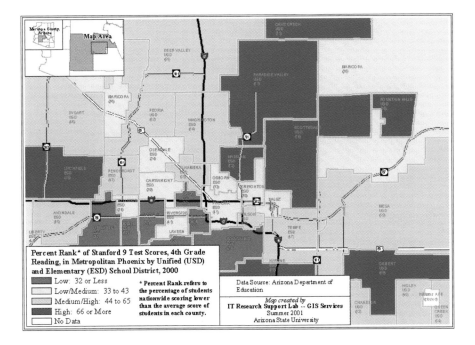

Percent Rank* of Stanford 9 Test Scores, 4th Grade
Reading, in Metropolitan Phoenix by Unified (USD)
and Elementary (ESD) School District, 2000

Low: 32 or Less
Low/Medium: 33 to 43
Medium/High: 44 to 65
High: 66 or More
No Data

* Percent Rank refers to
the percentage of students
nationwide scoring lower
than the average score of
students in each county.

Data Source: Arizona Department of
Education

Map created by
IT Research Support Lab -- GIS Services
Summer 2001
Arizona State University

Map 5-8. Highway Expenditures Have Supported the Region's Core

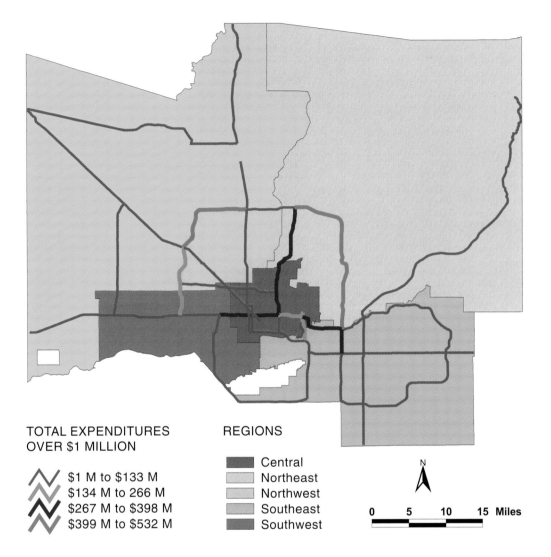

TOTAL EXPENDITURES
OVER $1 MILLION

$1 M to $133 M
$134 M to 266 M
$267 M to $398 M
$399 M to $532 M

REGIONS

Central
Northeast
Northwest
Southeast
Southwest

N

0   5   10   15 Miles

Map 6-1. Major Roads Built in the Pittsburgh Region, 1900–80

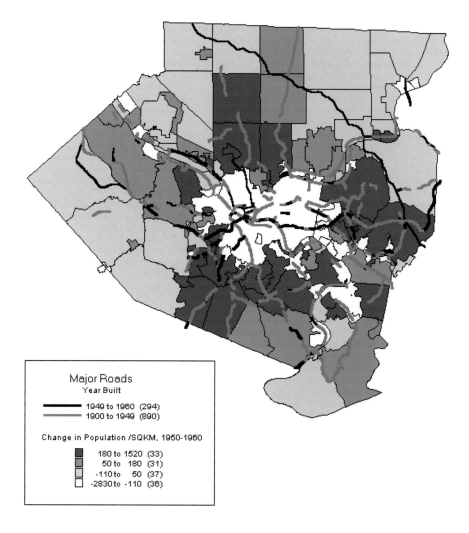

Source: U.S. Census Bureau and road segment data from the Southwestern Pennsylvania Commission.

Map 6-2. Change in Pittsburgh MSA Municipal Population, 1980–2000

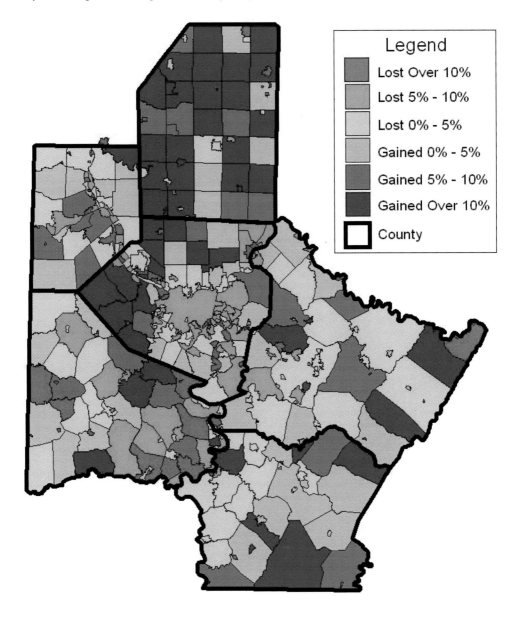

Source: 1990 and 2000 Decennial Census, Bureau of the Census, U.S. Department of Commerce.

Map 6-3. Employment Change by Zip Code in the Pittsburgh MSA, 1998–2002

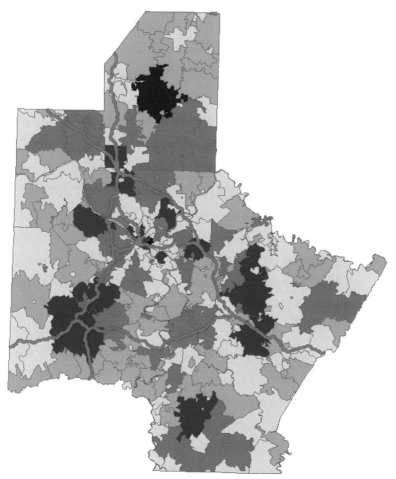

Employment Change by Zip Code, 1998-2002

- -608 - 0
- 1 - 100
- 101 - 1,000
- 1001 - 3,500
- 3,501 - 8,000

Source: Pennsylvania Department of Labor and Industry, Quarterly Census of Employment and Wages, Employment Security (ES-202) database.

Map 6-4. Map of Monongahela Valley Economic Development Strategy

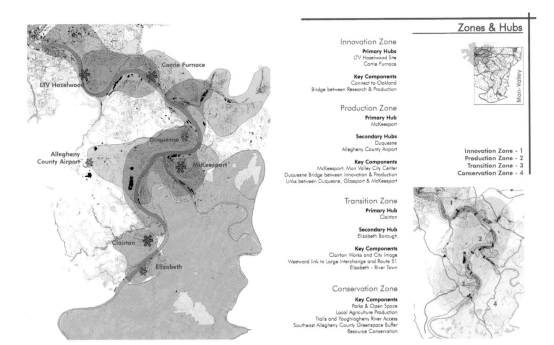

Source: Allegheny County, Department of Economic Development, for the Mon Valley Economic Development Strategy. Tripp Umbach & Associates (lead consultant) and Perkins Eastman Architects.

CHAPTER 3

Los Angeles:

Region by Design

Jennifer Wolch, Pascale Joassart-Marcelli,
Manuel Pastor Jr., and Peter Dreier

How did public policies shape America's most iconoclastic city-region
. . . or did they?

Los Angeles is often viewed as the grand exception in American
urbanism—the city that "breaks the rules." Diverse, fragmented, polarized, and ungovernable, a metropolis without geographic center or unifying civic culture, southern California is often described as having
grown without benefit of planning or policy. But some analysts have
recently challenged these views. Missing from the debate about southern
California is any systematic analysis of how federal, state, and local
public policies have shaped the region, especially during the post–World
War II period.

In this chapter we examine how public policy has contributed to the
region's development.[1] We argue that public policies have often promoted L.A.'s intertwined dilemmas of urban sprawl and the deteriora-

The authors are grateful to the University of Southern California's Southern California
Studies Center (SC2) and the National Science Foundation Program in Geography and
Regional Science for funding the research reported here. We also thank Michael Dear of
SC2 and Bruce Katz of the Brookings Metropolitan Policy program for their advice and
continued support. We are most indebted to our colleagues on the Building the Sustainable
Metropolis project whose work is reported here: Carolyn Aldana, Gary Dymski, Steve
Erie, William Fulton, Eugene Grigsby, Genevieve Giuliano, Enrico Marcelli, Juliet Musso,
and Stephanie Pincetl. Research assistance by Brooke Zobrist and GIS support from Ale-
jandro Alonso was invaluable. Finally, we are grateful to Michael Murashige for his edito-
rial assistance, and to Janet Pack for her comments and suggestions.

1. Hise (1997); Scott and Soja (1996).

tion of older communities, and that, in the process, they have undermined the region's sustainability by creating deep-seated and overlapping social, economic, and environmental problems.[2]

In this way, L.A.'s story is not unlike that of other major metropolitan regions in the United States. But southern California's unique geography—its topography, hazards, and climate, its far-flung polycentric urban form, as well as its demographic diversity, byzantine system of governance, dispersed power structures, and dynamic economy, can make interpreting the region as well as designing and executing specific planning objectives very difficult indeed. Differences between southern California and other metro areas also mean that current nationwide calls for "smart growth" policies may need some alteration to effectively moderate inequities, slow sprawl, and promote more livable communities in the southern California region.

We first sketch the context for post–World War II development in the region, shaped, as it was, by geographic setting, economic base, political culture, and infrastructure. Then we describe the basic regional trends linked to two major and interrelated problems facing the region—metropolitan inequality and sprawl. Third, we assess the role played by public policies implemented at various levels of government. And last, we consider broad policy alternatives that hold promise for reshaping the region's future.

Building Southern California

More than 16 million people live in the 177 cities, five counties (Los Angeles, Orange, Riverside, San Bernardino, and Ventura), and 35,000 square miles that make southern California the second-largest metropolitan area in the United States. Although the urbanized portion is much smaller, it is still large by comparison—about 14,000 square miles. But southern California's natural environment did not predispose it to house such a large population.

The varied and extreme topography, climate, and river systems make it an improbable site for a major urban region.[3] The area's Mediterranean climate produces hot, dry summers and winters with low average

2. Sustainability refers to the ability of economic, social, and political systems to meet the needs of the present without compromising the ability of future generations to meet their own needs through excessive or inappropriate use of natural resources. This analysis is based on a set of detailed case studies by a team of scholars assembled by USC's Southern California Studies Center.

3. Schoenherr (1992).

Table 3-1. Population in Southern California Counties, 1870–2020 (forecast)
Thousands

Year	Los Angeles	Orange	San Bernardino	Riverside	Ventura	Total
1870	15	n.a.	4	n.a.	n.a.	19
1880	33	n.a.	8	n.a.	5	46
1890	101	14	25	n.a.	10	151
1900	170	20	28	18	14	250
1910	504	34	57	35	18	648
1920	936	61	73	50	28	1,150
1930	2,209	119	134	81	55	2,597
1940	2,786	131	161	106	70	3,253
1950	4,152	216	282	170	115	4,934
1960	6,011	709	501	303	199	7,724
1970	7,042	1,421	682	457	378	9,981
1980	7,478	1,932	893	664	530	11,496
1990	8,863	2,411	1,418	1,170	669	14,531
1998	9,214	2,722	1,635	1,479	732	15,782
2020 (forecast)	10,885	3,526	2,456	2,676	924	20,467

Source: California Department of Finance (2004).
n.a. = not available.

precipitation but intense storms that can cause flooding. Beneath the region lie faults that can generate devastating earthquakes.[4] Steep landslide-prone mountains surround the coastal plain, creating a barrier to offshore air currents and causing inversion layers that trap air contaminants, giving Los Angeles its reputation as one of the world's smoggiest cities. And periodic hot, dry winds, topographic features, and fire-adapted vegetation promote wildfires that chronically threaten the region, increasing risks of floods, landslides, and debris flows.[5]

In 1870, only 15,000 people lived in Los Angeles County. But between 1870 and 1880 the population doubled and then tripled to 90,000 between 1880 and 1890 (see table 3-1), following completion of government-subsidized transcontinental rail lines. Most migrants came from the Midwest in search of wealth and the region's edenic environment, while native-born "Californios," Chinese laborers, and other people of color were harshly marginalized from social and economic life.

By 1900, 170,000 people lived in L.A., and as small centers emerged in outlying counties, the population swelled to 250,000. Between 1900

4. Sherman and others (1998); Federal Emergency Management Agency (FEMA), www.fema.gov/nr/nr_0106.htm (1998).
5. Sherman and others (1998).

and 1920 the population soared as a result of agricultural expansion, boosterism and town building, land speculation, and anti-union policies to attract business. In addition, a business-controlled public sector—encouraged by Progressive reforms—engineered large-scale infrastructure projects vital for urban growth.[6] The Los Angeles Aqueduct promoted the development of Los Angeles as an "infinite suburb"; the Metropolitan Water District removed constraints to growth by building the Colorado River aqueduct;[7] flood-control projects "regulated" the area's rivers and permitted floodplain development;[8] and civic leaders built the nation's largest storm drain system with massive federal subsidies to handle urban surface runoff into the Pacific Ocean.[9]

An extensive transportation infrastructure, also fundamental to growth, included a complex system of ports, airports, and surface transportation. The federally subsidized Ports of Los Angeles and Long Beach helped move the regional economy from land speculation toward industry. A decentralized airport system, which initially included several airports linked to aircraft manufacturers and military installations that later became general airports, is now anchored by Los Angeles International Airport (LAX), one of the largest in the world.[10] By the early twentieth century, the nation's largest metropolitan transit system—the Pacific Electric Red and Yellow Car companies—with 1,500 miles of tracks, linked a relatively small downtown to lower-density suburbs. Land speculators created streetcar systems to inflate agricultural land values by improving accessibility to downtown employment. Thus transit infrastructure investments made by private parties, rather than government, led initial waves of exurbanization.

Despite rapid growth in the number of passengers, traction companies often operated under losses and were replaced by automobiles, universally considered the way of the future. Cars reinforced existing patterns of dispersed residence and employment. Between 1919 and

6. Erie (1992).
7. Davis (1995).
8. The Los Angeles Drainage Area Project, for instance, with seventeen debris basins, three major flood control dams, forty-eight miles of channelization, and more than one hundred bridges, kept flood waters at bay and allowed development of the foothills. See Keil and Desfor (1996).
9. Efforts to control or eradicate nature to facilitate development also permeated public policies for dealing with the region's natural hazards. Once declared disaster areas, parts of the city affected by floods, fires, or other "acts of nature" routinely attract public funds to subsidize rebuilding in the very same high-risk zones, and to underwrite additional hazard control projects. See Davis (1996, 1998).
10. SCAG (2000, pp. 76–78).

1929, auto registrations skyrocketed to one car for every three residents. Powerful lobby organizations, the automobile, bus, and tire industries, public officials, and consumers, who perceived cars as more efficient or profitable, all demanded auto infrastructure rather than continued investment in rail transit. By the 1960s, buses had replaced the last Red Cars.

Between the two World Wars, the region's population roughly doubled, with L.A. County reaching 2.7 million. The region recovered faster from the Depression than the rest of the nation. Its key industries, such as automobiles and related sectors, continued to grow, making southern California the largest auto market and biggest branch-plant auto-manufacturing zone in the country. Aircraft and movie production also expanded, and new industries such as chemicals, apparel, and furniture emerged. A continuous belt of factories soon extended from downtown L.A. to the ports at Long Beach and San Pedro. By 1940 manufacturing employment growth rates in Los Angeles were among the highest in the nation. But residential and labor markets became increasingly divided by race, limiting the access of workers of color to the region's better-paying jobs.

World War II (and later conflicts in Korea and Vietnam) prompted the Department of Defense to exploit the region's existing aircraft manufacture and Pacific location, producing a regional concentration of defense-related industries. Population grew to almost 10 million by 1970 as workers migrated in for good defense jobs. The resulting boom in home building urbanized the San Fernando Valley and the outlying counties, especially Orange County, where population grew tenfold between 1940 and 1970. Most of the region's large cities also suburbanized (see map 3-1).

In an effort to protect themselves from rising tax rates and to escape communities of color in the older urban centers, as well as a result of suburbanization, nearly sixty cities incorporated between 1940 and 1960, enabled partly by the ease of contracting with county governments for urban services. From 1970 to 1990, the two eastern counties (Riverside and San Bernardino) quickly urbanized, fueled in part by Proposition 13 and other tax limitations that encouraged land-extensive retail development.[11]

---

11. Proposition 13 limited property tax revenues to cities, stimulating them to seek other revenue sources such as sales taxes and fees. This led many jurisdictions to encourage retail development in order to reap sales tax revenues.

Map 3-1. Phases of Urbanization in the Los Angeles Region, Pre-World War II through 1990

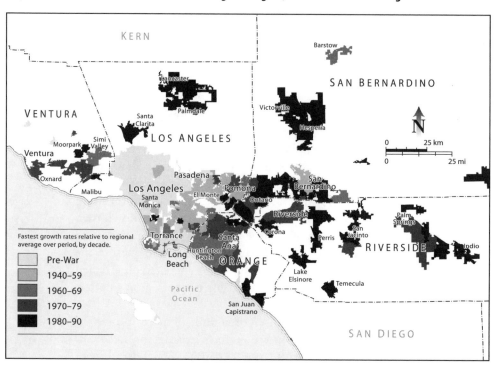

Immigrants from Asia, Europe, and especially Mexico and other parts of Latin America arrived during the 1980s and 1990s. Although some new immigrants settled in central areas, many went directly to suburbs with concentrations of immigrants and ethnic businesses. However, by the 1990s most population growth was due to natural increase rather than immigration.[12] The region is expected to add over 6 million residents and to top 20 million persons by 2020.

Recent growth has also been driven by infrastructure projects. Massively expanded port facilities act as a linchpin for the region's global trade, in turn fueling development of a large, decentralized logistics sector linked to rail facilities and trucking and stimulating warehousing and trade industry expansion. Beginning in the 1960s, the Los Angeles World Airports (LAWA), L.A. city's airport enterprise district, acquired Ontario and Palmdale airports. Major plans are under way to increase LAX's capacity to serve global travelers.[13] By the 1980s, rail transit also

12. SC2 (2001).
13. Erie, Kim, and Freeman (1999).

returned to the public agenda, spurred by L.A.'s downtown business community; the result is a controversial system of fixed and light-rail lines around downtown and to suburbs that cost more than $6 billion and is often described as both inefficient and inequitable.[14]

Since the 1970s the region's political culture has also become increasingly fragmented. The dominance of Los Angeles—both city and county—has waned. Since Proposition 13, subregions and cities have had to compete for jobs and tax revenues. And the region has resisted attempts to strengthen regional government. Until the 1960s, L.A. was governed by a small group of cohesive, conservative elites. Since then, the region's business and corporate leadership has become fragmented and less politically effective. At the same time, counties and cities have become far more racially diverse and economically polarized. Community-based organizations as well as labor unions have grown in number and influence, creating a complex political landscape. Yet in this increasingly mixed political climate within and across cities, the outlying counties do tend to share one political perspective: an aversion to being seen as part of Los Angeles.

Recent Regional Trends

Southern California's population expanded over 40 percent between 1980 and 2000, growing from 11.5 to 16.4 million. Los Angeles, the largest county with more than 9.5 million people, grew by more than 2 million residents (27 percent). Orange County grew by 47 percent and Riverside and San Bernardino Counties—the so-called Inland Empire—more than doubled in population, adding almost 1.7 million. As a result, Los Angeles County has become far less dominant than it was a century earlier. By 2040, population in the outlying counties is expected to equal that of L.A. County, and thus the region's population will be more evenly distributed.

Population Dynamics

The city of Los Angeles is by far the largest municipality in the region, with almost 4 million residents. The region also includes eight other cities with populations over 150,000, the largest being Long Beach (452,905) in L.A. County and Santa Ana (314,990) in Orange County.[15] Most of the fastest-growing cities—some that grew more than 100 per-

14. LAMTA (2001).
15. SCAG (2000, p. 16).

Map 3-2. Population Change in the Los Angeles Region, 1980–2000

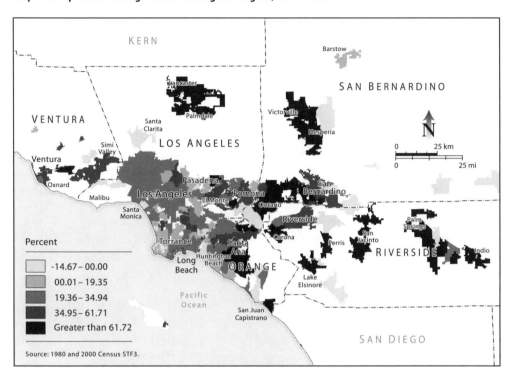

Source: 1980 and 2000 Census STF3.

cent between 1980 and 2000—were on the region's fringe, however (see map 3-2). Only a few older, affluent cities remained stable in terms of population.

Today, as table 3-2 illustrates, southern California exhibits extraordinary racial diversity, and is in fact one of the most diverse in the nation, or a "melting pot metro."[16] The distribution of populations of color shifted significantly between 1980 and 2000, yet remained relatively concentrated, as illustrated for the Latino population in map 3-3. The most affluent communities remain predominately white. In 2000 almost half of the region's cities still had majority white populations, with percentages higher in outlying counties.[17] At the same time, Latino-majority cities in 1980 had become overwhelmingly Latino by 1990, underscoring trends toward increasing racial separation at the municipal level.[18]

16. Frey (2001).
17. Myers and Park (2001).
18. Fulton, Glickfeld, McMurran, and Gin (1999).

Table 3-2. Ethno-Racial and Foreign-Born Composition and Change in Southern California Counties, 1980–2000

Percent

	Los Angeles	Orange	Riverside	San Bernardino	Ventura	Region
	Proportion of population by race or ethnicity in 2000					
White	31.09	51.26	51.04	44.00	56.75	39.01
Black	9.47	1.50	5.98	8.79	1.79	7.33
Asian	11.81	13.48	3.57	4.57	5.24	10.27
Latino	44.56	30.76	36.21	39.16	33.42	40.30
Other	3.06	3.00	3.20	3.48	2.80	3.09
	Percentage point change, 1980–2000					
White	−21.78	−26.91	−22.87	−28.99	−15.64	−21.79
Black	−0.26	0.64	4.03	6.06	0.35	0.99
Asian	7.43	10.62	3.04	3.78	3.26	7.00
Latino	22.86	20.70	28.16	29.46	18.39	23.47
Other	1.86	1.96	2.53	2.56	1.85	2.01
	Percent foreign-born					
1980	22.26	13.31	9.96	7.70	12.67	18.50
2000	36.24	29.86	19.01	18.64	20.70	30.95
Change (1980–2000)	13.97	16.55	9.04	10.94	8.03	12.45

Source: Census (STF3), 1980; (SF4), 2000.

These trends must be understood alongside immigration trends. By 1990 the region was home to almost a quarter of the nation's immigrants.[19] More than one in four residents were foreign-born, more than half arrived after 1985, and 80 percent emigrated from Asia or Latin America. In Los Angeles County by 1990, one in three residents was foreign-born.[20] Poverty rates among immigrants, especially new immigrants, increased between 1980 and 1990.[21]

Land Consumption and Population Density

Despite southern California's image as a sprawling metropolis, land consumption rates have been relatively low compared to other metro-

19. Myers (1996).

20. Studies of the distribution of adult undocumented Latino immigrants in Los Angeles County reveal their high concentration in the older core communities, but also in the San Fernando Valley and Pomona in the eastern San Gabriel Valley. In these places they constituted between 15 and 30 percent of the total population. See Marcelli (1998, pp. 17–20).

21. Myers (1999, p. 157).

Map 3-3. Latino Population Change in the Los Angeles Region, 1980–2000

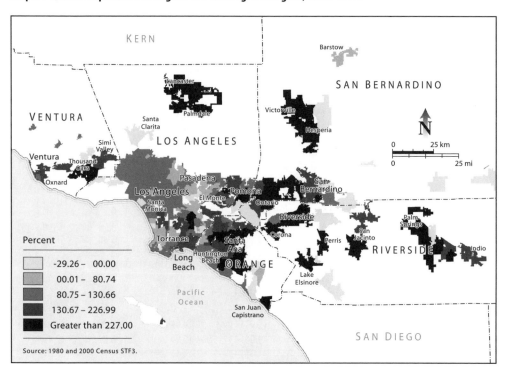

Source: 1980 and 2000 Census STF3.

politan areas, and population densities are high, prompting descriptions of "dense sprawl."[22] Between 1970 and 1990 the urbanized area increased faster than population, as determined using the U.S. Census definition of "urbanized area" based on population density.[23] But a better definition is one based on land actually devoted to urban uses, as measured by the National Resources Inventory (NRI).[24] Using this measure of urbanized land, between 1982 and 1992 regional population grew by almost 25 percent, while urbanized land increased only about 20 percent. Southern California was one of only two large metro areas where population grew faster than urbanized land.[25] By 1997 the Los

22. This term was coined by William Fulton.

23. Orfield (2000, p. 31).

24. This study measures density as the population of a metro area divided by the amount of urbanized land in that area; urbanized land, in turn, is measured as actual land devoted to urban settlement as determined by the National Resources Inventory (NRI), not as a function of population density (the basis of census definitions of "urbanized land"). See Fulton, Pendall, Nguyen, and Harrison (2001).

25. Ibid.

Map 3-4. Change in Population Density in the Los Angeles Region, 1980–98

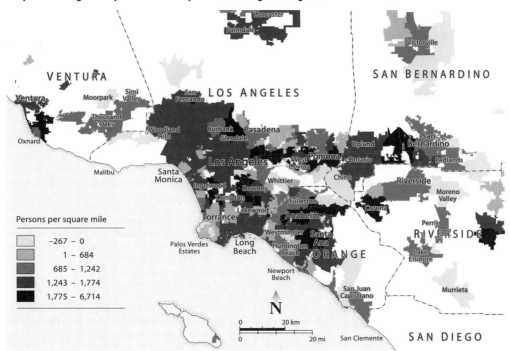

Persons per square mile

▢	−267 – 0
▨	1 – 684
▨	685 – 1,242
▨	1,243 – 1,774
■	1,775 – 6,714

Angeles region had attained a density of 8.31 persons per urbanized acre—higher than the New York region.[26] Thus, although in 1980 population per square mile ranged from a high of 1,855 in L.A. County to lows of 90.8 in Riverside and 44.5 in San Bernardino Counties, a large portion of these two counties is Mojave Desert, so populated parts of these outlying counties were already quite dense. Densities subsequently increased dramatically throughout the region (see map 3-4).

Residential development in outlying areas such as Orange County has become increasingly dense, now up to about ten to twelve units per acre, from the traditional ratio of six or seven units per acre. More people live in the older urban areas, however, mainly because of larger households among immigrant families and doubling up by the poor. Between 1990 and 2000, household size in the region increased approximately 7 percent, from roughly 2.9 to about 3.1 persons per household.[27] Density in the "hub" cities of central Los Angeles County increased dramatically,

26. Ibid. (p. 6).
27. SC2 (2001).

from about 7,500 persons per square mile in 1975 to about 12,000 persons per square mile in 1995.[28]

This trend is likely to continue because, despite relatively high densities, the sheer size of the region and its rapid population growth meant that more than 400,000 acres of land were urbanized between 1982 and 1997,[29] leading to a shortage of developable land in the region. Significant portions of undeveloped land are either too steep or ecologically sensitive, or are farmlands, state and national forests, or lands protected by conservation efforts through the Endangered Species Act.

Housing

Southern California's housing stock totaled 5.3 million units in 1990. Over time, as household size grew, more intensive use of older housing has resulted in an increase in substandard housing and rapidly escalating rates of overcrowding. While the housing stock grew quickly during the 1980s, recession in the early 1990s slowed new construction until the mid-1990s.

Between 1980 and 1998, growth in total housing units in Los Angeles County lagged far behind population growth (13 percent versus 28 percent) and led to overcrowding and severe affordability problems. In 1998 the average southern California household spent 37 percent of pre-tax wages ($15,500) on housing (one of the highest figures in the nation). About 14 percent of households were burdened with severe housing costs (twice the national average) and 15 percent suffered from overcrowding (twice as high a percentage as any other major metropolitan area). The homeownership rate (49 percent) is lower than in any U.S. metro area except New York and well below California and U.S. averages. According to the National Low-Income Housing Coalition, a worker must earn two to three times the minimum wage to afford an average one-bedroom apartment in metropolitan Los Angeles. Almost half of poor renters must pay either more than half their income for rent or live in an extremely inadequate housing unit.[30] Again, this is one of the highest figures in the country.[31]

28. Fulton, Glickfeld, McMurran, and Gin (1999).
29. Fulton, Pendall, Nguyen, and Harrison (2001, p. 5).
30. The city of Los Angeles has especially severe problems with inadequate housing units. The Blue Ribbon Citizens' Committee on Slum Housing findings, released July 28, 1997, reported more than 150,000 substandard apartments in the city of Los Angeles—about one out of seven rental units in the city. See http://www.cityofla.org/LAHD/slumhsg.pdf.
31. SC2 (2001).

Map 3-5. Rent as a Percentage of Income in the Los Angeles Region, 1999

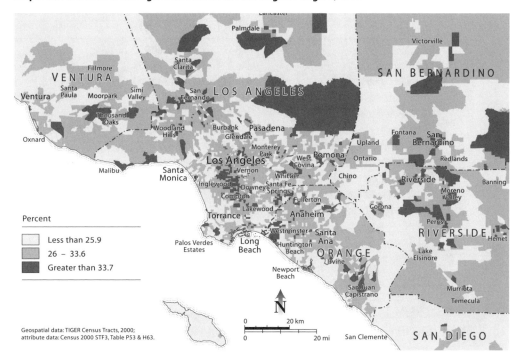

Percent

- Less than 25.9
- 26 – 33.6
- Greater than 33.7

Geospatial data: TIGER Census Tracts, 2000;
attribute data: Census 2000 STF3, Table P53 & H63.

The affordability index—the share of households that can afford a median-priced home—had fallen to 34 percent in Orange County and 39 percent in L.A. County by the end of the 1990s.[32] Although rental affordability—measured by the percentage of income spent on rent—was worse in central Los Angeles and Orange counties, affordability problems were still widespread (see map 3-5). According to the American Housing Survey, for example, in L.A. County, 45 percent of all renters paid more than they could afford in 1985, and this share rose to 49 percent by 1995—before the post-recession rent escalations.

Industrial Expansion

Southern California's economy, as measured by employment, more than tripled in size during the second half of the twentieth century. Like the United States overall, postwar southern California was characterized by rapid growth of durable manufacturing industries such as automobiles, tires, aerospace, and defense. The 1970s brought dramatic

32. SCAG (2000, pp. 49–51).

Table 3-3. Industry Composition in Southern California, 1950–90
Number employed

Industry	1950	1970	1990
Agriculture	88,571	60,900	126,718
Construction	146,232	195,500	465,731
Manufacturing	459,115	1,012,000	1,350,376
Transportation and public utilities	150,301	248,900	458,758
Wholesale trade	98,327	173,700	340,182
Retail trade	362,836	641,100	1,095,395
Financial and real estate services	102,008	227,900	541,247
Business services	74,298	174,200	420,764
Personal services	138,848	158,500	245,970
Professional services	199,499	673,800	1,425,524
Public administration	96,949	198,600	232,127
Other	68,721	91,500	194,104
Total	1,985,706	3,856,600	6,896,897

Source: 1960, 1970, and 1990 Public Use Microdata Sample (PUMS) from Scott (1996, tables 8-1, 8-2, and 8-3, pp. 217–19).

changes, with an increase in services (especially business services) and a decline in the share of manufacturing (see table 3-3)—though less dramatic than in other parts of the country because of a new wave of reindustrialization of mostly nondurable manufacture and trade. With this shift, middle-class, typically unionized, blue-collar manufacturing jobs were replaced by low-wage, nonunionized labor, thereby increasing regional poverty and inequality.

The early 1990s recession hobbled southern California's economy. With almost 500,000 jobs lost between 1990 and 1994, this drastic downturn exacerbated the proliferation of low-wage work and increased income disparities. Only in mid-1997 did the region recover its prerecession job level.[33]

Accompanying this restructuring, economic activity shifted from central cities and old industrial zones to outer suburbs. Between 1950 and 1970, manufacturing spread southeast, eventually reaching northern Orange County and stimulating the first wave of suburbanization. Later, in the 1980s and 1990s, while new technology and business and financial services clusters developed in Orange and Ventura counties and in the northwestern part of San Fernando Valley, traditional blue-collar areas of southeastern Los Angeles County declined rapidly. Meanwhile,

33. California Employment Development Department (2004).

Table 3-4. Annual Employment by County, 1983–2003

Number employed

Year	Los Angeles	Orange	Riverside and San Bernardino	Riverside	San Bernardino	Ventura
1983	3,549,400	878,300	465,700	...	...	181,200
1984	3,670,200	941,300	495,700	...	...	188,700
1985	3,765,300	987,000	536,700	...	...	197,600
1986	3,865,200	1,030,600	574,400	...	...	205,200
1987	3,964,700	1,077,800	610,900	...	...	217,300
1988	4,046,400	1,138,100	...	282,600	365,100	229,700
1989	4,124,800	1,164,500	...	295,900	393,200	237,800
1990	4,149,500	1,179,000	...	321,700	413,400	247,000
1991	3,992,600	1,150,800	...	322,700	418,900	246,000
1992	3,813,600	1,133,300	...	325,800	425,700	244,100
1993	3,716,800	1,122,700	...	332,000	423,800	245,000
1994	3,710,400	1,133,800	...	341,500	431,300	251,100
1995	3,754,500	1,158,000	...	355,300	446,400	254,300
1996	3,795,700	1,191,100	...	366,300	458,500	255,300
1997	3,872,000	1,240,700	...	388,400	474,800	260,000
1998	3,951,300	1,305,700	...	412,200	491,600	270,000
1999	4,010,200	1,352,500	...	441,600	518,700	281,100
2000	4,079,800	1,396,500	...	466,500	543,600	294,300
2001	4,082,000	1,420,800	...	484,300	566,400	299,000
2002	4,034,600	1,411,000	...	508,900	575,100	301,000
2003	3,998,100	1,432,400	...	526,700	581,400	304,000

Source: California Employment Development Department (2004).

Riverside and San Bernardino counties benefited from an increased rate of industrialization and rapid retail growth. Not surprisingly, given the accelerated population growth and housing development in those areas, construction also increased in the four outlying counties, especially Riverside.

The early 1990s recession affected the region in different ways, with Los Angeles and, to a lesser extent, Orange County suffering the biggest losses (see table 3-4). Although the majority of the region's jobs are still found in Los Angeles County, an increasing share is located in outlying areas. Indeed, the Los Angeles–Long Beach Primary Metropolitan Statistical Area had one of the nation's most decentralized employment patterns by the late 1990s, with only about 7 percent of all jobs located within a three-mile radius of downtown (compared to about 45 percent in New York, 26 percent in Boston, and 19 percent in Chicago). Even

Map 3-6. Job Density in the Los Angeles Region, 1990

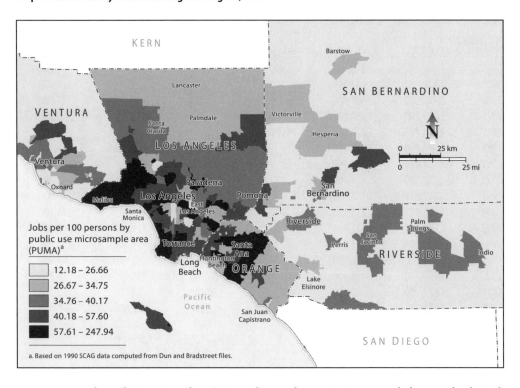

a. Based on 1990 SCAG data computed from Dun and Bradstreet files.

though Los Angeles County hosts the nation's seventh largest high-tech industrial base, measured in terms of per capita high-tech jobs, Orange and Ventura Counties surpass Los Angeles in average per capita high-tech output: $9,180 and $5,081 compared with L.A.'s $4,520.[34] This suggests a concentration of high-tech activity in suburban areas and, indeed, in the early 1990s many areas of Los Angeles County lost high-tech employment to outlying counties.

Despite high unemployment in the region's older areas, job density (jobs per 100 persons) remains high, especially in inner Los Angeles County and northern Orange County (see map 3-6). In some areas the number of jobs available exceeds the total population. However, these area's neighborhoods often suffer from high poverty because the jobs available do not correspond to local residents' skills and job growth is slow or even negative.[35] In downtown and East Los Angeles, for example, there were more than 200 jobs per 100 residents, but total jobs

34. U.S. Conference of Mayors and National Association of Counties (2000).
35. Pastor and Marcelli (2000).

decreased by almost one-fifth between 1990 and 1994. This contrasts with areas in outlying counties, where job density was often below fifty jobs per 100 persons while job growth was over 30 percent. Surprisingly, the former central areas continued to experience rapid population growth (although at a lower percentage rate) than outlying counties, leading to a growing absolute spatial mismatch between labor supply and demand in those zones.

Inequality, Poverty, and Welfare

In the 1980s and 1990s, southern California experienced both the best and worst with respect to the well-being of workers and households. Regional median household income rose from $18,730 in 1980 to $37,302 in 1990, but was largely unchanged in the first half of the 1990s.

INCOME INEQUALITY. An analysis by Pastor shows that, in 1980, median household incomes were substantially higher in Orange and Ventura Counties ($22,557 and $21,236 respectively) than in Los Angeles County and the Inland Empire (from $16,000 to more than $17,000).[36] Over the decade these differences increased. Despite the recession, by 1995 Orange County's estimated median household income reached $48,701, while incomes in Los Angeles declined between 1990 and 1995.[37] Median income for households in the top 20 percent of the income distribution in 1995–98 was more than seven times that for the bottom 40 percent (see table 3-5). Moreover, the income gap grew over the 1990s despite economic recovery. While the top 20 percent of the income distribution added over $5,000 in income (in 1998 dollars) between the two periods, the lowest 40 percent of the distribution actually saw a decline in their real incomes.

36. Pastor (2000).

37. This analysis uses annual data from the March Supplements of the Current Population Survey (aggregated into a 1991–94 period in which the region experienced a sharp recession and a 1995–98 period characterized by postrecession job growth). We compare median income for those households in the top 20 percent of the region's income distribution with the median household income of those in the bottom 40 percent. One standard way to track distribution involves calculating the share of total income accruing to the top tier of households and comparing this with the share accruing to the bottom tier. Unfortunately, in the 1991–94 period, because the highest incomes in the region are arbitrarily "top-coded," calculated shares would understate the income going to the wealthiest residents in those years. In the second period, the top code is the average of the highest incomes; this yields a correct calculation for total income accruing to the wealthiest, but comparing either shares or averages in the two periods is problematic. Choosing wide income bands and focusing on medians sidesteps this problem.

Table 3-5. Median Household Income by Selected Group in the SCAG Area, 1990s

Average of median income in 1998 dollars

Group	1991–94	1995–98
Bottom 40 percent	15,180	14,807
Top 20 percent	101,812	106,839
Ratio (top 20:bottom 40)	6.71	7.22
Los Angeles County		
White	44,708	47,577
Black	25,918	26,804
Latino	24,983	24,742
Asian	42,822	40,206
All	34,668	35,152
Rest of SCAG		
White	49,834	48,094
Black	35,999	30,593
Latino	31,317	32,460
Asian	40,580	49,278
All	42,791	43,001

Source: U.S. Census Bureau, Current Population Survey, March Supplements (1991–98).

Racial income inequality grew during the 1990s, especially between white and African American and Latino households. Asian households, despite poverty rates roughly twice those of white households, are not far behind in median income, in part because Asian households tend to be larger, with greater numbers of income earners, but low per capita income. Although regionwide median household income rose by nearly $1,000 for whites, it rose only modestly for Asians and fell for African Americans and Latinos. Los Angeles County has the greatest racial income inequality.

The transformation of southern California's economy and the resulting bifurcation of employment opportunities underlie these widening income gaps. Specifically, three sorts of "mismatches" help to explain these dynamics: a skills mismatch between job seekers' skills and the available employment, a spatial mismatch between job seekers residing in job-poor areas and the location of job growth, and a social mismatch between job seekers and the social networks that lead to higher-wage employment.[38] Latinos and African Americans disproportionately live in

38. While the higher educational attainment of whites helps to explain some of the racial disparity in income, it does not fully explain the growing disparities because the educational levels of the workforce have been rising over time.

areas where the early 1990s recession caused the highest job losses (mostly L.A. County), while whites dominate in areas where job growth continued (mostly Orange, Riverside, and Ventura Counties). Recent research shows that social networks pay off for southern California's white workers but do less for other groups. Though Latinos often have contacts to secure employment, these contacts typically lead them to low-wage work that does not always reflect their skills and provides limited upward mobility.

The burst of small businesses throughout the region may drive growth, but such firms rarely pay high wages or provide health insurance. For example, the percentage of households in which at least one member has health insurance declined from 66.3 percent between 1990 and 1994 to 63.9 percent between 1995 and 1998, with the rate in L.A. County nearly 9 percent lower than that in the rest of the region.

POVERTY. Poverty increased during the 1980s in all southern California counties except Ventura. Official poverty rates were particularly high in L.A. County—over 15 percent in 1990—but the Inland Empire also had double-digit rates. Poverty rates fell marginally over the decade in a few cities, with the sharpest drops in several San Gabriel Valley and southwest Riverside County cities, formerly rural areas that suburbanized over the decade. But far more cities experienced increased poverty rates. And disturbingly, poverty also rose among working people. Whereas in 1990 over 52 percent of the poor lived in households with at least one full-time worker, by 1998 this number had risen to 57 percent. By 2000, a quarter or more of the population of many of the region's cities were living below 150 percent of the federal poverty threshold (see map 3-7).

Moreover, poverty concentration increased between 1980 and 1990. One standard concentration measure—the proportion of poor living in high-poverty tracts—shows that 41 percent of people below 150 percent of the official poverty threshold lived in high-poverty census tracts in southern California in 1990, compared with 33 percent in 1980.[39] Percentages were predictably higher in Los Angeles County, where the proportion grew from 41 percent in 1980 to 48 percent in 1990. Despite the fact that highly concentrated poverty is less common in the other counties, it nevertheless increased rapidly between 1980 and 1990, and increased again between 1990 and 2000.

39. High poverty areas are defined as those tracts with proportions of population in poverty greater than one standard deviation above the mean regional poverty rate, or above 38 percent. See Jargowsky and Bane (1991).

Map 3-7. Poverty Rate in the Los Angeles Region, 2000 (by city)

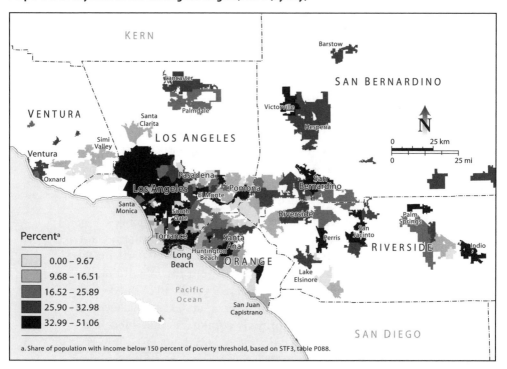

a. Share of population with income below 150 percent of poverty threshold, based on STF3, table P088.

The passage of the Personal Responsibility and Work Opportunity Act in August of 1996 drastically contracted the public safety net. The impact of these changes in welfare policy is most severe in Los Angeles County, especially central Los Angeles, where most welfare recipients reside. The next downturn in the economy will likely have a devastating impact on new entrants to the labor force, leading to greater unemployment but no safety net. Given welfare reforms and a severe shortage of affordable housing, homelessness is a serious problem in southern California.

Fiscal Characteristics of the Region's Cities

Like many other metropolitan areas, southern California has a highly fragmented governmental structure. In 1997 the region was made up of five counties, 177 cities, and more than 1,100 special districts. The fiscal choices available to local lawmakers are severely constrained by state constitutional restrictions, most notably property tax restrictions contained in 1978 "tax revolt" measure Proposition 13.[40] As a result of

40. Musso (2004).

Proposition 13 and subsequent measures, the property tax is effectively limited to 1 percent of market value, assessed value growth is capped, and voter approval is required for any tax increases.[41] Revenues from the fixed 1 percent property tax rate are allocated by the county to cities and other local governments primarily on the basis of state formulas created in 1978. The constrained fiscal environment raises questions about whether the fiscal system promotes efficient service delivery and a reasonably equitable distribution of regional fiscal resources, and whether cities in the region have sufficient fiscal capacity—the hypothetical ability of a local government to generate revenues for public services relative to the need for such services.[42] These questions are especially important for poor cities that suffer from a combination of a low tax base with greater needs associated with poverty concentration, and aging infrastructure and housing stock.

EFFICIENCY, EQUITY, AND THE CHANGING COMPOSITION OF CITY FINANCES. Musso shows that between 1982 and 1997 reforms allowed cities to become *less* reliant on traditional municipal financing sources (such as sales and property taxes) and *more* reliant on other taxing sources and fees (see table 3-6).[43] Fees and utility taxes are more efficient than sales taxes because they are user-based, cannot be "exported" to nonresidents, and do not lead to perverse land-use incentives. However, because they are regressive they may exacerbate income disparities.[44] The reduced dependency of cities on sales tax revenues, however, has not eliminated fierce competition among cities for auto malls and other sales tax revenue producers, hence keeping the practice of fiscal zoning common in the region. Cities in Orange County receive a somewhat higher share of revenue from sales taxes than the rest of the region, and in Los Angeles County dependence on the sales tax is much more variable.

FISCAL CAPACITY AND DISPARITY. Low fiscal capacity can contribute to disinvestment in physical infrastructure and human capital

41. An increase in special-purpose taxes, those that are earmarked for particular purposes, requires two-thirds voter approval. General-purpose taxes, those that are not identified with a particular use, require majority voter approval. Because the property tax rate is restricted to 1 percent, the common bases for increased taxes include transient occupancy, business taxes, and utility taxes.

42. ACIR (1987). Also see Ladd and Yinger (1989).

43. Musso (2004).

44. To the extent that cities have homogeneous populations, such user fees would not have a regressive impact *within* a city. Nonetheless, income variation *across* cities would imply that fees have a regressive regional impact.

Table 3-6. Source of City Revenue in Southern California, 1982 and 1997
Percent

Source	1982	1997
Property tax	13	11
Sales tax	17	12
Other taxes	15	20
Fees	14	24
Federal aid	12	9
State aid	10	11
Other revenue	19	14

Source: California State Controller's Office, Annual Reports of Financial Transactions Concerning Cities of California, 1982 and 1997.

and lead to cycles of economic decline. Within metropolitan regions, fiscal disparities can fuel the flight of firms and wealthier residents from high-tax or service-poor cities to fiscally advantaged suburbs. These fiscal incentives further encourage segregation and increase the gaps in fiscal capacity between the higher-income coastal counties and the Inland Empire. Substantial fiscal disparities can also be horizontally inequitable to the extent that residents of jurisdictions with lower fiscal resources pay a higher proportion of their income for a given public service package or receive a poorer package of services given a particular tax rate.[45]

In 1982 per capita fiscal capacity was $502 for the region, with a low of $384 in San Bernardino and a high of $516 in both Los Angeles and Orange Counties. For the purposes of this analysis, Musso assessed total fiscal capacity by calculating a "representative" income burden measure for discretionary revenues to which intergovernmental grants, sales tax revenues, and property tax revenues were added.[46] Conceptually this index measures the revenue a city would raise if it were to collect discretionary taxes, fees, and other revenues at a percentage of personal income equal to the regional average rate, adjusted upward for the intergovernmental grants, sales tax, and property tax allocated to the municipality under state law.[47]

45. Ladd and Yinger (1994).
46. Musso (2001).
47. Because of data deficiencies Musso was unable to take into account nonresidential economic activity, or the extent to which taxes are exported out of the jurisdiction. Differences in the nonresidential property tax base across communities will be reflected in the measure to the extent that they are reflected in higher property tax allocations.

In the 1980s and 1990s per capita incomes of older coastal and hill-side communities increased while the interior counties of San Bernardino and Riverside attracted middle- and working-class residential growth that generates a lower tax base. Thus, by 1997, the average per capita fiscal capacity for the region had risen to $641, with the largest increases having occurred in Orange, Los Angeles, and Ventura Counties. Conversely, fast-growing San Bernardino and Riverside dropped considerably ($449 and $477 respectively), defying the conventional wisdom of "trickle-down" exurbanization by which newly developing suburban communities are wealthier and have higher capacity to provide basic services.[48]

Examining fiscal capacity and fiscal effort (the ratio of actual revenues to fiscal capacity) for cities in the region reveals a similar pattern, with the older coastal suburbs generally enjoying relatively high fiscal capacity and low effort.[49] This advantage results from high household incomes alongside lower levels of poverty and newer and better-maintained housing stock, streets, city facilities, and basic infrastructure—all of which reduce the costs of service provision (see map 3-8). In contrast, poorer, older suburbs in central Los Angeles County, as well as some developing Inland Empire residential communities, have relatively low fiscal capacity but high fiscal effort. These older economically distressed cities, with large poor populations, deteriorating housing stock, and aging facilities and infrastructure, must exert disproportionate fiscal effort just to maintain adequate urban services, while newer working-class cities in the Inland Empire may have inadequate fiscal capacity to provide new infrastructure to support population growth.

Transportation

Between 1980 and 2000 the region made major transportation investments, including a subway, light-rail lines, and an interurban commuter rail system. Most of the largest projects were located in Orange

48. Reinforcing this picture of growing fiscal disparities among cities, the Gini coefficient, which varies from 0 (if fiscal capacity is completely evenly distributed) to 1 (if one city captured all of the fiscal capacity for the region), increased during the study period, from 0.16 in 1982 to 0.20 in 1997.

49. To the extent that taxes are exported in part or in whole, as they would be if taxes on nonresidential economic activity were shifted to consumers, fiscal burden will be shifted outside of the jurisdiction. It should be noted that the communities experiencing substantial fiscal effort, older suburbs and newly developing communities, are primarily residential and hence are probably not able to export much of their fiscal burden.

Map 3-8. Fiscal Capacity and Effort in the Los Angeles Region, 1997

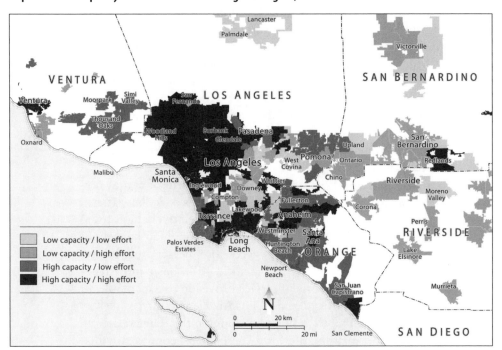

County, along its north-south axis, and in northern L.A. County and the Inland Empire.[50]

Additions to transportation system capacity and population growth fueled part of the increase in total auto vehicle miles traveled (VMT) as well as per capita VMT. After small reductions following the early 1990s recession and new capacity expansions, regionwide daily VMT grew by 19 percent between 1994 and 1997. This increase dramatically outstripped population growth as auto users drove more miles.[51] Between 1982 and 1999 VMT increased by 65 percent in Los Angeles and 123 percent in the Inland Empire, while over the same period in those areas population increased 27 and 56 percent respectively. In Los Angeles County, hours of delay per capita per year rose from thirty-one in 1982 to fifty-six in 1999, resulting in increased air pollution and more than 1.1 million gallons of wasted fuel, for a total delay-related

50. As part of these investments, 500 miles of high-occupancy vehicle (HOV) lanes were constructed by 1999, mostly in southern L.A. and Orange Counties. See SCAG (2000, pp. 73–76).

51. See SCAG (2000, pp. 73–76).

cost of almost \$12.5 billion—the highest in the nation. In the Inland Empire, annual hours of delay per person rose from six in 1982 to thirty-eight in 1999.

At the same time, total public transit trips declined from their 1985 high, despite a 12 percent increase during the 1990s. And the rate of transit use fell from thirty-four transit trips per thousand population in 1990 to thirty-two in 1997, despite heavy investment in transit in L.A. County.[52] By century's end, 93 percent of all regional commuters were still using cars.[53] The reasons for the stubborn dominance of the car in L.A. despite investments in transit are complex (as they are in many other urban regions). Radial transit systems focused on downtown cores do not adequately serve a polycentric metropolis burdened by severe jobs/housing imbalances; many bus systems are overcrowded, outdated, and perceived as unsafe; and segregation of land uses in relatively low-density suburbs makes driving unavoidable.

Environmental Quality

Industrialization, vehicular traffic, climate, and topography have all contributed to the deterioration of the region's ambient environment. By the mid-1970s, the region's air quality exceeded federal lead standards for the entire year and federal ozone standards for almost half the year. Despite recent reductions in both mobile and point-source emissions, the South Coast Air Basin (which excludes only Ventura County) remains the nation's most polluted. The region also has pollution "hot spots," especially near large-scale refineries and chemical plants. Moreover, the region exports its air pollution by appropriating massive amounts of energy from more than twenty U.S. and Canadian power plants, such as the coal-fired Navajo Generating Plant in Arizona, which emits 250 tons of sulfur dioxide daily. Air toxics, diesel emissions linked to expansion of heavy-duty trucking, the popularity of sport utility vehicles, and high traffic densities all threaten the region's environment.[54]

Widespread fears about groundwater contamination arose in the 1970s and 1980s when contaminated wells in the San Fernando and San Gabriel Valleys were declared federal Superfund sites. By the late 1990s, 40 percent of southern California's wells were contaminated.[55] Well contamination and air pollution are both closely related to the sheer volume

52. SCAG (1999, p. 71).
53. SCAG (2000, pp. 73–76).
54. Hricko, Preston, Witt, and Peters (1999).
55. SC2 (2001).

of solid waste the region produces—50,000 tons of garbage per day in Los Angeles County alone. Although landfilled solid waste declined during the early 1990s recession, volumes subsequently increased as the region recovered. Many cities have not complied with the state's 1989 Integrated Waste Management Act, which mandated a 25 percent reduction in the 1990 levels of solid waste by 1995 and a 50 percent reduction by 2000.[56] As in many metropolitan areas, illegal dumping and seepage of toxic wastes from industrial facilities and storage tanks contaminate groundwater and soils, leaving vacant "brownfields" too costly to clean up. Although the health effects of many environmental contaminants are not completely understood, failure to meet federal standards for ozone and fine particulates is estimated to cost the region $9.4 billion in health-related expenses annually. The entire region faces unhealthful exposure, but the probability of dying from air pollution varies across counties, from an estimated 55 deaths for every 100,000 residents in Orange County to 79 in L.A. County and 122 in the Inland Empire.[57] According to Morello-Frosch, Pastor, and Sadd, people of color have higher lifetime cancer risks due to air pollution from all sources than whites (64 versus 49 deaths for every 100,000).[58] Race is consistently related to the distribution of risks, even when controlling for income and residential location near industrial, commercial, and transportation land uses. This suggests that people of color are more apt to live near more polluting land uses, such as freeways with high volumes of diesel traffic and heavy emitters of industrial toxic waste (see figure 3-1).

Poor air and water quality also severely damage plant and animal communities. By 1995 only 16 percent of the region's wilderness remained as a result of urbanization.[59] Only 10 percent of the state's species-rich coastal sage scrub habitats, once prevalent in southern California, remain. Similarly, local wildlife populations were decimated by lost habitat and blocked movement corridors.[60] Salmon, antelope, and grizzly bears are locally extirpated, while species such as brown pelicans, gnatcatchers, and Stephen's kangaroo rats are severely endangered by pollution or development.[61] In Los Angeles County alone, there were

---

56. SCAG (2000, p. 58).
57. SCAG (2000, pp. 55–58).
58. Morello-Frosch, Pastor, and Sadd (2001, table 2, p. 564).
59. Davis (1996, p. 179).
60. Wolch, Gullo, and Lassiter (1997).
61. Nichols and Young (1991); Beatley (1994).

Figure 3-1. Estimated Lifetime Cancer Risk from Ambient Hazardous Air Pollutant Exposures, Southern California, 1990

Lifetime cancer risk per 100,000 population (percent)

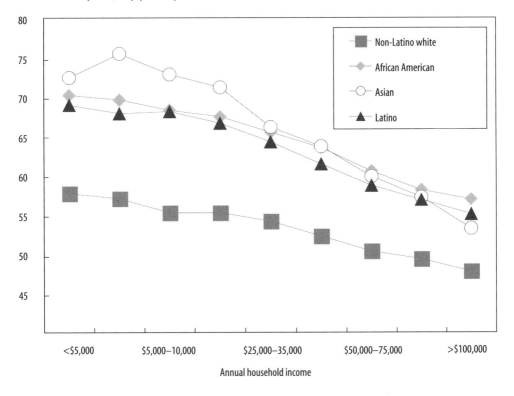

Annual household income

twenty-five animals and twenty-two plants either on state or federal threatened and endangered species lists or proposed for listing in 2000.

Shaping the Region with Public Policy

Southern California's rapid demographic, economic, social, political, and environmental transformations since World War II have produced a complex metropolis characterized by a rapidly growing and diversifying population that is becoming more dense and continues to consume urban fringe land; insufficient infrastructure leading to overcrowded schools and housing and major traffic congestion; rising ethno-racial and income polarization linked to economic restructuring, welfare reforms, and local fiscal relations; and severe environmental stresses that are unevenly distributed by race and location and that endanger native plants and animals. These characteristics are not simply the result of individual actions. They are closely linked, directly or indirectly, to public policies.

Federal Expenditures in Southern California

Despite devolution, which in some policy arenas involved reductions in federal funding to lower-level governments, the federal government continues to spend billions of dollars that find their way to local areas. Between 1994 and 1996 the federal government spent an average of $77.4 billion per year in southern California—almost 25 percent of the gross regional product. Of that amount, $12.3 billion was allocated to antipoverty programs, including individual welfare payments and housing subsidies, as well as place-based housing, education, and health projects. The allocation of these funds to cities is critical at a time when many local governments must cope with escalating demands for infrastructure and urban services linked to rising poverty on the one hand, yet are limited in their ability to raise revenues on the other.

A recent study analyzed federal spending in southern California categorized into redistributive (or antipoverty) and nonredistributive (or other) expenditure, and adjusted to per capita annual averages for two periods (1983–85 and 1994–96) in order to reflect larger trends in fiscal federalism.[62] Results indicate that real per capita federal spending in southern California decreased almost 4 percent between 1983–85 and 1994–96 (see table 3-7). However, the reduction was largely driven by sharp defense spending cuts. Redistribution expenditures more than doubled because even by the mid-1990s the economy had not fully recovered from the 1990s recession—so poverty remained higher than in the early part of this period. Changes in specific programs were more extreme and often explain the variation in the broader categories. For example, both Medicare and Medicaid increased rapidly during the 1983–96 period as real health care costs rose and the uninsured population exploded in southern California. Infrastructure-building, environmental, and anticrime efforts also increased dramatically. Some unique events affected spending: the explosive response to the beating of Rodney King in 1992 influenced redistributive programs; the 1994 Northridge earthquake and local floods increased disaster assistance and the

62. The analysis uses the Consolidated Federal Funds Reports (CFFR) from 1983–84 to 1996–97, the Annual Reports of Financial Transactions Concerning Cities of California for 1981–82 and 1996–97, and the 1980 and 1990 population censuses. For further details on the methodology used for this analysis, see Joassart-Marcelli, Musso, and Wolch (2000) and Joassart-Marcelli and Musso (2001).

Table 3-7. Federal Expenditures by Type in Southern California Cities, 1983–83 and 1994–96

Expenditure	1983–85 (dollars)	1994–96 (dollars)	Change (percent)
Nonredistributive	5,537.69	4,682.73	−15.44
Retirement	1,689.76	1,832.11	8.42
Social Security and other retirement	1,070.56	1,028.37	-3.94
Medicare and related	469.02	703.48	49.99
Retirement for veterans and families	150.18	100.26	-33.24
Other spatial	608.98	1,392.96	251.95
Highways and related	41.59	53.98	29.77
Other infrastructure	35.49	17.22	-51.48
Assistance for disaster and environment	318.04	642.26	101.94
Crime	0.66	5.26	697.56
Housing-related tax benefits	213.20	674.25	216.25
All other	3,238.95	1,457.66	−55.00
Transfers to families and veterans	1.71	2.27	32.65
Direct business	6.91	12.48	80.50
Direct payments: Post Office	0.00	0.00	0.00
Procurement: defense	2,293.99	722.27	−68.51
Procurement: civilian	357.78	214.26	−40.11
Procurement: Post Office	13.48	32.72	142.72
Salaries and wages: military and defense	261.08	150.75	−42.26
Salaries and wages: other civilians	100.30	99.76	−0.54
Salaries and wages: Post Office	151.80	146.38	−3.57
Research	37.30	56.79	52.25
Arts	0.04	0.39	863.01
Other health	14.13	15.96	12.98
Other grants	0.43	3.62	739.36
Redistributive	368.71	982.08	166.36
Individual transfers	288.02	798.75	177.33
Food stamps	26.34	85.08	222.94
Redistributional grants	94.22	220.90	134.45
Medical assistance	92.98	285.34	206.88
Unemployment	5.64	13.85	145.74
Supplemental Security Income	62.53	115.49	84.68
Redistribution to veterans	6.30	0.00	−99.96
Earned-income tax credit	0.00	78.08	-
Spatial programs	80.69	183.33	127.21
Housing and other space-related transfers	6.00	122.92	1,948.92
Housing and community development	59.51	36.96	−37.89
Education	3.82	4.55	19.05
Health	11.36	18.91	66.43
Total	5,906.40	5,664.81	−4.09

Source: Joassart-Marcelli, Musso, and Wolch (2004, table 7.1, p. 200).

Table 3-8. Federal Redistributive and Nonredistributive Expenditures by County, 1983–85 and 1994–96

1996 dollars per capita

County	1983–85			1994–96		
	Redistributive	Nonredistributive	Total	Redistributive	Nonredistributiove	Total
Los Angeles	431.38	5,716.29	6,147.67	1,086.06	3,968.47	5,054.53
Orange	182.62	5,386.57	5,569.19	567.97	5,789.79	6,357.75
Riverside	348.95	3,899.92	4,248.87	655.35	3,211.15	3,866.50
San Bernardino	350.72	4,023.77	4,374.49	789.16	2,977.43	3,766.59
Ventura	236.06	3,901.77	4,137.83	651.72	4,678.19	5,329.91

Source: Data derived from analysis presented in Joassart-Marcelli, Musso, and Wolch (2004).

spatial allocation of environmental funds.[63]

GEOGRAPHIC PATTERNS IN FEDERAL FUNDING. Not surprisingly, Los Angeles County received the largest absolute share of federal dollars channeled to the region, and its mix included a disproportionately large share of redistributive funds. But as illustrated in table 3-8, on a per capita basis the picture looks different. Orange County residents received much higher levels of expenditures than other counties, especially Riverside and San Bernardino, whose low averages actually declined over the period. Orange County averages are driven largely by infrastructure spending, while, overall, Los Angeles County figures reflect a higher level of redistributive expenditure because of its greater proportion of poor households, and Riverside, with its large proportion of retirees, shows higher figures for retirement funds.

Still, these county patterns obscure sharp city-level differences (see map 3-9). Cities that attract below-average per capita amounts of both antipoverty and other federal funding ("weak antipoverty and weak other") include low-income inner suburbs in the old industrial belt running from south central Los Angeles County through the Inland Empire and selected working-class suburbs in the outlying counties. By contrast, L.A. City, coastal cities, and scattered cities in outlying suburbs received more than average federal expenditures per person ("strong antipoverty and strong other"). On a per capita basis, federal funds tended to go disproportionately to cities with lower poverty rates, which only deepens metropolitan inequality. Indeed, people in the richest 20 percent of the region's cities (those with the lowest poverty rates) received on average almost twice as much as people in the poorest 20 percent of cities. This is largely due to the allocation of nonredistributive expenditures,

63. Dreier and Rothstein (1994).

Map 3-9. Federal Expenditure Patterns in the Los Angeles Region, 1994–96

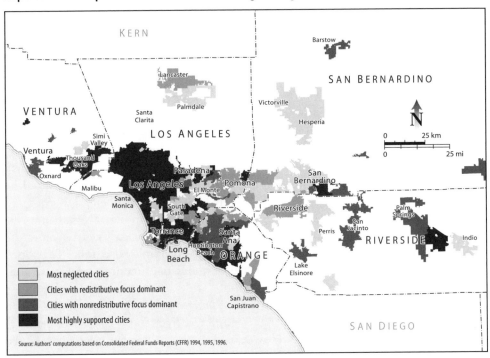

Source: Authors' computations based on Consolidated Federal Funds Reports (CFFR) 1994, 1995, 1996.

which constitute over 80 percent of all federal spending and seem to favor wealthier cities. However, on a per capita basis, federal antipoverty expenditures are targeted to the poorest communities. These amounts have risen over time, although faster in wealthier cities, indicating that growth in antipoverty expenditures has been disproportionately directed to poor individuals living in nonpoor cities.[64]

EXPLAINING THE DISTRIBUTION OF FEDERAL EXPENDITURES. To test whether the allocation of federal funds targets poor cities and alleviates fiscal disparities in the region, Joassart-Marcelli, Musso, and Wolch modeled per capita federal expenditures by city as a function of socioeconomic (including poverty rates), fiscal (including fiscal capacity), demographic, and institutional variables.[65] The results indicate

64. Growth in antipoverty funds may have gone disproportionately to wealthier cities because city agencies and nonprofit service organizations there are less overwhelmed and better able to help residents apply for and receive subsidies. Also, poorer cities may have a growing share of working poor and immigrant residents, who may not be eligible for many forms of assistance.

that, as expected, poverty is a crucial determinant of redistributive funds allocation. However, while its impact on the distribution of other funds was insignificant in the 1983–85 period, it became negative in the 1990s, suggesting that nonredistributive expenditures—the largest share of federal funds—increasingly favor cities with lower poverty rates.[66] The study also found that both discretionary local fiscal capacity and fiscal effort had a positive influence on the allocation of redistributive federal funds to southern California cities. Thus redistributive federal expenditures fail to alleviate fiscal disparities and to the contrary often help cities that can more easily afford to help themselves (for example, those that can provide matching funds for federal and state programs).

The relative institutional strength of individual cities, measured by whether they have their own charter (as opposed to being incorporated under the state's general legislation), also seems to play a significant role in attracting antipoverty funds. Southern California's charter cities are typically older and have a more diverse economic base, more developed civic culture, a fuller complement of municipal functions, and more nonprofit social welfare organizations. They are therefore better equipped to compete for nonformula-funded federal antipoverty programs.[67]

Correlation analyses suggested a negative relationship between race variables and spending. However, after controlling for other characteristics such as socioeconomic status, these variables became insignificant in the regressions, except that the proportion of Latinos had a negative impact on the allocation of nonredistributive expenditures in the early 1980s. Nonredistributive expenditures, which include retirement spending, were also positively influenced by the proportion of people older than sixty-five. Finally, population growth had a negative impact on the amount of nonredistributive expenditures. This finding indicates that the allocation of federal funds may not necessarily go to cities with the highest need for infrastructure development and new services.

65. Complete regression results are available in Joassart-Marcelli, Musso, and Wolch (2004). Comparable regression models with slightly different data provide similar results in Joassart-Marcelli and Musso (2001).

66. Because a significant proportion of redistributive expenditures is allocated to cities based on a prediction equation including poverty as one of the predictors, there is a potential endogeneity problem linked with regressing redistributive expenditure on poverty. In an attempt to solve this problem two-stage least-squares regressions were used to explain the distribution of redistributive expenditures with an instrumental variable for poverty. The poverty instrument is predicted using median income, proportion of African Americans, and proportion of Latinos. These variables seem to predict poverty rather well given the high R^2 obtained (0.7438 in 1990). Regressions of nonredistributive expenditures use ordinary least squares (OLS) methods.

67. Wolch and Geiger (1983); Joassart-Marcelli and Wolch (2001).

To further test whether federal expenditures equalize or exacerbate disparities characteristic of southern California's urban fiscal landscape, total per capita federal expenditure and capacity to raise other revenues were added to discretionary local fiscal capacity. A comparison of the coefficients of variation for fiscal capacity with those for the total figures between cities makes it clear that federal expenditures did not help to equalize fiscal capacity among cities grouped according to their poverty rates in either of the two periods. Indeed, coefficients of variation more than tripled once federal expenditures were taken into account, suggesting that the allocation of federal funds exacerbates local fiscal disparities instead of reducing them.

In sum, federal spending is unevenly distributed across municipalities. Although redistributive funds go to the poorest cities, the majority of funds do not. Therefore some affluent cities receive the largest share of federal expenditures while some of the most fiscally strapped ones receive less-than-average per capita shares. These spending patterns serve to deepen rather than equalize fiscal disparities between cities—an unintentional but real effect of federal expenditure policies in southern California—while failing to address the problems of poorer cities, typically located in the urban core and older industrial suburbs.

Lost Opportunities for Regional Transportation Planning in Southern California

Before the 1970s, most transportation planning was highway planning, funded largely by federal and local sources. The Highway Trust Fund, established to construct the Interstate Highway System, was supported by the federal fuel tax and highway-related excise taxes. It provided an 80 to 90 percent federal match for highway construction. Beginning in the 1970s, when funding for public transit increased rapidly, a special tax fund was established in California. Federal transit subsidies came from the general fund and were therefore vulnerable to national political objectives and the state of the economy. In the 1980s the Reagan administration reduced direct transit subsidies and shifted the fiscal burden to state and local governments. The 1982 federal fuel tax increase for the first time earmarked some of the tax for public transit and gave more flexibility to regions to use highway funds for transit. But overall levels of federal support for transportation dwindled.[68]

In response, local governments passed major tax measures for transportation (for example, Proposition A in 1980 in Los Angeles, which

68. Giuliano (2004).

created a half-cent local sales tax measure, and Proposition B in 1988, in Orange, Riverside, and San Bernardino). Moreover, localities began to require developers to contribute to new transportation infrastructure expenditures.

DEVOLUTION IN SOUTHERN CALIFORNIA. According to a study by Giuliano, the 1991 ISTEA (the federal Intermodal Surface Transportation Efficiency Act) and its follow-on TEA-21 (Transportation Equity Act for the 21st Century) marked a new direction in transportation funding and planning, restructuring highway finance.[69] ISTEA provided for flexible funding between modes and linked transportation planning with air quality management. Furthermore it mandated that comprehensive Regional Transportation Plans (RTPs) and short-range, project-specific Regional Transportation Improvement Programs (RTIPs) be developed and approved by the metropolitan planning organization (the Southern California Association of Governments, SCAG, in southern California), thus moving some planning responsibility to the regions.

This provided an opportunity for SCAG to become a powerful force for regional transportation planning. But SCAG chose to devolve much of the transportation planning process to its constituent counties and to major operating agencies (such as the Los Angeles County Metropolitan Transportation Authority [MTA] for transit and Caltrans for highways). Thus county transportation commissions now program all transportation money (including federal and state funds). The RTPs and associated RTIPs are thus developed "bottom-up," and SCAG's only role is to negotiate disagreements and ensure consistency between plans.

Giuliano explains this decentralized process by reference to three major factors: the lack of significant support for regional planning in California; the increased importance of local funding, which inevitably translates to increased local control; and a complex funding system that politicizes the planning process, reduces accountability, and limits understanding of RTIP details to very few agencies.[70]

CONSEQUENCES OF DEVOLUTION. According to Giuliano, ISTEA and decentralized transportation planning have had two important consequences.[71] First, local residents in southern California pay an increas-

69. Ibid.

70. For example, in county RTIPs prepared during the 1982–97 period, there were 263 funding sources: 78 for transit, 93 for highways, and the remainder for local arteries. Of these sources, 121 were federal, 45 state, and 97 local. Several funding sources overlapped or were renamed, replaced, or eliminated over the years, making such a budgeting and planning exercise truly challenging.

Figure 3-2. Transportation Funding, by Source, for Southern California

Billions of dollars

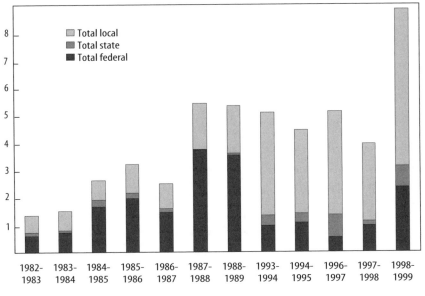

Source: Giuliano (2004, figure 5.1, p. 157).

ingly large share of the cost of transportation infrastructure (see figure 3-2). Shifting infrastructure costs to local residents has efficiency benefits, but comes at the expense of equity. Because the major source of local funds is a sales tax—regressive and weakly related to travel needs—a greater proportional burden falls on lower-income households. Second, the five counties have been free to pursue very different transportation investment programs (see table 3-9). While transit investment dominated in Los Angeles, especially in the 1990s, the outlying counties—especially Orange—invested almost exclusively in highways and local roads. Although they arguably began the decade with pressing needs for additional highway and road capacity, these counties did not develop a range of transportation choices designed to reduce automobile dependence or promote more compact development.

MTA AND THE BUS RIDERS UNION STRUGGLE. Los Angeles County provides transit services to residents of other counties, but also promotes downtown Los Angeles as the region's central hub. The MTA, L.A. County's transportation commission, runs a bus fleet and three rail

71. Giuliano (2004).

Table 3-9. Regional Transportation Expenditures in Southern California Counties, 1996–97

Transportation mode	Los Angeles	Orange	Riverside	San Bernardino	Ventura	Entire region
Transit						
Total (dollars)	2,739,407	221,141	104,664	186,894	33,216	$3,285,322
Share (percent)	77	17	22	32	32	55%
Highways						
Total (dollars)	113,606	1,034,683	278,684	304,959	43,279	$1,775,211
Share (percent)	3	79	59	53	41	30%
Local street						
Total (dollars)	683,697	46,589	87,989	86,457	27,822	$932,554
Share (percent)	19	4	19	15	27	16%
Total (dollars)	3,536,710	1,302,413	471,337	578,310	104,317	$5,993,087
County share (percent)	59	22	8	10	2	100%

Source: Giuliano (2001, adapted from figure 1, p. 7).

operations, channels funds to sixteen suburban municipal bus operators, and also created MetroLink, a regional commuter rail with five lines converging in downtown. In their effort to reduce auto congestion and associated pollution, MTA expenditures during the 1990s favored rail-line riders (including commuters from outlying areas) over severely neglected central L.A. County bus riders. Although in 1992 buses carried 94 percent of all MTA riders (mostly low-income people of color), only about 30 percent of MTA's $2.6 billion capital and operating budget went to buses, leading to severe overcrowding on key routes—up to 140 percent of capacity.[72] In contrast, the three rail lines carried less than 6 percent of riders, mostly white and affluent, but received 71 percent of the budget. Each rider on a MetroLink train received a $41 subsidy in 1994; a bus rider received $1.17. And in 1994 security expenditures per rider were forty-three times higher on rail lines than on MTA buses. MTA has been further criticized for spending inequalities that caused disparities in fares and service quality: for example, lines with a higher share of passengers of color got lower subsidies, and suburban bus operators, with mostly white ridership, received higher MTA subsidies than its own bus riders. These disparities led the Bus Riders Union (BRU), a grassroots organization expressly formed to represent poor (often immigrant) bus riders, to initiate a federal civil rights suit that claimed discrimination against transit riders of color. The suit resulted in a consent

72. Statistics in this section are derived from the "Summary of Evidence, Labor Community Strategy Center V. MTA," from the federal consent degree requiring the MTA to address the court's finding of discriminatory disparate impact on citizens of color. See www.igc.org/lctr/smmry2.html.

decree that forced the MTA to alter its fare policies, purchase additional buses, and extend service, but controversy over implementation and MTA compliance continues.

In sum, devolution of ISTEA authority to counties increasingly limits the federal role in transportation planning and promotes locally tailored RTIPs. While outlying counties targeted funds to highways and local roads, Los Angeles County emphasized transit that favored affluent suburban commuters over low-income bus riders of color, fueling political battles and lawsuits over transportation service equity, without appreciably affecting the overall share of transit riders.

The Housing Affordability Crisis and Subsidizing Suburbanization

The scarcity of new suburban housing affordable to low-income households has deepened regional patterns of racial and economic polarization. As shown in table 3-10, in 42 percent of all census tracts in Orange County and in 48 percent of all census tracts in other southern California counties median home prices exceeded 30 percent of median household income (the standard criterion for affordability) in the tract in 1990.[73] In lower-income areas, affordability problems are even more severe, and federal housing policies have supported housing polarization by disproportionately promoting homeownership for white families in suburban areas. Redevelopment policies have been unable to alleviate affordability problems and thus have failed to stop the movement of poor and middle-income individuals in search of cheaper housing to outlying areas.

FEDERAL HOMEOWNERSHIP POLICY AND RACIAL/SPATIAL INEQUALITY. Federal policy has long supported homeownership, and therefore suburbanization, by allowing homeowners to deduct their mortgage interest and property taxes from their taxable income. Aldana and Dymski estimated tax benefits in southern California counties for all homeowners in 1990 and for owners of homes purchased in 1997 alone (see table 3-11).[74] Homeowner mortgage deductions on homes purchased in 1997 range from 6.6 times (in Los Angeles County) to 20 times (in Orange County) the total value of subsidized housing expenditures, illustrating the imbalance in housing policies.

73. Aldana and Dymski (2004).
74. The former estimates are based on 1989 interest rates and the number of years that 1990 homeowners had resided in their current homes; the latter are 1998 tax deductions reported under the Home Mortgage Disclosure Act. See Dymski and Aldana (2001).

Table 3-10. Housing Affordability and Median Income in Southern California Counties, 1990

County	Tracts with median rent:income ratios of 30 percent or more (percent of total)	Median income of tracts with rent:income ratios of less than 30 percent (dollars)	Median income of tracts with rent:income ratios of greater than 30 percent (dollars)	Difference in median income between tracts with a rent:income ratio of greater and less than 30 percent (percent)
Los Angeles	49.8	40,078	29,393	−26.7
Orange	41.9	49,073	38,974	−20.6
Riverside	56.1	32,319	29,079	−10
San Bernardino	48	34,145	27,453	−19.6
Ventura	49.6	40,626	46,035	13.3

Source: Aldana and Dymski (2001, table 1).

Table 3-11. Estimated Mortgage Interest, Property Tax Deductions, and HUD Housing Assistance in Southern California Counties, 1990 and 1998
Dollars

County	1990 property tax and mortgage interest tax deductions	1998 HUD housing assistance expenditures	1998 property tax and and mortgage interest deductions for homes purchased in 1997	Percent due to conventional loans, 1998
Los Angeles	3,670,843,029	55,883,211	368,067,621	79.7
Orange	1,547,740,910	8,748,051	175,603,953	87.0
Riverside	675,332,801	3,170,452	58,979,550	56.4
San Bernardino	664,847,100	5,108,828	54,097,846	48.1
Ventura	453,503,479	3,482,313	43,005,819	86.8

Source: Aldana and Dymski (2004, tables 3.1, 3.3, pp. 105, 108).

According to Dymski and Aldana, federal policy has also underwritten and exacerbated racial redlining and thus segregation.[75] Explicit racial lending criteria governing Federal Housing Administration/Veterans Administration (FHA/VA) assessment procedures increased racial segregation in the region, and despite reform efforts, mortgage lending is still characterized by racial disparities. Logistic regression models on 1996–98 conventional and FHA/VA loan data suggest that African Americans are at a significant disadvantage in obtaining conventional loan approval, their approval rates being from 57 to 71 percent below those of white applicants with the same income, debt, and other characteristics considered by lenders. Latino applicants in every county (except Ventura) were also at a disadvantage, having lower approval rates, all

75. Dymski and Aldana (2001).

Figure 3-3. Minority Disadvantage in Home-Purchase Loan Market, Los Angeles County, 1996–98

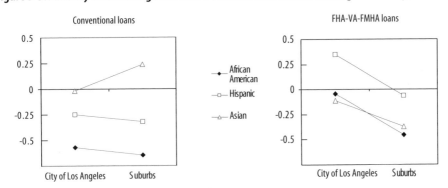

Source: Aldana and Dymski (2001, figure 1). The figures represent proportional disadvantage relative to white applicants with the same income and loan/income levels based on a logit model of loan approval.

other things being equal. Racial disadvantages linked to FHA/VA loan approval are smaller. Disadvantages for Latino applicants are not statistically significant, and while African American applicants remain subject to statistically significant levels of disadvantage, they are nevertheless lower than for conventional loans (24 to 48 percent below white approval rates). Within Los Angeles County, the extent of disadvantage for applicants of color was significantly greater for FHA/VA loan applications in suburban areas than in the city of Los Angeles (see figure 3-3), while in outlying counties they are at a greater statistical disadvantage in upper-income than in lower-income areas.

FEDERAL LOWER-INCOME HOUSING AND SPATIAL INEQUAL-ITY. A pattern of concentrated poverty is reinforced when direct federal and state investments in low-income housing are disproportionately targeted to older inner-area suburbs and central cities and excluded from more affluent communities through NIMBY campaigns. In turn, such poverty contributes to suburban flight and fringe expansion. Aldana and Dymski's analysis of federal low-income units and dollar outlays in 1998, aggregated by census tracts grouped according to their percentage of poor population, indicates that in three of the four counties analyzed, lower-income units and outlays are highest in the poorest census tracts.[76] In Orange County only small shares of lower-income subsidized housing are located in the two most affluent groups of census tracts (see table 3-12). In contrast, 1998 mortgage interest deductions for homes purchased in 1997 disproportionately flowed toward the lowest-poverty

76. Aldana and Dymski (2001).

Table 3-12. Poverty, Lower-Income Housing, and Mortgage Interest Deductions in Southern California Counties, 1990 and 1998[a]

County	1990 poverty tract quartiles (percent of poor)	Lower-income housing				Mortgage interest tax deduction on 1998 home purchase	
		No. of units	Percent	Outlays (dollars)	Percent	Total (dollars)	Percent
Los Angeles	3.5	6,288	5.9	3,265,705	5.8	166,813,393	45.3
	7.8	15,587	14.5	7,969,107	14.3	103,968,560	28.2
	15.2	32,361	30.2	17,752,259	31.8	63,858,566	17.3
	31.4	53,014	49.4	26,896,140	48.1	33,427,102	9.1
Total		107,250	100.0	55,883,211	100.0	368,067,621	100.0
Orange	2.2	2,145	12.7	1,120,588	12.8	82,644,786	47.1
	4.4	1,705	10.1	970,564	11.1	36,774,948	20.9
	7.6	6,809	40.3	3,327,384	38.0	38,956,575	22.2
	18.6	6,254	37.0	3,329,515	38.1	17,227,644	9.8
Total		16,913	100.0	8,748,051	100.0	175,603,953	100.0
Riverside	5.1	1,020	12.4	355,843	11.2	27,701,625	47.0
	8.8	2,270	27.7	804,754	25.4	15,016,722	25.5
	13.8	2,050	25.0	853,990	26.9	9,959,859	16.9
	25.0	2,860	34.9	1,155,865	36.5	6,301,344	10.7
Total		8,200	100.0	3,170,452	100.0	58,979,550	100.0
San Bernardino	3.9	1,611	13.9	707,091	13.8	20,488,122	37.9
	9.3	2,489	21.5	1,052,405	20.6	15,182,826	28.1
	14.9	3,001	26.0	1,392,679	27.3	12,541,983	23.2
	30.1	4,462	38.6	1,956,653	38.3	5,884,915	10.9
Total		11,563	100.0	5,108,828	100.0	54,097,846	100.0

Source: Aldana and Dymski (2004, table 3.2, p. 107).

a. Figures are distributed by census tract quartiles based on 1990 percentage of population in poverty.

areas, revealing that subsidies go to affluent neighborhoods. If mortgage deduction tax expenditures for all homes (not just new purchases) were to be taken into account, they would swamp low-income housing subsidies, in all southern California counties.

REDEVELOPMENT POLICIES AND THEIR IMPACT ON AFFORDABLE HOUSING. Although California first enacted redevelopment legislation in 1945, only in 1976 did redevelopment law require that 20 percent of tax increment revenues from redevelopment projects go to affordable housing. According to Grigsby, from 1986 to 1997 the seventy-two cities with redevelopment agencies in Los Angeles County produced only 20,505 affordable housing units.[77] Virtually all were produced by just ten cities; Los Angeles City's redevelopment agency alone created over 60 percent (11,750 units). On average, the number of new units (13,716) surpassed rehabilitated units (11,793).

As Grigsby shows, unlike publicly assisted housing, in general, redevelopment agency–sponsored housing is not concentrated in the center of the county. Even in the city of Los Angeles, low-income redevelopment financed housing tends to be spread out across a number of locations.[78] But several cities experienced a net loss of housing due to redevelopment. Almost 2,000 units were lost in Los Angeles County between 1996 and 1997, and fifty-seven cities with redevelopment agencies provided little or no new affordable housing. Therefore, contrary to redevelopment law's intent, redevelopment has limited impact on the region's affordability crisis.

Legal Immigrants and the Suburbanization of Southern California

New immigrants historically settled first in central cities, later moving to suburbs as they became upwardly mobile. Since U.S. immigration law gives preferential status to those with family members already legally residing in the United States, continued settlement of immigrants in urban core areas with large foreign-born populations might be expected. Moreover, because immigrants typically find jobs and housing through social networks, they often elect to settle where family, friends, and conationals reside.

While most new arrivals do settle in older central communities of southern California, Marcelli shows that an increasing *share* of all immigrants now plan to move immediately into suburbs (see map 3-10).[79] Los Angeles County continued to receive slightly more than two-thirds of all legal permanent residents (LPRs) intending to reside in southern California, but this tendency weakened between 1990 and 1996.[80] The share planning to reside in Los Angeles County fell from 76 to 68 percent, while Orange, San Bernardino, and Ventura Counties experienced slightly increased shares and Riverside County's roughly doubled from 2.6 to 5.1 percent.

Those areas attracting the largest numbers of LPRs did have higher proportions of foreign-born persons than other areas, reflecting needs

77. Grigsby (2000).
78. Grigsby (2000).
79. Marcelli (2004).
80. Immigration and Naturalization Service (INS) data on the intended place of residence of new legal permanent residents (LPRs) for 1990 to 1996 were aggregated from zip codes to PUMAs (public use microsample areas) to be matched with the 1990 Census PUMS (public use microdata sample).

Map 3-10. New Adult Legal Permanent Residents in the Los Angeles Region, 1990–98 (by public use microsample area, PUMA)

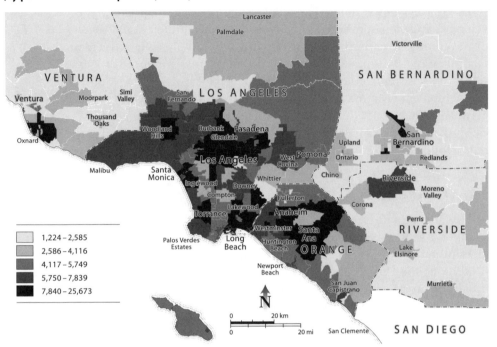

for public transportation, affordable housing, job and language training programs, and other antipoverty services. However, most new LPRs go to areas with relatively low antipoverty expenditures. Moreover, employment-based immigration policies that favor workers whose skills help to address domestic labor shortages may be promoting suburbanization since new immigrants disproportionately select communities with employment opportunities and rapid job growth. Thus policies that attract immigrants better prepared for economic success may have promoted this decentralization.

To the extent that suburban immigrants are wealthier than those who remain in central cities, this dynamic may intensify poverty concentration and intraregional disparities. Further, new suburban immigrants could indirectly reinforce exurbanization by "pushing" other decentralizing residents to leapfrog over suburbs with increasingly immigrant populations, to homogeneous white suburbs.

Table 3-13. Total Real Contributions by Acre-Foot of Water Delivered in
Southern California Counties, 1929–96

Dollars

Region	1929–70	1971–96	1929–96
City of Los Angeles	1,669.83	473.28	793.69
Rest of L.A. County	452.52	337.01	368.25
Orange County	229.37	312.57	289.63
Riverside County	199.34	290.84	269.92
San Bernardino County	655.01	290.64	334.84
San Diego County	211.25	261.62	250.54
Ventura County	439.36	333.53	340.12

Source: Erie, Freeman, and Joassart-Marcelli (2004, figure 1.7, p. 56).

Regional Water Supply Policies for Southern California Suburbs

Very little of southern California's staggering population growth could have occurred without a supply of cheap imported water. In the late 1920s, Los Angeles and several other major cities in the region joined in creating the Metropolitan Water District (the Met) to acquire Colorado River water. Now the agency's service area covers most of southern California. In the 1950s the Met approved the remarkable Laguna Declaration, pledging to find a permanent water supply and provide water to anyone within its service area who requested it. Then, in the 1960s, the state's voters approved the State Water Project, designed to bring water from northern to southern California, to be distributed by the Met.

From 1929 to 1970 the Met financed its water supply infrastructure through property taxes. Los Angeles City and, to a lesser degree, the other twelve founding Met members supported most capital costs of regional infrastructure that would later provide water to newer suburbs at a much lower cost than that levied on older jurisdictions. Thus by shouldering most of the water supply cost through their payments—or what the Met terms "contributions," which cover both capital and operating costs—Los Angeles City and County effectively subsidized suburban development (see table 3-13). Since 1929, L.A. has drawn 8 percent of total Met water deliveries but paid 17 percent of total Met financial "contributions" from member districts while, for instance, San Diego received 26 percent of total water delivered but paid only 18 percent of the financial contributions.

One reason for this suburban subsidy is that L.A., with access to its own cheaper water, used less Met water than envisaged, while newer members of the Met, in Orange and San Diego Counties, depended more heavily on Met supplies. For example, L.A. City, which paid the highest unit costs for Met water, consumed far less per capita and also less in absolute quantity than Orange and San Diego Counties during the 1929–70 period, even though its average population during these years was far larger. Second, tax-financed general obligation infrastructure bonds tended to be approved by voters. Third, the city received benefits from this arrangement—more votes on the Met board and first rights to Met water during droughts. Fourth, although L.A. representatives dominated the Met, they implemented policies favoring suburban expansion because, as part of the region's pro-growth leadership, they were committed to continued real estate development and municipal expansion.[81]

Water subsidies led the way for suburban growth in the region. Before 1970, when the Met altered its pricing system, L.A. City paid heavily for Met water but grew at a 2.2 percent average annual rate. Orange and San Diego Counties, in contrast, paid little for Met water while averaging annual growth rates of up to almost 12 and 14 percent respectively.[82] The same relationship holds for all twenty-seven Met agencies: member areas with deeper water subsidies grew faster than areas with lower rates of subsidy. After 1970 outright subsidies paid by L.A. were eliminated, but the Met's basic goal remains to ensure that water supply does not constrain growth. In addition, outlying areas closer to the Colorado Aqueduct have successfully obtained a point-to-point pricing system that lowered their costs, while new agricultural-to-urban water transfers herald a new era of water for suburban growth. Nevertheless, lawsuits over water availability have halted major fringe developments and may ultimately alter the Met's policy course.

Federal and State Habitat Conservation Planning and Limits to Suburbanization

The federal Endangered Species Act (ESA) was the tool of choice for environmentalists attempting to protect species in southern California until the 1990s, when its cumbersome, expensive, slow, and piecemeal nature spurred the development of Natural Community Conservation Planning (NCCP) directed by the California Department of Fish and

---

81. Gottlieb (1988).

82. Clearly Los Angeles City and County grew more slowly but from much larger bases than those of the other counties, and thus some differential in growth rates would be expected.

Game. NCCP was initially designed to protect the California gnat-catcher's coastal sage scrub habitat in advance of potential development and listing.[83] Yet according to Pincetl, with participation voluntary, collaboration was limited, so although some landowners and governments voluntarily complied, six months after the creation of the NCCP program, more than 2,000 acres of the gnatcatcher habitat had still been destroyed.[84]

Federal intervention created institutional arrangements to make the NCCP process viable. U.S. Interior Secretary Bruce Babbitt declared the gnatcatcher a threatened species and issued special regulations requiring those interested in developing its habitat to participate in California's NCCP negotiation process. Subsequent NCCP regulations permit development of up to 5 percent of the land in each designated coastal sage scrub subregion and required individual landowners seeking to develop more to demonstrate that their property is not gnatcatcher habitat.[85] Thus, although technically voluntary, the NCCP was clearly energized by the federal ESA.

Since 1991, NCCP collaborative groups have developed eleven subregional conservation plans (amounting to subregional land-use planning) that involve 6,000 square miles in southern California. Thus far, some 150,000 acres have been preserved, and NCCP plans are now incorporated into city and county general plans.[86] Thus NCCP represents a rare example of regional consensus building around an environmental agenda being translated into local land-use policy.

Still, results have been mixed. San Bernardino County has done little to advance species protection. Urbanized Los Angeles has crept north, but the county has avoided systematic habitat protection.[87] In central Orange County, NCCP efforts appear relatively successful at preserving coastal sage scrub, but the U.S. Fish and Wildlife Service allowed the construction of a toll road through the preserve.[88] And in southern Orange County, NCCP progress is stalled because the major landowner will not participate. But the comprehensive Riverside County Integrated

83. Codified as chapter 10 of division 3 of the California Fish and Game Code (2800 et seq.) per Introduction to NCCP General Process Guidelines (http://ceres.ca.gov/CRA/NCCP/).

84. Pincetl (2004).

85. Marks, Gearin, and Armstrong (2004).

86. Gail Presley, California Department of Fish and Wildlife, telephone conversation with Stephanie Pincetl, May 18, 2000.

87. Landis (1993).

88. Presley (2000).

Plan (RCIP), covering land use, habitat, and transportation, complements its Habitat Conservation Planning efforts.[89] In addition, market incentives were devised, allocating tradable credits to any landowner who dedicates land within the plan area to the reserve system devised to protect the endangered Stephen's kangaroo rat—an important innovation in an area where fragmented land ownership renders negotiations difficult.

In sum, the federal Endangered Species Act and state NCCP program have preserved habitat and protected open space, stimulating subregional land-use planning and putting a brake on sprawl. Time and money, however, may constrain success. State and federal financial support will be crucial, and incentives may be required to overcome the limits of its voluntary nature.[90]

Local Growth Management Policies

Despite ESA and NCCP efforts, growth management ultimately remains under local control. According to a study by Joassart-Marcelli, Fulton, and Musso, between 1989 and 1992 more than half of southern California cities adopted new measures designed to manage growth, such as land-use tools, incentive programs, and development restrictions (see table 3-14).[91] However, between 1995 and 1998 this proportion fell to less than a quarter, with no clear connection between growth management activity in the two periods.[92] One-third of all growth management activity in the period 1995–98 involved some form of zoning restriction; most often these restrictions were associated with rising housing prices and exclusionary practices.[93] Not surprisingly, then, the sharpest declines were in commercial restrictions.

While environmental protection and efforts to preserve community character may explain the initial increase in growth management, recent declines are harder to understand given the region's simultaneous densi-

89. Information about the basis for the plan, including population projections, is found at www.rcip.org/stakeholdertext.htm.

90. For example, Fish and Game and the federal Fish and Wildlife Service have agreed to shoulder 50 percent of the land acquisition costs for the San Diego NCCP, estimated at over $200 million for 27,000 acres. See Presley (2000).

91. Joassart-Marcelli, Fulton, and Musso (2004).

92. The study drew on the 1992 Levine-Glickfeld Growth Control Survey (see Fulton, Glickfeld, McMurran, and Levine, 1999) combined with a 1998 UC Berkeley and California Department of Housing and Community Development survey directed by John Landis. City level variables from the 1980 and 1990 Censuses of the Population and 1982 and 1997 Controller's Reports supplemented these data.

93. Wolch and Gabriel (1985); Ladd (1998); Pendall (1999).

Table 3-14. Growth Management Activity in Southern California Cities, 1989–92 and 1995–98

	Number of cities		Percentage of cities	
Type of growth management measure	1989–92	1995–98	1989–92	1995–98
Residential building permit cap	2	2	1.67	1.67
Commercial building permit cap and restrictions	12	1	10.00	0.83
Adequate public facilities requirement (residential)	13	4	10.83	3.33
Adequate public facilities requirement (commercial)	11	4	9.17	3.33
Urban limit lines	1	1	0.83	0.83
Growth management element in general plan	14	2	11.67	1.67
Rezoning of residential development area	2	9	1.67	7.50
Downzoning of residential development area	24	10	20.00	8.33
Residential building floor-area restrictions	30	5	25.00	4.17
Simple majority vote requirement	0	2	0.00	1.67
Super-majority vote requirement	0	0	0.00	0.00
Other measures to control development	20	7	16.67	5.83
Any measure (at least one)	60	28	52.5	24.2

Source: Joassart-Marcelli, Fulton, and Musso (2001, adapted from figure 9.3, p. 261).

fication and urban expansion. Joassart-Marcelli, Fulton, and Musso argue that these trends reflect a shift in fiscal imperatives brought by the early 1990s recession for cities facing the twin pressures of Proposition 13's fiscal constraints and the growing local burden of service provision.[94] Their analysis of changes in growth management activity between 1989–92 and 1995–98 indicates that cities involved in growth management are typically neither the fastest growing nor the most dense. They usually enjoy greater fiscal capacity, lower poverty and unemployment, higher proportions of white residents, and lower proportions of immigrants and Latinos. However between 1989 and 1992, housing characteristics seem to have been the most important influences on growth management activity. Cities with lower vacancy rates but good housing conditions (that is, higher property values and less overcrowding) tended to adopt growth restrictions, while other sorts of city characteristics were not critical. In the second period, though, socioeconomic, institutional, and fiscal characteristics became very important. Cities with high poverty and unemployment rates were much less likely to adopt growth management measures. While fiscally healthier cities were more likely to approve such measures, those with higher shares of revenue from sales taxes were less likely to do so.

94. Joassart-Marcelli, Fulton, and Musso (2004).

Thus wealthier cities often used growth management to maintain fiscal strength and to avoid inflows of poorer residents, while poorer communities that suffered most from the recession saw development as central to job creation and housing improvement and rolled back growth management efforts. This dynamic not only fails to support regional environmental protection and shared prosperity; it also promotes exurbanization and the concentration of poverty and unemployment.

Toward a New Regionalism in Southern California

There are no signs that the southern California growth juggernaut is slowing. In its wake lie stark contradictions. While growth has produced financial gains for a few, poverty and privation persist for many more. While more people of color are becoming economically mobile and purchasing homes, many remain disadvantaged in the mortgage and labor markets. Cool, leafy suburbs sit right next to hot, high-density neighborhoods without a tree in sight. And despite strenuous efforts to clean up pollution and curb low-density development, rapid growth continues to produce environmental degradation, habitat loss, and species endangerment.

These dynamics have been shaped by public policies that, rather than supporting the image of an unplanned region, have profoundly influenced the region at every level of government. Our studies reveal that some public policies have promoted growth, exurbanization, economic inequality, and racial segregation, while others have increasingly constrained local development choices. Many such policies are rarely conceived as "urban," but they may more powerfully shape our metropolitan areas than well-known urban initiatives such as community development block grants or empowerment zones. Efforts to address the region's critical problems cannot reverse the cumulative impact of policies in place for decades. But if we are to level the playing field for cities and people in southern California and to contain environmental degradation, it is critical for federal, state, and local governments to remove perverse incentives that drive undesirable metropolitan outcomes.

From the perspective of governance, perhaps the single largest barrier to resolving the problems facing southern California is its pervasive fragmentation. Even major federal policies that explicitly mandate regional planning have largely failed to engender a powerful regionalism, despite having other beneficial impacts. "Stealth regionalism" under the guise of the Endangered Species Act, for example, has become a force for regional planning, but only in some parts of the metropolis and only for land-use management. This leaves major problems that can only (or most effectively) be addressed on a regional scale that is virtually untouched. Southern California's geographic scale, history of home rule, and economic, political, and social fragmentation exacerbate the failures of traditional regional governance. Even solutions advocated by "new regionalists," such as central city–inner suburb coalitions to promote regional tax base sharing, are most improbable here, where the very terms of reference (central city, inner-ring suburb) do not apply.

What, then, should be done in southern California? Many policies we assessed originated at the federal level, are deeply entrenched, and have powerful constituencies. But because so many federal policies fundamentally structure the "rules of the game" for metropolitan regions, it is crucial to revise or remove those that have deleterious urban consequences. Funding formulas could be changed to promote fiscal equalization, and regulatory powers could be expanded or modified to promote regional cooperation and integrated planning. At the state and local levels there is also latitude, for example, to require additional affordable housing in affluent communities and to eliminate the perverse incentives for fiscal zoning and beggar-thy-neighbor municipal competition for sales tax revenues.

Our research suggests that three interacting strategies are critical to allowing the region to resolve its long-standing problems: an equity-based regionalism, a focus on greater sustainability, and a coordinated "smart-growth" agenda. Equity-based regional planning seeks to raise wages, ensure health care coverage for all workers, provide affordable housing close to job opportunities, and expand the use of tax credits for low-wage workers and their households. This approach, pursued by community-based organizations (CBOs) and labor groups, starts from the recognition that making connections to larger regional dynamics and opportunities may offer the best avenue out of economic deprivation and inequality.[95] Another key element of shared prosperity is to use the idea of a common future to commit business to reducing poverty as a way to improve the business climate. Because business cooperation is critical, it sets the parameters for viable social policy, especially in a new economy that values skills, networks, and industrial niches. Indeed, new evidence suggests that metropolitan regions that pay more attention to reducing central city poverty, city and suburban differentials, and inequality actually grow faster.[96]

95. Pastor, Dreier, Grigsby, and Lopez-Garza (2000).
96. Pastor, Dreier, Grigsby, and Lopez-Garza (2000).

Despite widespread awareness of the environmental challenges facing southern California, the region still lacks a coherent agenda for how to use resources for everyday life. Such an agenda would involve tracking regional sustainability, establishing resource consumption and pollution benchmarks, and setting goals for the future. An important step would be to add sustainability criteria to standard environmental impact reports (EIRs), making determinations based at least partly on a proposed project's impact on overall sustainability goals. Cities and counties could create local sustainability programs that set targets for environmental remediation, pollution reduction, and conservation. They could also develop "green" building and landscaping codes, and support emergent "green" industries that enhance energy efficiency, restore local ecosystems, reduce waste, and encourage ecological restoration of local rivers.

A smart-growth agenda for the region would involve an entirely new framework as well as some specific policy approaches. Smart growth requires equitable regional policy goals for housing and transportation that will accommodate growth in keeping with a unified vision for the region's future geographic scale. The region must begin tracking land supply, setting large-scale goals, integrating land use and transportation planning, and linking natural resources and protection efforts; given that the regional council of governments currently lacks real power, new collaborative and cross-cutting organizational structures may need to be created to carry out these crucial tasks. Southern California might also follow Maryland's example regarding policies that direct infrastructure and other state spending to built-up areas by earmarking state funds to encourage smart-growth planning and development, to provide incentives for urban land recycling and infill development, and to create high-density, transportation-oriented developments. Finally, for smart-growth initiatives to address the realities of economic and social inequality (in addition to environmental and efficiency concerns), organizations representing low- and moderate-income people—including CBOs and labor unions—must be included in the planning process.

References

Advisory Committee on Intergovernmental Relations (ACIR). 1987. *Measuring State Fiscal Capacity.* Washington: ACIR.

Aldana, Carolyn, and Gary Dymski. 2001. "Urban Sprawl, Racial Separation, and Federal Housing Policy in Southern California." University of Southern California, Southern California Studies Center.

———. 2004. "Urban Sprawl, Racial Separation, and Federal Housing Policy." In *Up against the Sprawl: Public Policy and the Making of Southern California*, edited by Jennifer Wolch, Manuel Pastor Jr., and Peter Dreier, pp. 99–119. University of Minnesota Press.

Beatley, Timothy. 1994. *Habitat Conservation Planning.* Washington: Island Press.

California Department of Finance. 2004. "Population Projections by Race/Ethnicity, Gender and Age for Children for California and Its Counties, 2000–2050." Sacramento (www.dof.ca.gov/html/demograp/dru_publications/projections/p3/p3.htm [May]).

California Department of Fish and Game. 2004. "Natural Community Conservation Planning" (http://ceres.ca.gov/cra/nccp/[August]).

California Employment Development Department. 2004 (www.edd.calmis.ca.gov [August]).

City of Los Angeles. 1997. "Report of the Blue Ribbon Citizens' Committee on Slum Housing." Los Angeles Department of Housing, July 28 (http://calmis.ca.gov/htmlfile/subject/indtab6:SIC.htm; and http://calmis.ca.gov.htmlfile/subjectindtable.htm [October]).

County of Riverside. 1999. "Riverside County Integrated Planning" (www.rcip.org/stakeholdertxt.html [August]).

Davis, Mike. 1995. "Water Pirates and the Infinite Suburb." *Capitalism, Nature, Socialism* 7: 81–84.

———. 1996. "Let Malibu Burn: A Political History of the Fire Coast." *LA Weekly*, Nov. 15, pp. 23–24, 27, 29–30, 32.

———. 1998. *The Ecology of Fear.* New York: Metropolitan Books.

Dreier, Peter, and Richard Rothstein. 1994, "Seismic Stimulus: The California Quake's Creative Destruction." *American Prospect* (Summer): 40–46.

Dymski, Gary, and Carolyn Aldana. 2001. "Subsidizing Sprawl: Federal Housing Policies for the Rich and the Poor." University of Southern California, Southern California Studies Center.

Erie, Steven P. 1992. "How the Urban West Was Won: The Local State and Economic Growth in Los Angeles, 1880–1932." *Urban Affairs Review* 27, no. 4: 519–54.

Erie, Steven P., and Pascale Joassart-Marcelli. 2000. "Unraveling Southern California's Water/Growth Nexus: Metropolitan Water District Policies and Subsidies for Suburban Development, 1928–1996." *California Western Law Review* 36: 267–90.

Erie, Steven P., Gregory Freeman, and Pascale Joassart-Marcelli. 2004. "W(h)ither Sprawl? Have Regional Water Policies Subsidized Suburban Development?" In *Up against the Sprawl: Public Policy and the Making of*

Southern California, edited by Jennifer Wolch, Manuel Pastor Jr., and Peter Dreier, pp. 45–70. University of Minnesota Press.

Erie, Steven P., Thomas P. Kim, and Gregory Freeman. 1999. "The LAX Master Plan: Facing the Challenge of Community, Environmental and Regional Airport Planning." University of Southern California, Southern California Studies Center.

Frey, William. 2001. "Melting Pot Suburbs: A Census 2000 Study of Suburban Diversity." Brookings Center on Urban and Metropolitan Policy.

Fulton, William. 1997. *The Reluctant Metropolis*. Point Arena, Calif.: Solano Books.

Fulton, William, Madelyn Glickfeld, Grant McMurran, and June Gin. 1999. "A Landscape Portrait of Southern California's Structure of Government and Growth." Claremont Graduate University Research Institute.

Fulton, William, Madelyn Glickfeld, Grant McMurran, and Ned Levine. 1999. "Growth Governance in Southern California." Claremont Graduate University Research Institute.

Fulton, William, Rolf Pendall, Mai Nguyen, and Alicia Harrison. 2001. "Who Sprawls the Most? How Growth Patterns Differ across the U.S." Brookings Center on Urban and Metropolitan Policy.

Giuliano, Genevieve. 2001. "Where Is the Region in Transportation Planning for Southern California?" University of Southern California, Southern California Studies Center.

———. 2004. "Where Is the 'Region' in Regional Transportation Planning?" In *Up against the Sprawl: Public Policy and the Making of Southern California*, edited by Jennifer Wolch, Manuel Pastor Jr., and Peter Dreier, pp. 151–70. University of Minnesota Press.

Gottlieb, Robert. 1988. *A Life of Its Own: The Politics and Power of Water*. New York: Harcourt Brace Jovanovich.

Grigsby, Eugene, III. 2000. "Redevelopment's Contribution to Affordable Housing in Southern California." University of Southern California, Southern California Studies Center.

Hise, Greg. 1997. *Magnetic Los Angeles: Planning the Twentieth Century Metropolis*. Johns Hopkins University Press.

Hricko, Andrea, Kim Preston, Hays Witt, and John Peters. 1999. "Air Pollution and Children's Health." In *Atlas of Southern California*, vol. 3, pp. 55–60. University of Southern California, Southern California Studies Center.

Jargowsky, P. A., and M. Bane. 1991. "Ghetto Poverty in the United States, 1970–80." In *The Urban Underclass*, edited by C. Jencks and P. E. Peterson. Brookings.

Joassart-Marcelli, Pascale, and Juliet Musso. 2001. "The Distributive Impact of Federal Fiscal Policy: Federal Spending and Southern California Cities." *Urban Affairs Review* 37: 163–84.

Joassart-Marcelli, Pascale, and Jennifer Wolch. 2003. "The Intrametropolitan Geography of Poverty and the Nonprofit Sector in Southern California." *Nonprofit and Voluntary Sector Quarterly* 32: 70–96.

Joassart-Marcelli, Pascale, William Fulton, and Juliet A. Musso. 2004. "Can Growth Control Escape Fiscal and Economic Pressures? City Policies before and after the 1990s Recession." In *Up against the Sprawl: Public Policy and the Making of Southern California*, edited by Jennifer Wolch, Manuel Pastor Jr., and Peter Dreier, pp. 255–77. University of Minnesota Press.

Joassart-Marcelli, Pascale, Juliet Musso, and Jennifer Wolch. 2004. "Federal Expenditures, Intrametropolitan Poverty, and Fiscal Disparities in Southern California Cities." In *Up against the Sprawl: Public Policy and the Making of Southern California*, edited by Jennifer Wolch, Manuel Pastor Jr., and Peter Dreier, pp. 195–224. University of Minnesota Press.

Keil, Roger, and Gene Desfor. 1996. "Making Local Environmental Policy in Los Angeles." *Cities* 13: 303–14.

Labor/Community Strategy Center v. L.A. County Metropolitan Transportation Authority. 1994. Summary of evidence (http://www.thestrategycenter.org/Decree/summary_of_evidence.html [August 16, 2004]).

Ladd, Helen. 1998. *Local Government Tax and Land Use Policies in the United States: Understanding the Links*. Northampton, N.Y.: Edward Elgar.

Ladd, Helen F., and John Yinger. 1989. *America's Ailing Cities*. 2nd ed. Johns Hopkins University Press.

———. 1994. "The Case for Equalization." *National Tax Journal* 47, no. 1: 211–23.

Landis, Betsey. 1993. "Significant Ecological Areas: The Skeleton in Los Angeles County's Closet?" In *Interface between Ecology and Land Use in California*, edited by J. E. Keeley. Los Angeles: Southern California Academy of Sciences.

Los Angeles Metropolitan Transit Authority (LAMTA). 2001 (www.mta.net).

Marcelli, Enrico. 1998. "Undocumented Latino Immigrants." In *Atlas of Southern California*, vol. 2, pp. 17–20. University of Southern California, Southern California Studies Center.

———. 2004. "From the Barrio to the 'Burbs? Immigration and the Dynamics of Suburbanization." In *Up against the Sprawl: Public Policy and the Making of Southern California*, edited by Jennifer Wolch, Manuel Pastor Jr., and Peter Dreier, pp. 123–50. University of Minnesota Press.

Marks, Mara A., Elizabeth Gearin, and Carol Armstrong. 2004. "The Experimental Metropolis: Political Impediments and Opportunities for Innovation." In *Up against the Sprawl: Public Policy and the Making of Southern California*, edited by Jennifer Wolch, Manuel Pastor Jr., and Peter Dreier, pp. 343–71. University of Minnesota Press.

Morello-Frosch, Rachel, Manuel Pastor, and James Sadd. 2001. "Environmental Justice and Southern California's Riskscape: The Distribution of Air Toxics Exposures and Health Risks among Diverse Communities." *Urban Affairs Review* 36: 551–69.

Musso, Juliet. 2004. "Metropolitan Fiscal Structure: Coping with Growth and Fiscal Constraint." In *Up against the Sprawl: Public Policy and the Making of Southern California*, edited by Jennifer Wolch, Manuel Pastor Jr., and Peter Dreier, pp. 171–94. University of Minnesota Press.

Myers, Dowell. 1996. *Immigration: Past and Future*. University of Southern California, Lusk Center for Real Estate.

————. 1999. "Upward Mobility in Space and Time: Lessons from Immigration." In *America's Demographic Tapestry: Baseline for the New Millennium*, edited by James W. Hughes and Joseph J. Seneca. Rutgers University Press.

Myers, Dowell, and Julie Park. 2001. "Racially Balanced Cities in Southern California, 1980–2000." Public Research Report 2001-05. University of Southern California, School of Policy, Planning and Development.

Nichols, Mary, and Stanley Young. 1991. *The Amazing L.A. Environment*. Los Angeles: Living Planet.

Orfield, Myron. 2000. *Los Angeles Metropatterns: Social Separation and Sprawl in the Los Angeles Region*. Minneapolis: Metropolitan Area Research Corporation.

Pastor, Manuel, Jr. 2000. "Regional Growth and Inequality." University of Southern California, Southern California Studies Center.

Pastor, Manuel, Jr., and Enrico A. Marcelli. 2000. "Men 'N the Hood: Skill, Spatial, and Social Mismatches among Male Workers in Los Angeles County." *Urban Geography* 12, no. 6: 474–96.

Pastor, Manuel, Jr., Peter Dreier, Eugene Grigsby III, and Marta Lopez-Garza. 2000. *Regions That Work: How Cities and Suburbs Can Grow Together*. University of Minnesota Press.

Pendall, Rolf. 1999. "Do Land Use Controls Cause Sprawl?" *Environment and Planning B: Planning and Design* 26: 555–71.

Pincetl, Stephanie. 2004. "The Preservation of Nature at the Urban Fringe." In *Up against the Sprawl: Public Policy and the Making of Southern California*, edited by Jennifer Wolch, Manuel Pastor Jr., and Peter Dreier, pp. 225–51. University of Minnesota Press.

Schoenherr, Allan A. 1992. *A Natural History of California*. University of California Press.

Scott, Allen J. 1996. "The Manufacturing Economy: Ethnic and Gender Division of Labor." In *Ethnic Los Angeles*, edited by Roger Waldinger and Mehdi Bozorgmehr, pp. 215–45. New York: Russell Sage Foundation.

Scott, Allen J., and Edward W. Soja, eds. 1996. *The City: Los Angeles and Urban Theory at the End of the Twentieth Century*. University of California Press.

Sherman, Douglas, and others. 1998. "Natural Hazards." In *Atlas of Southern California*, vol. 2, pp. 45–50. University of Southern California, Southern California Studies Center.

Southern California Studies Center. 2001. *Sprawl Hits the Wall: Confronting the Realities of Metropolitan Los Angeles*. In *Atlas of Southern California*, vol. 4. University of Southern California, Brookings Center on Urban and Metropolitan Policy.

Southern California Association of Governments (SCAG). 1999. *The State of the Region 1999*. Los Angeles.

————. 2000. *The State of the Region 2000*. Los Angeles.

Texas Transportation Institute. 1999. "Annual Urban Mobility Study." Texas A&M University System (www.mobility.tamu.edu).

———. 2001. "Annual Urban Mobility Study." Texas A&M University System (http/www.mobility.tamu.edu).

United States Conference of Mayors and the National Association of Counties. 2000. "U.S. Metro Economies: Leading America's New Economy" (http://www.mayors.org/citiesdrivetheeconomy/index2.html).

Wolch, Jennifer, and Stuart Gabriel. 1985. "Dismantling the Community-Based Human Service System." *Journal of the American Planning Association* 51: 53–62.

Wolch, Jennifer, and Robert K. Geiger. 1983. "The Distribution of Urban Voluntary Resources: An Exploratory Analysis." *Environment and Planning A* 15: 1067–82.

Wolch, Jennifer, Andrea Gullo, and Unna Lassiter. 1997. "Changing Attitudes toward California's Cougars." *Society and Animals* 5: 95–116.

CHAPTER 4

Philadelphia:

Spatial Economic Disparities

Joseph Gyourko and Anita A. Summers

Economic development and growth have varied widely across jurisdictions within the Philadelphia metropolitan area. The same is true for social conditions across the region. This is likely to make forging metropolitan solutions to urban and regional problems difficult, because they typically require a political consensus that itself is hard to establish in such circumstances. There is no doubt that the effort still needs to be made, but the extent of regional policies remains very limited. At this writing in 2004, large differences in fiscally burdensome socioeconomic conditions are primarily addressed at the federal and state levels. The evidence indicates that these large differences are not compensated for by intergovernmental aid, making certain locations in the metropolitan area fundamentally less attractive places for firms and households. The distortion of the location decisions of businesses and households is economically inefficient and helps foster growth and development patterns within the metropolitan area that are not efficient. One of the striking findings of our research is how little state aid flows, in particular, do to rectify this situation. We conclude that state and federal intergovernmental flow allocation formulas, as well as welfare, tax, and land-use policies, all could be revised to help promote more efficient regional growth and development. Intergovernmental fiscal flows, and their integral relationship to local tax effort (local taxes per capita as a percentage of per capita income), play a pivotal role in the socioeconomic contours of the metropolitan area.

The first four sections of this chapter describe and analyze the patterns of extant socioeconomic conditions throughout the Philadelphia metropolitan area and the factors contributing to them. In the first section we focus on broad patterns of growth, development, land-use patterns, and poverty. We document the often stark differences in economic and social conditions between the central city of Philadelphia and its suburbs, and among the suburbs themselves. We then report on an empirical analysis of the distribution of federal and state intergovernmental flows and local tax effort in relation to the distribution of poverty across the Philadelphia metropolitan area. The results show that the poorest jurisdictions tend to have the highest local tax effort, and that state and federal flows do not redistribute effectively to offset the extra costs of delivering public services to the poor. The fiscal playing field across locations is not level. We next go beyond the analysis of current flows and investigate capital spending on public infrastructure within the metropolitan area. State-level road and highway investments in particular are found to flow in relatively large amounts to the suburbs. We then report on an analysis of a policy—federal tax policy regarding owner-occupied housing—usually not considered to have important implications at the metropolitan level. However, this research concludes that the benefits of housing tax policy are very concentrated spatially, with a relatively few suburban areas reaping much of the benefit.

The final section summarizes the findings on city-suburban disparities in the Philadelphia Metropolitan Statistical Area (MSA) and makes suggestions for metropolitan policy that would result in more balanced and more efficient growth and development for the region.

Growth and Development Patterns

Past research on metropolitan areas has centered on comparisons among large cities (why are some large cities doing better than others?) and intrametropolitan analysis (comparisons of city and suburban patterns).[1] The analysis in this section focuses on the details of the suburban patterns of population, poverty, and growth. In the next section, the focus is on fiscal pressures and state and federal aid. In addition, most of the analysis in the subsequent sections centers on the Pennsylvania portion of the Philadelphia MSA, because recent data on state intergovernmental flows are not available for New Jersey. To enable this, we

1. The data and analysis in this section are drawn from Summers (2000).

Table 4-1. Selected Characteristics of the Central City and Suburbs in the Philadelphia MSA, 1990s

Characteristic	Central city		Suburbs	
Total population, 1996 (000s)	1,478.0	9.5	84.8	11.0
Total employment, 1996 (000s)	598.0	4.9	27.4	5.5
Percent living in poverty, 1990	19.8	4.7	35.0	5.5
Percent unemployed, 1990	9.7	3.6	16.4	4.8
Population density, 1996 (people per square mile)	10.5	2.5	8.1	2.5
Population change, 1990–96 (percent)	−6.8	7.3	−3.0	2.9
Household median income, 1990 ($000)	24.6	43.5	17.4	39.0
Median year housing built, 1990	1939	1960	1945	1958
Local tax revenue per capita, 1996 ($)	2,001.8	395.7	n.a.	n.a.
Total federal revenue per capita, 1994–96 average ($000)	8.0	3.8	6.6	4.6
Nonhighway state revenue per capita, 1995 ($)	140.0	15.7	n.a.	n.a.
Violent crime rate, 1996 (per 1,000 population)	15.3	2.1	31.4	2.9
Percent without high school diploma, 1990	24.4	12.2	30.3	14.8
Percent black, 1990	39.9	5.0	56.3	10.4

Source: U.S. Census Bureau (1990).

amassed a large data set on the 334 metropolitan civil divisions (MCDs) in the Philadelphia metropolitan statistical area (MSA). The full database is available from the authors.

The major central cities in the region have very different socioeconomic characteristics from their suburbs (see table 4-1). Poverty rates are five to six times higher in the central cities, unemployment rates are two to three times higher, housing is substantially older, crime rates are seven to ten times higher, and education levels are substantially lower. Population changes are negative in the city, yet strongly positive in the suburbs. Federal and state aid to cities is much larger than to the suburbs. However, numerous analyses have demonstrated that the volume of intergovernmental flows leaves cities with substantial poverty service costs that need to be met from their own local revenue sources.[2] The playing field for Philadelphia has not been made level with the surrounding local governments. Philadelphia uses much of its local tax revenues to provide services to the poor—an activity that belongs at higher levels of government. Table 4-1 documents the extent of the unevenness.

Population

There are several features of interest in the population dynamics of the Philadelphia MSA suburbs. An examination of the 236 MCDs in the

2. See, for example, Pack (1995); Summers (2000).

Pennsylvania part of the region shows that between 1980 and 1990 the largest suburbs grew the most, but in the next six years—1990 to 1996—they grew the least (see columns 1, 2, and 3 of table 4-2). The mid-sized municipalities are growing most rapidly. The lowest population quintile in the suburbs had the lowest household income and the highest poverty rates (see table 4-3, page 117), but apart from that, there was little variation across the other quintiles. The development of land for nonresidential use was consistently proportionately greater in the larger suburbs, as one might expect. But the proportion of land devoted to multi-family residential use had a much less consistent pattern. Municipalities with an average population of from 5,000 to 10,000 had double the proportion of the other size municipalities, except, of course, Philadelphia. The map of the region (see color plates, map 4-1) shows the geography of the population dynamics in a more striking fashion. Most of the growth is in the towns farther out from the center city of Philadelphia. Many closer-in suburbs are growing slowly or declining. Regression analysis sheds additional light on some of the major factors associated with the wide variation in population growth rates among the suburbs.[3] On average, the higher-growth suburbs have higher median incomes and they tax themselves relatively more. These communities want high levels of public goods and are willing to tax themselves to get them. They also are farther from Philadelphia and relatively small, and their housing stock is relatively new. Not specifically measured in these equations, but undoubtedly a significant factor in enabling these characteristics to emerge, is the greatly expanded suburban transportation network. A measurement of the specific location effects of this expansion would probably reduce the unexplained variation in population growth across the suburbs, though the positive effect of distance from the center city is almost certainly a reflection of the enabling effect of a stronger transportation network.

In sum, in the Philadelphia suburbs, population is expanding where the population is more affluent, is better educated, has access to more single-family dwellings, and is relatively small.

Land-Use Patterns

We also compiled detailed data on land-use patterns in 1970 and 1990 for each of the MCDs in the Philadelphia MSA. Our analysis focused on three aspects of land use: the dynamics of land-use changes

3. This and other regression analyses referred to in this chapter are available from the authors on request.

Table 4-2. Dynamics of Land Use by Population Quintile for the Philadelphia MSA, 236 Pennsylvania MCDs, 1970–1990

Quintile	*1* *Mean total population, 1990*	*2* *Mean percentage in residential use, 1970*	*3* *Mean percentage in residential use, 1990*	*4*[a] *Mean percentage change in percentage of residential use, 1970–90*	*5* *Mean percentage of nonresidential developed land, 1970*
1	1,391	19.08	22.94	20.20	14.03
2	2,896	22.01	26.14	18.78	15.29
3	5,120	20.38	23.43	14.99	13.53
4	9,418	27.30	32.96	20.76	18.45
5	26,660	31.63	37.46	18.45	19.42
Philadelphia	1,585,577	30.29	31.62	4.38	44.09

Quintile	*6* *Mean percentage of nonresidential developed land, 1990*	*7*[b] *Mean percentage change in percentage of nonresidential developed land, 1970–90*	*8* *Mean percentage of multi-family use, 1970*	*9* *Mean percentage in multi-family use, 1990*	*10*[c] *Mean percentage change in percent of multi-family use, 1970–90*
1	16.67	18.79	3.06	2.35	−23.24
2	19.08	24.78	4.77	5.74	20.16
3	17.61	30.21	3.98	3.50	−12.18
4	22.24	20.56	6.76	10.42	54.13
5	28.21	45.25	4.34	5.72	31.92
Philadelphia	47.82	8.46	22.28	25.82	15.90

Source: Authors' calculations.
a. [(Col. 4 − Col. 3) / Col. 3] x 100.
b. [(Col. 7 − Col. 6) / Col. 6] x 100.
c. [(Col. 10 − Col. 9) / Col. 9] x 100.

in relation to population size in the MCDs, the determinants of nonresidential land-use development in the MCDs, and the potential for growth under existing zoning ordinances.

The proportionate use of land for residential, nonresidential developed, and multi-family housing is shown in table 4-2. The percentages of land use in 1970 and 1990, and the changes over the twenty years between those two dates, are arrayed by population quintile. (City of Philadelphia data are shown for comparison purposes.) Residential land use, as one would expect, is larger in the suburban MCDs with higher populations. There is no clear pattern to the growth in proportions. Nonresidential developed land proportions are also higher in the more populated suburban MCDs, and there the rate of growth is sharply higher in the most populated ones. Together these data indicate an increased use of land for development, rather than for recreation, agriculture, and protection of wooded and vacant land, with the greatest pressures coming from the most populated suburban MCDs. In the four suburban counties in Pennsylvania, more than 185 acres were added to residential and nonresidential development between 1970 and 1990; and the amount of land devoted to agriculture, recreation, and vacant and wooded land declined by more than 200 acres. It is also of interest to note that the highest proportion of land allocated to multi-family use, and the biggest growth in this proportion, was in the MCDs with an average population of 9,500 (the fourth quintile), not in the largest or smallest quintiles. And declines in the proportions of land in multi-family use took place in the smallest 20 percent of MCDs averaging 1,400 persons, and in the 20 percent averaging 5,000.

The proportion of land developed for nonresidential use gives some indication of the role of commercial, industrial, and business activities in an MCD. The magnitude of these activities, which is described in the next section, is clearly relevant to the distribution of some intergovernmental flows. It is of interest, therefore, to gain insight into the characteristics of communities with higher proportions of land devoted to nonresidential development. Regression analysis indicates that the proportions are higher in MCDs that have older housing, have a higher proportion of land already in that usage, are closer to the center city, have emerged with higher local taxes per capita subsequently, have a higher proportion of their labor force employed in durable manufacturing, and receive more per capita state aid. The poverty rate underlies many of these factors. Where poverty rates are higher, housing is older, the MCDs are closer to Philadelphia City, and local taxes per capita are higher. If the poverty measure is taken as a surrogate for these factors, then the conclusion is clear that nonresidential land use is encouraged by less poverty. Even when the associated factors are explicitly in the regression, the role of poverty emerges, though less strongly, of course. Beyond that, nonresidential land use is encouraged by what is probably more permissive zoning in areas with older infrastructure, and by the stimulus of intergovernmental assistance and local expenditures in the provision of public services.

One of the most interesting questions relevant to land-use development is the extent to which communities have development plans that are constrained by binding zoning regulations. In 1994 the Delaware Valley Regional Planning Commission completed a study of five high-growth corridors covering nineteen MCDs in the Philadelphia MSA: Route 295 in Burlington County, N.J.; Route 322 in Chester County, Pa.; Route 322 in Delaware County, Pa.; Route 322 in Gloucester County, N.J.; and Route 130 in Mercer County, N.J.[4] They analyzed how much development could take place under existing zoning regulations in these major corridors and translated their conclusions into population and employment potential. They concluded that, over the next twenty years (by approximately 2018), the corridors could handle from 8 to 117 percent more people than forecast, and from 160 to 1,900 percent more employees than forecast. This magnitude of build-out is not what is forecast, but the figures suggest that, with this build-out potential, local communities have important choices to make. Their land-use policies, revised or left as they are, will define those choices.

If the combined effects of market forces and the political process are not producing the amount of open space in a township that the majority of citizens want, then the voters must make it known that they want policies such as conservation easements, purchase of development rights, and mandatory cluster development ordinances considered. Similarly, if traffic congestion exceeds what is "wanted," given the trade-offs, then traffic impact fees are a possible tool. If the citizens are concerned about rapidly mounting demands on public services and infrastructure because of rapid growth, then timed-growth ordinances and capital improvement programs may be appropriate policies. We do not have a systematic measure of what various suburban populations want. But that people and businesses are ready to pay a wide range of impact fees to live in suburban locations is clear.

In sum, rapid development of land is occurring in the suburban communities of the Philadelphia metropolitan area. Both residential and nonresidential development are most rapid in the bigger and more affluent communities, and development is boosted by the receipt of intergovernmental aid. But, at least in the areas of the major highway corridors, this growth is not running up against current zoning limitations.

4. Delaware Valley Regional Planning Commission (1994).

Table 4-3. Selected Characteristics of Philadelphia and Its Suburbs by Poverty Quintile, 1990

Quintile	1 Mean 1990 poverty rate (percent)	2 Mean 1980 poverty rate (percent)	3 Mean change in population, 1990–96 (percent)	4 Mean household income, 1990 (dollars)
1	1.40	3.57	12.77	54,624
2	2.43	4.05	8.26	48,578
3	3.67	4.86	7.43	44,425
4	5.23	6.61	6.45	37,618
5	10.71	10.22	1.48	31,957
Philadelphia	19.76	20.17	−6.79	24,603

Quintile	5 Mean unemployment rate, 1990 (percent)	6 Mean nonresidential developed land, 1990 (percent)	7 Mean percentage in multi-family use, 1990	8 Mean percentage of residential land in multi-family use, 1990
1	2.6	14.36	1.59	6.17
2	3.0	19.08	2.57	7.81
3	3.1	21.41	3.36	8.35
4	4.1	21.24	6.91	14.32
5	5.1	27.78	13.30	36.72
Philadelphia	9.7	47.82	25.82	81.93

Source: Authors' calculations.

Poverty

Not all suburbs are affluent; there is great variation in suburban poverty. There is one suburb with a poverty rate of 0.54 percent and another with a 26.6 percent poverty rate, about 6 percentage points higher than for the city of Philadelphia. Table 4-3 summarizes statistics on poverty in suburban areas and in relation to the city of Philadelphia. The first column presents the average poverty rate of suburbs arrayed in quintile order and for the central city of Philadelphia. The remaining data are averages for each of the poverty quintiles. Note that the mean poverty rate in the top suburban quintile is 10.7 percent, only one-half of Philadelphia's rate. As one might expect, the MCDs with the lowest poverty rates had the most rapid rates of population growth, the highest household income, and the lowest unemployment rates. They were also the communities with the lowest percentages of nonresidential developed and multi-family land use.

The geographic dispersion of poverty is shown in map 4-2 (see color plates). Poverty is concentrated in the city of Philadelphia, in Chester, and in a few other areas. An examination of the simple relationship between poverty rates in each Philadelphia MSA suburb and other characteristics of these suburbs indicates that higher poverty rates coexist with a higher proportion of multi-family dwellings, a higher proportion of land in nonresidential developed usage, a higher proportion of blacks, higher density, more violent crime, lower income, lower rates of population growth, and older housing.

There are no simple cause-and-effect implications of the coincidence of these characteristics; poorer people may be attracted to areas where housing prices are lower because the stock is older and more dense, for example. In fact, the strength and persistence of the interrelationships among these characteristics makes simple interventions in any one of them unsuccessful. That points to the preference for relying on a strong macroeconomy supplemented by policies designed to enable market forces to operate on a playing field that equalizes the fiscal burdens of poverty concentrations.

Studies of America's large cities uniformly find that cities with higher rates of poverty have lower rates of growth and are characterized by a relatively poorly educated labor force and more crime. A very interesting aspect of the analysis of the Philadelphia suburbs is that the directional association among the characteristics of communities with varying rates of poverty is the same as that in comparisons among large cities.

In research for this project, Ehrlich and Madden looked more carefully into the distribution and characteristics of the poor across the Philadelphia MSA.[5] They point out that though only 34 percent of the MSA's residents live in Philadelphia, 63 percent of the poor do, and that the differences in the family structure and employment characteristics between the suburban poor and the urban poor go well beyond those aggregate levels.

Ehrlich and Madden explore why the poor are concentrated in the city. Hypotheses abound: older housing is generally cheaper per square foot in the city; transportation costs are lower; there is greater access to poverty relief programs; housing discrimination or zoning restrictions may produce higher prices in the suburbs; higher-income households may prefer suburban locations; the suburban poor may be poor for

5. Ehrlich and Madden (2000).

shorter spells because their poverty is more often caused by temporary unemployment or marriage breakups than by lack of job skills.

Ehrlich and Madden conclude that race is the key differentiating characteristic between city and suburban poor, and that education and household structure do not account for the racial concentration disparities. Regardless of income, African Americans are disproportionately located in the city. The large difference between poverty rates in Philadelphia and its suburbs is explained primarily by this disproportion and then by the additional fact that African Americans have much higher rates of poverty than white households. The city poor also have characteristics that differ from those of the suburban poor. Poor city households have fewer retirees, more female heads, more unemployed, more welfare recipients, more adult high school dropouts, and more children. These differences suggest that different policies are needed to address the different dimensions of the poverty. Ehrlich and Madden also examined the variations across the Philadelphia suburbs in the locations of poor households. Their data indicate that African American suburbanites live in suburbs with higher density, lower average income, and greater poverty rates than do white suburbanites. The distribution of poor whites across the suburban map is much more even than the distribution of poor African Americans.

A question of great interest, addressed in the next section, is the extent to which federal and state intergovernmental flows are directed to these suburban communities in accordance with their poverty rates and consequent tax pressures. We discuss to what extent intergovernmental flows are redistributional and to what extent they level the fiscal playing field perceived by firms and households.

Fiscal Patterns

Much has been written documenting the fact that America's large cities bear significant redistributive burdens. Janet Rothenberg Pack estimates that, for large cities (defined as having over 300,000 in population) with average poverty rates of 20 percent, direct poverty expenditures are $36 per capita if they are structured as a city and $277 per capita if they are a city-county government.[6] Pack estimates that for every additional percentage point in a city's poverty rate there is an additional $27.74 per capita in indirect poverty expenditures. A high-poverty city with a 25

6. Pack (1995).

percent poverty rate would spend $166 more per capita on these indirect costs than a city with the average 19 percent poverty rate. For the city of Philadelphia, a research study estimated that over 7 percent of own-source revenues go to direct poverty services,[7] and almost half of the school district's own-source revenues go to educating poor children.[8] Thus it is clear that in large cities a material fraction of the poverty costs is borne by own-source revenues. Intergovernmental aid does not fully compensate them for the added costs of the poverty in their jurisdictions.

Does this also describe the situation in suburban jurisdictions? The most important result from our empirical effort to examine the factors associated with higher tax effort of MCDs is that communities with higher rates of poverty pay more taxes relative to their income. This suggests that individual suburbs, much like large cities with high poverty, fund poverty needs disproportionately out of own-source revenues. Further, intergovernmental flows are distributed in ways that do not offset the extra costs of additional poverty.

In sum, the data indicate that federal flows to poorer communities are larger, but not so much so that they fully offset the fiscal burdens associated with higher poverty. And, the data on state flows for Pennsylvania indicate that such aid is not higher for high-poverty areas.

State Intergovernmental Flows in the Pennsylvania Suburbs of the Philadelphia MSA

The scatter diagram of figure 4-1 tells a dramatic story. The per capita allocation of nonhighway state funds to the suburban MCDs bears no discernible relationship to their poverty rates in this simple comparison. There is no evidence of a redistributional effect, even when highway allocations (which are very lumpy) are omitted. Regression results take many more factors into consideration and support these conclusions with more precision. Moreover, if highway revenues are included, the results are very similar. Poverty does not appear to be a meaningful factor in the commonwealth's overall allocation of funds to the suburban MCDs in the Philadelphia region.

Building on the work by Raimondo, we conducted additional work to investigate the relationship between state intergovernmental flows to suburban MCDs and key political characteristics.[9] This work analyzed whether state aid flows are influenced by the share of the statewide

7. Summers and Jakubowski (1996).
8. Summers and Ritter (1996).
9. Raimondo (1983).

Figure 4-1. State Nonhighway Revenue per Capita versus Percent in Poverty in the Pennsylvania Portion of the Philadelphia MSA

Dollars per capita, 1996

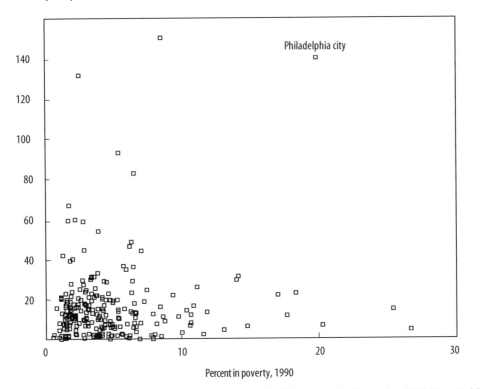

Note: Four MCDs were omitted because they were very distant outliers: West Conshohocken Borough (pop. 1,258), Marcus Hook Borough (pop. 2,545), Malvern Borough (pop. 2,944), and Ivyland Borough (pop. 498).

votes cast for the governor in the previous gubernatorial election, by the margin of victory that elected the governor, or by the voter participation rate in the MCD. The fundamental political question raised is: are voter choices in an MCD associated with the allocation of discretionary flows of state funds?

An econometric analysis of state revenue flows (measured with and without highway grants) reveals several relationships. The size of the MCD is a factor in the per capita flows: larger MCDs get more. Further, MCDs with a higher share of the statewide vote for the incumbent governor also receive higher revenue flows. It is not possible, therefore, to determine whether the relevant factor is size or political pressure. MCDs with a higher proportion of nonresidential developed land receive more funds, as do those that tax themselves more heavily. Various measures of tax effort are correlated with poverty rates, but whether poverty rates are included with these measures or examined excluding them, there is no evidence that the level of poverty is a factor in determining state flows to the Philadelphia MSA MCDs.

Federal Intergovernmental Flows in the Pennsylvania Suburbs of the Philadelphia MSA

We also calculated a disaggregated data set of federal flows to each MCD, separating out redistributive and nonredistributive flows.[10] There are two categories of redistributional funds: redistributional funds going directly to people, such as food stamps and Medicaid, and spatially related redistributional funds, such as assistance in housing and crime control going to a municipality with high poverty.

These data show that, unlike aid from the commonwealth, federal redistributional revenues are indeed correlated with local poverty rates, The dollar amounts of per capita federal redistributional funding intended to help poor people (directly) and poor communities (spatially) are closely related to the amount of poverty in the MCD (see figure 4-2).

It is interesting to dissect the factors, including poverty, that appear to be major determinants of these federal flows. Regression analysis indicates that the direct federal redistributional flows are overwhelmingly determined by poverty. Population density and the proportion of land area in business also are highly and positively correlated with these aid flows. Either measure of the intensity of land use is associated with a higher level of federal redistributive funds. The proportion of developed nonresidential land use is also highly correlated with tax effort (per capita local taxes as a percentage of per capita income). Both characteristics accompany larger federal redistributive flows. And slower-growth areas received more direct funds per capita. The fact that density measures and slower-growth measures result in additional funds going to the poor people in a community suggests that there is explicit recognition in the allocation formulas that, among suburban MCDs, the economic dynamics of the community and the concentration of poverty give rise to greater public service needs. Another way of describing this is to say that there is explicit recognition of the higher tax effort borne by poorer communities, shown by the significant tax

10. These were calculated with invaluable advice from our colleagues Wim Wiewel and Joseph Persky at the University of Illinois at Chicago.

Figure 4-2. Average Federal Redistributional Revenue per Capita in 1994–96 versus Percent in Poverty in 1990: Pennsylvania Portion of the Philadelphia MSA

Dollars per capita, 1994–96 average

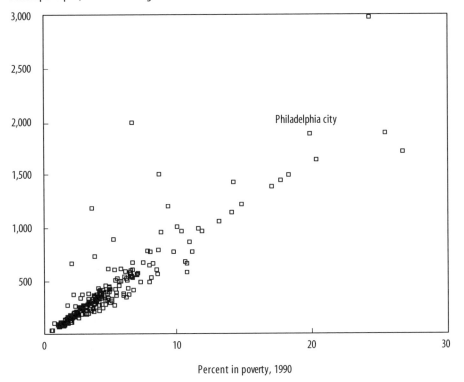

Percent in poverty, 1990

Note: Four MCDs were omitted because they were very distant outliers: West Conshohocken Borough (pop. 1,258), Marcus Hook Borough (pop. 2,545), Malvern Borough (pop. 2,944), and Ivyland Borough (pop. 498).

effort effects when the percentage of nonresidential land is omitted. There is no clear evidence that areas where a high percentage of voters voted for President Clinton received more per capita direct redistributional aid than other areas.

Analysis of federal spatially related redistributional funds shows some similar patterns: more aid went to the poorer and denser areas with high tax effort. However, there is no evidence that relatively slow population growth is a factor in these flows. To the contrary, the farther the MCDs are from the center city (correlated with high population growth), the greater the spatially related flows. The finding that these flows are higher in MCDs with lower voter turnout is a restatement of the very high correlation between general voter participation rates and levels of poverty and density.

The same regression analysis shows that other federal funds are negatively related to poverty. Federal nonredistributive flows in the suburbs are directed more to MCDs that are smaller, have slower population growth, put forth more tax effort, and are more densely developed. A simple regression between other federal funds and poverty shows no significant relationship. Once the size of the population is factored in, there is some evidence that MCDs that produced a larger share of the state vote for Clinton in 1992 received more federal per capita nonredistributional grants. These nonredistributional grants are much larger than the redistributional funds, so on net, total per capita federal revenues are not associated with poverty rates in the suburban communities. Figure 4-3 illustrates the widely varying flows to higher poverty jurisdictions.

Conclusions about Growth, Development, and Fiscal Patterns

The major conclusions from the analysis of the socioeconomic, land-use, and fiscal data for the suburban Pennsylvania MCDs of the Philadelphia MSA are as follows:

—Communities experiencing population expansion are the ones where the population is more affluent, resides more in single-family dwellings, and has a smaller population.

—Land-use data confirm the following: (1) increased absorption of land for development, with the greatest pressures coming from the most populated suburban MCDs; (2) the biggest suburban growth in multi-family use is in communities averaging 9,500 in population (not the largest of the noncentral-city MCDs); and (3) increased nonresidential land-use development is concentrated in municipalities characterized by less poverty, older infrastructure (as measured by housing age), and more intergovernmental aid. (The links here may be indirect. Nonresidential land use may be attracted to such areas by lower land prices; communities with these characteristics may court this type of development and may not zone it out.) But in the areas along major highway corridors, growth has not hit current zoning limitations.

—The characteristics associated with higher poverty are clear: higher population density, more violent crime, lower rates of population growth, older housing, lower average income, higher proportions of blacks, higher proportions of multi-family dwellings, and higher proportions of nonresidential developed land.

Figure 4-3. Average Federal Revenue per Capita versus Percent in Poverty in the Pennsylvania Portion of the Philadelphia MSA

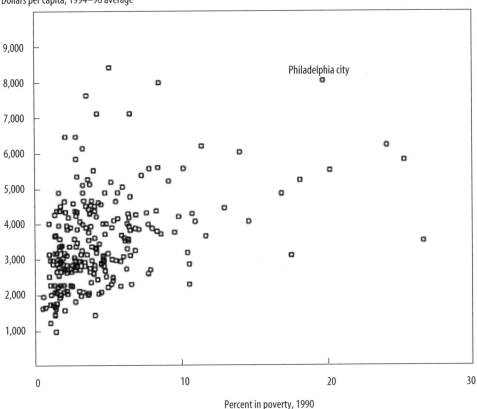

Dollars per capita, 1994–96 average

Percent in poverty, 1990

Note: Four MCDs were omitted because they were very distant outliers: West Conshohocken Borough (pop. 1,258), Marcus Hook Borough (pop. 2,545), Malvern Borough (pop. 2,944), and Ivyland Borough (pop. 498).

—Of the many factors that can account for the wide disparities in the poverty rates of the city and its suburbs, and for the disparities across the suburbs, race is the most important one.

—Poor communities exert higher tax effort. Their local tax burden relative to their per capita income is higher than in more affluent communities.

—State funding in Pennsylvania does not contribute to leveling the fiscal playing field among the Philadelphia suburbs. There is no discernible relationship between state funding and poverty rates.

—Federal redistributional flows are clearly redistributive across suburban communities. But federal nonredistributional expenditures are very large and are allocated on the basis of factors that result in flows that more than offset the redistributive flows.

—Neither state nor federal redistributional flows show patterns that could be clearly linked to political pressures. The measures of political pressure are closely related to factors, such as population size and density, that are elements of the distribution formulas, so it is not possible to assign causality to one set of factors over another.

Capital Spending on Highways and Sewerage

In a 1999 paper, Andrew Haughwout examined the spatial distribution of selected public works spending over the five-year period from 1987 to 1991.[11] The time span studied was chosen because it ends just as the city of Philadelphia entered a severe fiscal crisis. The city's restricted access to the credit markets makes much of the remainder of the 1990s an inopportune time frame in which to study infrastructure spending behavior. And, a multiple-year study period is necessary because of the lumpy nature of capital spending. That is, because capital expenditures often change radically from year to year, one needs to look at averages over time to gain an accurate picture of how infrastructure spending differs across localities.

Special attention was paid to the most capital-intensive functions: streets, highways, and sewerage, with a particular focus on roads because of the important role the Commonwealth of Pennsylvania plays in funding that function. The latter turns out to very important for the Philadelphia region because the state's direct spending behavior results in stark differences in implicit subsidies to suburban and central-city areas, with the suburbs being the winners in this process.

An analysis such as this is difficult because local government itself is so complex in Pennsylvania. In 1990 there were 5,158 local governments, ranking Pennsylvania second only to Illinois according to 1990 census data. All levels of government engage in capital spending, including special districts. Haughwout focused on general-purpose governments for a variety of data reasons, using the sample of Pennsylvania-based jurisdictions in Philadelphia County and its four

11. Haughwout (1999).

Table 4-4. Local Government Nonpoverty Spending: Philadelphia and Pennsylvania Suburbs of the Philadelphia MSA, 1987–91

Per capita 1991 dollars

Fiscal year	Capital		Operations and maintenance		Total	
	City	Suburbs	City	Suburbs	City	Suburbs
1987	73.04	43.74	941.37	379.17	1,014.42	422.91
1988	52.72	52.03	1,007.61	364.09	1,060.33	416.11
1989	46.05	68.24	1,012.54	395.19	1,058.60	463.43
1990	92.43	84.37	1,018.18	384.84	1,110.62	469.21
1991	59.16	70.11	1,007.27	401.35	1,066.43	471.46
Total	323.40	318.49	4,986.98	1,924.63	5,310.39	2,243.12
Average	64.68	63.70	997.40	384.93	1,062.08	448.62

Source: Reprinted from Haughwout (1999, table 2). Underlying data are from the *Annual Survey of Governments*, 1987–91 computer tapes.

Pennsylvania suburban counties from the *Annual Survey of Governments* for 1990.[12]

An overview of direct spending by local governments can be seen in table 4-4. Note that overall spending on nonpoverty functions was substantially higher in the city ($1,062 per capita) than in the suburbs ($449 per capita), but that there was virtually no difference in per capita capital expenditures. Hence high maintenance and operations spending in the city accounted for virtually all of the twofold difference in nonpoverty spending between the city of Philadelphia and its suburbs on average.

Other research by Haughwout finds that other central cities also tend to spend more on operations and maintenance than do their suburbs, but that the difference is especially large in Philadelphia.[13] The discrepancy is due largely to lower suburban spending in three areas: police and fire, government overhead, and transportation. The analysis that follows shows that Pennsylvania's extensive role in directly funding highways and roads is an important factor that largely accounts for the differences found here. In other capital-intensive functions (for example,

12. For this reason, sixty-five school districts in the metropolitan area were excluded from the analysis. There were data on too few districts in the primary data source, the *Annual Survey of Governments*, to allow for any meaningful analysis. Special districts and authorities were not examined because it is impossible to identify the geography of costs imposed by them. They often operate in multiple jurisdictions, and rely on a combination of user charges and subsidies, because they have no independent taxing power in Pennsylvania.

13. Haughwout (1998).

Table 4-5. Nonpoverty Capital Spending by Function in Philadelphia and Pennsylvania Suburbs of the Philadelphia MSA, 1987–91

Per capita 1991 dollars

Function	City	Suburbs
Transportation	22.44	19.97
Highways	7.03	18.85
Corrections	1.97	2.17
Government overhead	7.26	10.15
Parks and recreation	6.43	3.85
Police and fire	3.68	3.68
Sewerage	18.09	6.82
Solid waste	0.39	8.88
Miscellaneous	4.42	8.18
Total	64.68	63.70

Source: Reprinted from Haughwout (1999, table 3). Underlying data are from the *Annual Survey of Governments*, 1987–91 computer tapes.

sewers, parks, and recreation), Pennsylvania is more like other states in its funding role.

Table 4-5 illustrates that the similar per capita capital spending figures for the city of Philadelphia and its suburbs mask important differences in composition. In terms of direct local spending, roads are clearly more important in the suburbs,[14] with sewerage much more important in city direct spending on capital items.[15]

While differences in direct local spending are of interest in their own right, it is state or federal flows that are more likely to drive a wedge between the financial burden of expenditures and the benefits they generate. They can provide different effective subsidies to different parts of the region, thereby allowing those areas receiving larger subsidies to offer higher service levels at lower costs.

Table 4-6 reports data on this intergovernmental aid for two particularly capital-intensive functions—highways and sewerage. Both highway

14. Philadelphia provides transportation services that are unique within the region. For example, the city spent an average of $14 per capita on air and water transportation, which explains why transportation spending is so less concentrated on highways for Philadelphia proper.

15. Haughwout (1998) shows that this is not atypical based on a large sample of central cities and their suburbs. Also, census data do not identify whether intergovernmental aid supplements local capital or operating funds (see Gyourko and Sinai, 2003). Hence Haughwout (1999) focused on highways and sewerage, two notably capital-intensive functions, so the distinction is less important.

Table 4-6. Intergovernmental Aid for Highways and Sewers in Philadelphia and Pennsylvania Suburbs of the Philadelphia MSA, 1987–91

Per capita 1991 dollars

Project	City	Suburbs
Highways	19.84	12.93
State	17.06	12.72
Federal	2.79	0.21
Sewers	3.15	0.00
State	2.39	0.00
Federal	0.76	0.00

Source: Reprinted from Haughwout (1999, table 4). Underlying data are from the *Annual Survey of Governments,* 1987–91 computer tapes.

Table 4-7. Direct State Highway Spending in Philadelphia and Pennsylvania Suburbs of the Philadelphia MSA, 1987–91

Per capita 1991 dollars

Spending item	City	Suburbs
Capital	70.14	87.35
Operations and maintenance	12.81	35.29

Source: Reprinted from Haughwout (1999, table 6). Underlying data are from the State of Pennsylvania Department of Transportation.

and sewerage aid favor the city, from both state and federal sources. However, this is far from the whole story, since higher levels of government can provide roads and sewerage directly, not just through aid. Table 4-7 reports on such direct spending by the commonwealth of Pennsylvania. The state spent literally nothing directly on sewerage during the sample period, but highways are a very different story. As noted above, transportation spending is more centralized in Pennsylvania than in other states, and much of this direct state spending is done in the suburbs. The suburbs received more capital and operations spending, with $123 per capita being spent on average in the suburbs versus $83 per capita in the city. Over the five-year sample period, this represented about a $200 per capita difference that dwarfed the city's advantage in intergovernmental aid. Table 4-8 finishes the picture by reporting own-source local spending for highways and sewers. The suburbs tend to spend a lot more from their own sources on roads, with the city focusing more of its own-source revenues on sewerage.

Table 4-9 summarizes all the data in terms of annual average and five-year totals. The key point to take from this is that state direct and

Table 4-8. Own-Source Local Spending for Highways and Sewers in Philadelphia and Pennsylvania Suburbs of the Philadelphia MSA, 1987–91
Per capita 1991 dollars

Project[a]	City	Suburbs
Highways	19.47	42.60
Sewers	65.88	41.11

Source: Reprinted from Haughwout (1999, table 5). Underlying data are from the *Annual Survey of Governments*, 1987–91 computer tapes.

a. Figures include capital and operations and maintenance spending.

Table 4-9. Highway and Sewer Spending in Philadelphia and Pennsylvania Suburbs of the Philadelphia MSA, 1987–1991
Per capita 1991 dollars

Project and funding source[a]	Annual average		Five-year total	
	City	Suburbs	City	Suburbs
Highways	122.26	178.16	611.29	890.82
Local own-source funding	19.47	42.60	97.35	212.99
Local from aid	19.84	12.93	99.22	64.67
State	82.94	122.63	414.72	613.16
Sewers	69.03	41.44	345.16	205.55
Local own-source funding	65.88	41.44	329.42	205.55
Local from aid	3.15	0.00	15.73	0.00
State direct	0.00	0.00	0.00	0.00

Source: Reprinted from Haughwout (1999, table 6) based on his calculations from data in tables 3–5.

a. Figures include capital and operations and maintenance spending.

indirect highway spending averages $103 per capita in the city of Philadelphia and $136 per capita in the suburbs. This $33 per capita difference is important because the total dollars involved are so large. It translates into the suburbs receiving $641 million more state money than the city did over this time period.

The importance of this difference in state flows lies in the economic distortion it can create. The state is providing different effective subsidies to different parts of the metropolitan area, with the suburbs coming out on top on average, at least during the time period studied. The suburbs are made relatively more attractive to potential residents in the sense that they can provide higher service levels at lower costs. Depending upon when and how much of this difference is capitalized into land prices, location decisions can be affected, possibly resulting in "too much" economic activity ending up in the suburbs.

The importance of factors such as infrastructure investment to local economic development is a matter of debate within the economics profession. It is very difficult to distinguish cause and effect in this area. Stated differently, the debate is about whether infrastructure investment encourages job and population growth or whether the latter encourages the former. Our interpretation of what we consider the best recent research on this issue is that capital spending differences such as these can and do affect local economic activity.[16] Consequently, we believe that the playing field is tilted in favor of the suburbs in the Philadelphia metropolitan area, with population and employment growth higher in suburban areas because of spatially biased roadway investments in particular.[17]

The Spatial Distribution of Owner-Occupied Housing Tax Benefits in the Philadelphia Area

It is well known that owner-occupied housing is favored in the tax code and that the benefits are skewed toward higher-income households. What is not known is the extent to which these benefits are skewed across space, not merely income. Given the extent of residential sorting by income that exists in many parts of the United States, one might also expect substantial redistribution to occur across locations. Gyourko and Sinai have estimated the gain or loss to each census tract that would result if the current tax treatment of owner-occupied housing were taxed in a more theoretically ideal manner with the revenue saved returned to taxpayers via a national lump-sum transfer.[18] Their work documents where benefits flow. In other words, they examine how much tax benefits would change in different localities if the tax code were changed. Gyourko and Sinai do not estimate the ultimate economic impact of any

16. Haughwout (1999).

17. We should note that differences in own-source spending are of much less concern in this respect. They do not represent an explicit financial subsidy from one set of taxpayers to another. In fact, Tiebout (1956) famously argued that such differences could be efficiency-enhancing if they reflect differences in preferences for publicly provided goods packages.

18. Gyourko and Sinai (2003). The more theoretically ideal tax is a Haig-Simons tax. This is one in which the homeowner's implicit rental income is taxed. Of course, a proper accounting then allows the owner to deduct the remainder of expenses, including maintenance costs and depreciation. See Gyourko and Sinai (2003) for the details.

such change in the tax code, although their work does report a range of possibilities according to whether program benefits are capitalized into land values.[19]

Tract-level data from the STF3 files of the 1990 Census are used to estimate the subsidy or tax benefit afforded owner-occupiers by the current code.[20] The procedure includes an underlying imputation of itemization status and itemization amount.[21] Tract data are then aggregated to the level of individual political jurisdictions. While Gyourko and Sinai report data for the entire nation, our focus here is on the Philadelphia region.

The gross value of benefits is estimated to be quite large for the nation as a whole: $159 billion in 1990 dollars. Much of this, $102 billion, or 64 percent, derives from the untaxed return on home equity. All owners receive some benefit from this component, because one does not have to itemize to receive it. Another $43 billion, or 27 percent, of the total arises from the deductibility of mortgage interest. This is less than the 35 percent of house value that is debt financed because some owners do not itemize, thereby receiving no benefits from mortgage interest on the margin. The remaining $15 billion is due to the deductibility of local property taxes. Gross benefits per owned unit are fairly large, averaging $2,725. On a per household basis (including renter and owner households), gross benefits are $1,765. Note that this also represents the per household cost needed to fund the program if it were to be self-financing. Thus net benefits should be calculated as gross benefit less the $1,765 average program cost.

The accompanying figures focus on the Philadelphia Primary Metropolitan Statistical Area (PMSA), which includes the following five counties: Bucks County, Chester County, Delaware County, Philadelphia County (which is conterminous with the city of Philadelphia), and Montgomery County. There were nearly 1.4 million households in the five-county region in 1989; approximately 780,000 of them were in the four suburban counties. The propensity to own is high throughout the region, with 74 percent of suburban households owning and 62 percent of households in the city of Philadelphia owning.[22]

19. See Gyourko and Sinai (2003).

20. STF3 is Summary Tape File 3 from the decennial census, in which data are organized in several geographic breakdowns.

21. The interested reader should see Gyourko and Sinai (2003) for details.

22. In this subsection, only the city of Philadelphia is considered the "central city." All tracts outside the Philadelphia city limits are considered the "suburbs." Chester and Norristown are considered central cities by the Census Bureau. To focus on distinctions with

The aggregate value of tax-code-related benefits to owners within the Philadelphia PMSA is estimated to be $2.7 billion in 1989. Of that amount, 84 percent, or nearly $2.3 billion, accrued to suburban owners. The other 16 percent, or $0.4 billion, accrued to city of Philadelphia owners. Within the central city of Philadelphia, a relatively high 69 percent of aggregate value is due to the value of untaxed imputed rent. This is because house values are so low in the city that many owners there do not itemize.

Of the 161 census-designated places in the five-county region, the typical owners in 121 of these communities received benefits in excess of the $1,765 mean program cost. There were 504,938 owned units in these jurisdictions, containing 53 percent of the 946,726 owned units in the PMSA. The small suburban communities of Rose Valley and Woodside had the highest net benefit flows on a per owner basis, with each owner receiving over $9,000 in housing-related tax benefit value. In the city of Philadelphia, the per owned unit benefit figure was only $1,166, indicating that the typical owner there suffered a negative net flow once the mean program cost of $1,765 is accounted for. While the cities of Philadelphia and Chester had the largest negative net benefit flows in aggregate terms, it also is useful to know that many suburban communities are in a similar position. In fact, the typical owner in thirty-nine smaller communities, mostly suburbs in southern Delaware and Bucks counties, receives a net negative transfer under the program. Owners in four low-income, low-housing-value communities (Chester, Darby, Colwyn, and Marcus Hook) received less than $1,000 per owner in gross benefit flow, indicating a net benefit flow in excess of $700 per owner-occupier in those jurisdictions.

Naturally, communities with plentiful rental units also tend to have relatively large negative net flows under the program, as an examination of the Philadelphia city data shows. The 224,192 renter households in the city paid over $395 million in program costs ($1,765 x 224,192 = $395,698,880). In Philadelphia's case, its owners on average received $599 less than the average program cost (or $1,765 − $1,166), so there was an added cost of about $224 million. In aggregate, Philadelphia's renters and owners funded nearly $620 million of housing-related tax benefits costs for nonresidents (including those outside of the metropoli-

the much larger central city of Philadelphia, we group together all areas outside the Philadelphia city limits. Where appropriate, we make comments on other designated central cities such as Chester.

tan area). This was nearly 23 percent of the PMSA's $2.7 billion in total tax expenditures.

While Philadelphia experiences by far the largest net outflow under the program, the city of Chester and inner-ring suburbs such as Darby are far bigger losers on a per household basis. In Chester, homeowners received only $673 on average in benefit value, $1,092 less than mean program costs. Owners in Darby were only slightly better off, receiving $851 in benefit value per household. And the sizable renter populations in both communities paid $1,765 per household.

A graphical presentation of the data down to the census tract level is a very useful way to capture the spatial distribution of the net benefit calculations (see color plates, maps 4-3 through 4-6, and figures 4-4 and 4-5). Map 4-3 plots average household income by census tract in the city of Philadelphia and the four Pennsylvania suburban collar counties. In this and all other figures, the thickest bold outline marks the Philadelphia city boundary. The medium-thick lines mark the boundaries between the suburban counties, and the thinnest black lines identify census tract boundaries. The tracts with the highest mean incomes are shaded the darkest. It is apparent from this figure that there is a heavy concentration of poorer households within the city of Philadelphia, although the suburbs in southern Delaware County also contain a large number of relatively poor tracts. Map 4-4 then plots median house value by census tract. This picture looks very much like map 4-3, reflecting the well-known high correlation between income and house value.

At the tract level, the significant disparities in tax benefits per owner-occupied housing unit can be seen in map 4-5. Because the value of benefits is driven largely by household incomes and house values, the shading in 4-5 looks similar to that in maps 4-3 and 4-4. Only a handful of tracts in Philadelphia have mean per owner benefit values above $3,000. The suburbs to the west of Philadelphia in Delaware County also tend to have low tax benefit levels, as do areas in southern Bucks County. It also is apparent that tax benefits are small on the metropolitan fringe in Chester, Montgomery, and Bucks Counties. Average benefits per owner tend to be above $6,000 in a broad swath of middle-ring suburban areas stretching across the entire metropolitan area. A handful of tracts along the so-called Main Line in suburban Montgomery County average over $12,000 per owned unit.

The wealthy suburban tracts reap most of the value of aggregate tax benefits as well, as can be seen in map 4-6 (see color plates). Obviously, the aggregate totals are driven not just by the benefit value per owner household, but also by the number of owners. Both tend to be low in the city of Philadelphia, where the vast majority of the city's census tracts receive well under $1.25 million per year in housing-related tax benefits. The darkest shaded tracts to the west of the city constitute the Main Line in suburban Montgomery and Delaware Counties. These tracts, along with a large swath of tracts in western Bucks County, reap over $10 million per year in aggregate tax benefit values.

While a simple visual inspection of these figures shows how spatially concentrated housing-related tax expenditures are, figures 4-4 and 4-5 highlight how skewed the distribution of subsidies is. Figure 4-4 plots the percentage of tracts achieving different levels of tax benefit value per owner. Roughly 10 percent of all tracts have per owner tax benefit levels above $6,000, while about 45 percent of all tracts have subsidies below $2,000. Cumulative aggregate tax expenditures are reported in figure 4-5. The top 5 percent of tracts receives roughly the same amount of aggregate subsidy as the bottom 60 percent: about $500 million in tax expenditure, or nearly 25 percent of the $2.7 billion total.

Equity issues aside, the policy importance of these results depends on just how much of the benefits are capitalized into land values. If capitalization is not complete, and there is good reason to think it would not be on the urban fringe where plenty of farmland is available for development, the redistribution from city to suburbs may encourage households to move out of center cities. Just as with infrastructure spending, location decisions may be inefficiently distorted. And in metropolitan areas such as this, in which suburbs appear to benefit at the expense of the central city, valuable agglomeration benefits may be lost.

Policy Implications

The overarching conclusion of this chapter is that there are significant economic and social disparities between the central city of the Philadelphia MSA and its suburbs that are deeply etched into structures of the regions. This should not be interpreted as implying that all economic disparities are bad, especially in terms of efficiency. Indeed, no serious economist believes everyone should be paid the same, that all investments should reap the same return, or that all communities should have the same income level or housing stock. In general, economic efficiency requires that differences in talent, performance, and risk be rewarded differently.

However, the research for this project suggests that city and suburban communities with high poverty concentrations remain relatively high-

Figure 4-4. Tax Benefit per Owner-Occupied Unit by Tract, Philadelphia MSA, 1989

Thousands of dollars

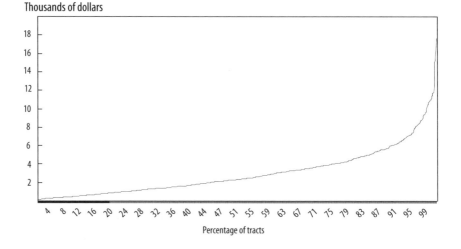

Percentage of tracts

Figure 4-5. Cumulative Tax Benefits, Philadelphia MSA, 1989

Billions of dollars

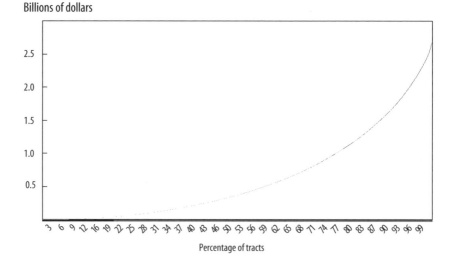

Percentage of tracts

cost places in which to live and work, notwithstanding large means-tested monetary and in-kind flows to the poorer residents of these locali-ties. Not only do intergovernmental aid flows not level the disparities between fiscal capacities and public service needs, but public capital spending and federal tax policy related to owner-occupied housing also tend to favor the better-off suburban areas. Consequently, the location decisions of some firms and middle-class (and above) households are distorted, leading to unbalanced and inefficiently allocated growth and development throughout the region. In this situation, policy can be changed to foster a more efficient outcome. While many focus on equity as a motivator for redistribution, we focus on the consequences of current policy for economic (in)efficiency in urban areas. These are not well known or well understood. More specifically, our analysis showed and implied the following:

—For the Philadelphia area, as considerable research has shown for the large cities, federal and state intergovernmental aid does not fully offset the variations in the costs of providing services for the poor. State aid from the Commonwealth of Pennsylvania is not directed toward poorer areas; however, federal distributive aid is directed in this fashion, but the much larger part of federal aid that is not redistributive more than offsets it. This almost certainly means that the location decisions of some businesses and households are being distorted, leading to an inefficient allocation of economic activity across the region. Unless there is clear evidence that there are sufficient differences in the efficiency with which suburban MCDs deploy intergovernmental flows (and their own resources), the analysis here points strongly to the need for substantial revision in the criteria for commonwealth aid, and for the introduction of redistributive components to the large federal block grants. Measures of government expenditure efficiency should, of course, be part of the revised distribution formulas so that better-run governments are rewarded and the least well run are provided with incentives to improve. Leveling the fiscal playing field across communities in the metropolitan area should also include a (re)consideration of current housing tax policy, the use of differentiated poverty policies in cities versus suburbs, and a review of infrastructure investment policies (especially by the commonwealth).

—The suburban poor and the city poor in the Philadelphia metropolitan area differ in many important ways, indicating that poverty programs should be tailored to specific groups. The fact that the city poor include relatively fewer retirees, more female-headed households, more unemployed, more welfare recipients, more high school dropouts, and larger families suggests that more emphasis should be placed on job search and training and child care in aiding the transition back into the labor force.

—Current policy on public capital spending should be reexamined so that it does not lead to even more unbalanced growth and development. In this respect, the beginning-of-the-century decision by Pennsylvania's

Department of Transportation to begin a major expansion and upgrade of the Route 202 corridor in suburban Philadelphia is immediately relevant. If carried to its logical conclusion, the Route 202 project will provide a new ring road in the region. The magnitude of the impact of a ring road on the spatial distribution of economic activity could be quite large. It is difficult to imagine how this investment would not shift the economic center of the region further west toward the King of Prussia area absent a countervailing investment in the city of Philadelphia. Indeed, the appropriate policy response would be to provide a more equal quality of public infrastructure investment across locations (on something like a per capita basis) so that fiscal policy does not inadvertently make one location more attractive than another and thereby distort firm and household location decisions.

—Finally, certain other policies that may not be considered urban in nature should be examined to determine if they also play an inadvertent role in distorting the fiscal playing field across communities. We examined federal tax policy with respect to owner-occupied housing and found that its benefits were intensely spatially skewed toward a relatively few suburban areas. The point here is not to undo a federal policy that undoubtedly was imposed for other reasons, but to highlight that all sorts of policies can distort the fiscal playing field across communities in any metropolitan area. An economically efficient metropolitan policy is one that reduces those distortions so that location decisions are not artificially biased toward one part of the region.

In sum, our analysis suggests that both the federal and state governments need to give much more serious attention to expenditure-neutral revisions of their grant and aid programs that take into account the spatial biases inherent in the current system. In addition, we believe that any restructuring of programs should include an element that promotes local public efficiency. Well-run jurisdictions should be rewarded. The overarching goal should be one in which policy does not tilt the fiscal playing field toward or away from Philadelphia or its suburbs. While this undoubtedly will involve some redistribution of resources, its aim should be to enhance efficiency by eliminating current incentives for unbalanced growth and development. What needs to be avoided is public policy that, even unintentionally, distorts the location decisions of businesses and families by making one area a fundamentally more attractive place in which to live and work than others. If well implemented, the policy paths suggested above would help create a stronger and less divided metropolitan area.

References

Delaware Valley Regional Planning Commission. 1994. *Land Use in the Delaware Valley, 1970–1990.* Analytical Report 2. Philadelphia.

Ehrlich, Steven R., and Janice F. Madden. 2000. "Where Are the Poor in the Philadelphia Metropolitan Area?" Working Paper. Philadelphia: University of Pennsylvania (January).

Gyourko, Joseph, and Todd Sinai. 2003. "The Spatial Distribution of Housing Related Tax Benefits in the United States." *Real Estate Economics* 31, no. 4.

Haughwout, Andrew. 1998. "Local Capital Spending in the U.S. Metropolitan Areas." *Public Works Management and Policy* 3, no. 1 (July).

———. 1999. "An Analysis of Public Investment in the Philadelphia Metropolitan Area." Unpublished paper.

Pack, Janet R. 1995. "Poverty and Public Expenditures." Working Paper 197. Wharton Real Estate Center, University of Pennsylvania (October).

Raimondo, Henry. 1993. "The Political Economy of State Intergovernmental Grants." *Growth and Change* (April).

Summers, Anita A. 2000. "The Philadelphia Metropolitan Case Study." Working Paper 328. Zell/Lurie Real Estate Center at Wharton, University of Pennsylvania (March).

Summers, Anita A., and Lara Jakubowski. 1996. "The Fiscal Burden of Unreimbursed Poverty Expenditures in the City of Philadelphia." Working Paper 238. Wharton Real Estate Center, University of Pennsylvania (August).

Summers, Anita A., and Garrett Ritter. 1996. "The Costs to Large Cities of Educating Poor Children." Draft Working Paper. Wharton Real Estate Center, University of Pennsylvania (August).

Tiebout, Charles M. 1956. "A Pure Theory of Local Expenditures." *Journal of Political Economy* 64 (October).

U.S. Census Bureau. 1990. *Census of the Population and Housing, 1990.* Summary Tape File (STF) 3F. Washington.

CHAPTER 5

Phoenix:

Dealing with Fast Growth

Arizona State University Research Team

Phoenix is often viewed as the quintessential Sunbelt metropolis: young, fast-growing, auto-centered, and sprawling. While some facets of the stereotype are accurate, the complete picture of metropolitan Phoenix is more complex. In some notable ways, metropolitan Phoenix's story is one of success. For example, in comparison with other urban regions, the Phoenix metropolitan area is fairly compact with relative equity between its core city and its suburbs. Prospectively, however, the challenges are great. The desert landscape is changing and some educational and economic divides are obvious; plus the mechanisms available to cope with problems may be insufficient to handle many rapidly evolving situations.

The members of the Arizona State University Research Team included Mary Jo Waits, associate director, Morrison Institute for Public Policy; Tina Valdecanas, senior research analyst, Morrison Institute for Public Policy; Mark Muro, senior research analyst, Morrison Institute for Public Policy; Len Bower, economist; Elizabeth Burns, professor, ASU Department of Geography; William Fulton, president, Solimar Research Group; Rebecca Gau, senior research analyst, Morrison Institute for Public Policy; Patricia Gober, professor, ASU Department of Geography; John Hall, professor, ASU School of Public Affairs; Alicia Harrison, research associate, Solimar Research Group; Kent Hill, assistant research professional, ASU Department of Economics; Glen Krutz, assistant professor, ASU Department of Political Science; Tom Rex, research manager, ASU Center for Business Research; Scott Smith, support systems analyst, ASU Department of Information Technology; Christina Kinnear, graduate assistant, Morrison Institute for Public Policy; Laura Valenzuela, graduate assistant, Morrison Institute for Public Policy; and Jamie Goodwin-White, graduate assistant, Morrison Institute for Public Policy.

Perhaps what stands out most when one examines the region's development is that Phoenix has grown along a different model than either East Coast or Sunbelt metropolitan areas. Consequently, the challenges facing the region should not necessarily be approached with the same tools and remedies that have been used in other regions. For example, contrary to the experiences of other regions:

—*Density is increasing.* Given residents' dependence on cars, most people would not expect the Phoenix region to be showing increases in population density from its core to its edges. But it is—making it one of only a handful of large areas in the country to do so. Population grew 263 percent between 1960 and 1990, while the urbanized area expanded 199 percent during the same period. By contrast, metropolitan Atlanta consumed nearly twice as much land as metropolitan Phoenix to accommodate approximately the same number of people.

—*The region's center is holding.* Employment remains concentrated in the metropolitan Phoenix core, and both population and employment rose in the heart of the metropolitan area in the 1990s, although the rate of expansion was less robust than in other parts of the region.

—*The region's core city and its major suburbs are quite balanced.* In keeping with the vitality of its center, there are no glaring disparities between the center (the city of Phoenix) and the next largest cities—at least in terms of housing values, jobs, and retail activity.

—*Metropolitan Phoenix consists of a relatively small number of municipalities.* Unlike many East Coast metropolitan areas that are divided into several dozens of small suburban municipalities, there are only twenty-four cities and towns in the Phoenix region (see color plates, map 5-1). Eighty-two percent of the region's population lives in either the city of Phoenix or one of the five large suburbs. This political map stands in stark contrast to a metropolitan region such as Chicago or Los Angeles that must contend with a few hundred separate jurisdictions each.

Nevertheless, the Metropolitan Phoenix region is also confronted with extraordinary challenges.

—*Residential development is moving outward swiftly.* Between 1993 and 1998, the urban edge advanced nearly one-half mile per year. In the southeast, the fringe pushed out an average of three-fourths of a mile each year.

—*Metropolitan Phoenix is using up its agricultural and desert land.* Calculations from aerial photographs show that between 1975 and 1995 some 40 percent of all agricultural land and 32 percent of all undeveloped desert land was lost to urbanization. Moreover, according to Maricopa Association of Government (MAG) projections, if the region continues to develop according to planned land-use patterns, the metropolitan region could encompass an area roughly 100 miles square.

—*A regional divide exists by race, poverty, and schools.* For years, the sections north and northeast of downtown Phoenix, including Scottsdale, have been affluent areas with attractive housing, good schools, and enviable amenities. Also for years, poor whites and low-income minorities have been concentrated in neighborhoods in the central and southern portions of the city of Phoenix.

—*The region's rapid growth disturbs the majority of residents.* In 1999 a Morrison Institute quality-of-life survey indicated that 80 percent of residents were "concerned" or "very concerned" about the region's growth. Most dramatically, nearly half reported that they would leave Phoenix tomorrow if they could.

Behind the Trends

As the following pages suggest, metropolitan Phoenix is where it is today—with its good and bad points—because of its special attributes, national factors, and policy choices.

SPECIAL ATTRIBUTES. The Phoenix region has been able to grow fast and add people, jobs, and opportunities in large part because of its good climate and many other highly sought-after natural amenities. In surveys, residents consistently cite climate, the environment (especially the beautiful desert scenery), and lifestyle as the region's major attractions.

TIMING AND NATIONAL TRENDS. The transformation of the region into a metropolis of almost 3 million took place almost entirely after World War II in the automobile era. The real estate crash of the late 1980s and the national recession that occurred at about the same time also influenced Phoenix's current form. The "bust" slowed decentralization and encouraged several years of more cautious in-fill development at a time of phenomenal population growth. In addition, metropolitan Phoenix's growth industry was affected significantly by the tight financial markets created by the virtual collapse of savings and loan institutions. The result was moderated development and a slowdown in home construction.

PUBLIC POLICY. The region is also doing well today because of yesterday's foresight; it is not all about destiny and "good genes." In the 1980s, for example, the state prepared for mega-growth with the passage of the highly acclaimed Groundwater Management Act and the Urban Land Management Act, which protect two of the state's critical resources. A highly efficient, compact, grid-based arterial road system also limited congestion in the region. However, a freeway system was built relatively late in the development process and appears to have kept employment relatively constrained to central areas. Through annexation strategies, the cities have had the luxury of being able to grow physically instead of being hemmed in by neighboring jurisdictions. More recently, metropolitan Phoenix cities have acted with boldness by independently focusing on urban revitalization, open-space protection, and a system of multi-tiered impact fees—higher on their fringes—to shape development patterns and help pay for community growth.

Looking to the Future

But none of this means that the Phoenix region does not have its problems or disturbing trends or that the region will not suffer from past public policy choices. Indeed, given the conditions and the trends that have emerged in recent years, metropolitan Phoenix faces a series of challenges that will require important and potentially divisive policy choices. These include: looming transportation and land-use conundrums; state trust land questions; growth agendas in the smaller cities; fixing the schools of the core; conflicting views on sprawl and density; a regional authority dilemma; an on-and-off relationship with Washington; tensions that surround state support of metropolitan Phoenix; and water's changing role.

These challenges are great, but not insurmountable. Just as the metropolitan Phoenix community has been able to avoid the pitfalls of the traditional growth model through a combination of special attributes, timing and national trends, and public policy, the direction it takes in the future will depend on the same three factors. Although not much can be done to control the timing of external influences, steps can be taken to ensure that efficient growth is supported while the high quality of life is maintained. The challenge is to do so in a comprehensive way.

Growing Up in the 1950s to 1970s

Metropolitan Phoenix's development has taken place almost entirely in the post–World War II era of cars, particularly since 1970. The metropolitan area's population almost tripled between 1950 and 1970, growing from approximately 332,000 to 971,000. Most of the early postwar growth occurred in the city of Phoenix, with the city's population increasing more than fivefold between 1950 and 1970, adding 477,000 to reach a total population of 584,000. At the same time, the city's land area expanded from 17 to 190 square miles.

Today the metropolitan area is the fastest growing large metropolitan area in the nation. The Census Bureau ranked the region as the fourteenth largest in area—approximately the same size as Cleveland, Minneapolis, and San Diego—with more than 3 million people in 2000. (According to the Census Bureau, the "Phoenix metropolitan area" consisted only of Maricopa County until 1990 Census results became available, when Pinal County was added. For historical consistency, and because little of Pinal County is part of the Phoenix urbanized area, references in this chapter to the Phoenix metropolitan area include only Maricopa County unless otherwise noted.) (See color plates, map 5-2.)[1]

Many of the settlement patterns that are still important in the region today were established early on. The presence of the Maricopa and Phoenix railroads ensured that the city was a hub in East–West trade routes. As a result, by the turn of the twentieth century, a pattern was developing in which the southern edge of town consisted of warehouses, railroad yards, industrial areas, and low-quality housing where the non-Anglo population tended to live. A more expensive residential quarter was established to the north and northeast of downtown Phoenix because of views, a cooling summer breeze, and other amenities. During the postwar period, the northeast remained the "preferred quarter" of the region, although other parts grew more rapidly as housing construction for working- and middle-class residents accelerated in the northwest and southeast areas.[2]

Throughout the early development years of the twentieth century, agriculture was a large part of the economy. In 1941 two major air force bases opened, and many war-related industries remained in the region and encouraged growth in manufacturing, primarily in aerospace and

1. Other geographic units occasionally referred to include: (1) Phoenix urbanized area. This geography closely follows the developed area, but only decennial census data are produced for urbanized areas. Discussions of population density use this geography, which in 1990 was only 8 percent of the county's land area. (2) The Maricopa Association of Governments (MAG) defines a planning area that includes the current developed area plus land projected to be largely developed by 2020. It is about one-fifth of the county's land area. (3) The Central Arizona–Phoenix Long-Term Ecological Research project defines a study area larger than the MAG planning area, but still substantially smaller than Maricopa County. It is used in discussions of land use.

2. Rex (2000a).

electronics. Motorola sited several facilities in the Phoenix area, beginning in 1949, and planted the seeds of the region's burgeoning electronics manufacturing sector. Manufacturing continued to dominate the region's production, although the service industry steadily increased as tourism grew. By the late 1960s the area's industrial mix was similar to the national average as reflected in Commerce Department data—as it still is today.

Phoenix in 1970

The year 1970 marked a turning point for metropolitan Phoenix, thus making it an appropriate base year for this study. A newly mature economy, the baby-boom generation aging into their twenties—the prime age for making long-distance moves—and the end of the 1969–70 recession led to a spurt in population and job growth that continued for the next thirty years.

In broad terms, the region's growth during this period was characterized by outward expansion of residential areas tempered by a limited transportation system and concentrated employment centers. As had historically been the case in the Phoenix region, most of the newly urbanized land was converted from agricultural cultivation, although newly cultivated agricultural land more than made up for losses to urbanization.[3] The region's cities were connected mostly by a grid-based arterial street system—the legacy of agricultural service roads along land survey section lines. Only forty miles of urban freeways were built from 1957 to 1968 as part of the region's Interstate Highway System, with a proposed regional plan for the construction of an additional 215-mile freeway system to be completed by 1980. Although these projects were well under way by 1970, the system contained important gaps, with segments of Interstate 10 lacking a connection through central Phoenix until 1985.[4]

POPULATION AND DENSITY BEGIN TO INCREASE. Verging on 1 million people in 1970, metropolitan Phoenix began to emerge as one of the nation's largest metropolitan areas. The city of Phoenix was still the most populous city in the metropolitan area by far, with 584,000 residents or about 60 percent of the region's residents, and continued to grow rapidly throughout the decade at an average rate of 5.6 percent a year. At the same time, the outlying cities were experiencing similarly

3. Rex (2000a).
4. Burns, Matranga, and Valenzuela (2000).

rapid growth. By 1970, Mesa and Tempe to the southeast, and Scottsdale to the northeast, had populations of approximately 60,000 each.

In general, population densities across the region were not much different in poor neighborhoods than in affluent ones. Population density was highest in the city of Phoenix; density dropped gradually and consistently away from the core, with a high of 5,000 residents per square mile within one mile of the downtown center and less than 2,500 six miles from the center. Higher-density pockets were also found in the central portions of Glendale, Scottsdale, Tempe, and Mesa.[5]

EMPLOYMENT WAS STRONGLY CONCENTRATED AT THE CORE. The lack of a comprehensive freeway network and dependence on an arterial street system tended to concentrate employment in a fairly compact area. In 1970 major industrial employers were clustered along a diagonal (formed largely by the route of the railroad and U.S. 60) from northwest to southeast of downtown Phoenix and along a corridor of North Central Avenue. By 1970 all of the major office buildings in the region were concentrated in downtown Phoenix, or more specifically, along North Central Avenue, creating an emergent high-rise district one mile north of downtown. Large shopping centers were located in east Phoenix and Scottsdale.

Primarily because they needed large tracts of land, the largest industrial employers located in several areas outside the central city across the region. Other major employment centers included Arizona State University in downtown Tempe and the state capital west of downtown Phoenix.

HOUSING DENSITY REMAINED UNIFORM, BUT POVERTY WAS CLUSTERED. Much like employment, the pattern of residential growth was constrained by the arterial grids and the high cost of extending the region's water network. New home development in 1970 was located primarily in fast-growing areas north and northwest of central Phoenix and in the traditionally affluent section to the northeast. Retirement communities began to proliferate in the southeast quadrant of the region and, to a lesser extent, in the northwestern part of the region. Low home values and low rents were concentrated in central and south Phoenix.

Despite this familiar pattern, there were some surprises in the way housing was geographically distributed—surprises that provide some insight into the atypical (by traditional standards) nature of the Phoenix

5. Rex (2000a).

region as an emerging Sunbelt metropolis. First, the affluent area to the northeast at this time was not the exclusive preserve of single-family homes. Rather, the area had a slightly higher share of multi-family units than in other parts of the metropolitan area, giving those areas more diversity in housing type than one might expect. Meanwhile, the lower-priced housing areas in south-central Phoenix were not disproportionately multi-family or renter-occupied, though the housing stock was older than the metropolitan average.

Although housing density was relatively uniform across the metropolitan area, poverty was concentrated in several areas. Most of south Phoenix suffered from poverty rates of 20 percent or more, while the most extremely poverty-stricken neighborhoods (rates of 40 percent or more) were scattered in central Phoenix and south to the Salt River. Moreover, the region's poverty tended to be concentrated among non-Anglo minorities, most notably within the Hispanic population. In 1970, Hispanics constituted 12 percent of the total population, but accounted for more than 25 percent of the population in the poor neighborhoods in south-central Phoenix, and more than 50 percent of the population in the most extreme poverty clusters.[6] Not surprisingly, educational attainment was lower and female-headed households were more common in these neighborhoods.

LAND OWNERSHIP PATTERNS AFFECTED URBAN FORM. The geography of the metropolitan Phoenix area was influenced by a combination of topographical boundaries (low and high mountains) and by state and federal land ownership. While the mountains to the south and west of the metropolitan were not substantial enough to form a barrier to future growth, the north and east were hemmed in by a large rugged mountain range. Three Indian reservations blocked urban expansion to the east and south. In addition, several large public parks within the metropolitan area were protected from any development.

The federal government owned or controlled more than half of the land in Maricopa County, including military bases. The state government owned 12 percent of the land in Maricopa County. These trust lands were acquired by the state from the federal government at the time of statehood and account for approximately 15 percent of the land (some 275 square miles) in the Maricopa Association of Governments (MAG) planning area.[7] Much of this land was just north and northwest

6. Rex (2000a).

7. Maricopa Association of Governments (MAG) was formed in 1967 and provides regional planning and policy decision guidance in the areas of transportation, air quality,

of the outer edge of the Phoenix metropolitan area. The state constitution mandated that these lands be managed to support the state's education system.

Thus by 1970 it was evident that Phoenix was developing differently from the classic metropolitan model of urban poverty and suburban affluence. In summary:

—The region was growing rapidly but remained relatively compact and had not yet experienced a major loss of agricultural land.

—Auto-oriented, the Phoenix region depended on arterial streets to provide access to centralized employment centers, but the lack of a freeway system curbed gross outward expansion.

Although distinct affluent and poor sections existed, they did not differ substantially in average household size, age distribution, employment rate, or population density. Thus although there were poor and affluent neighborhoods in 1970, their differences on a number of socioeconomic characteristics were not as pronounced as elsewhere in the nation. Educational achievement was, however, a major exception.

—The predominance of federal, state, and Indian land ownership in the region limited the spread of development to some degree.

Coming of Age: Phoenix after Thirty Years of Explosive Growth

Growth affects every dimension of the region's identity, including its population, employment, transportation arrangements, land-use patterns, and social landscape. The explosive growth experienced by the metropolitan Phoenix region since 1970 has done much to shape the model of development. The region's story conforms to neither the "traditional" model of urban development nor the popular image of Sunbelt growth.

In the traditional model, most often associated with older East Coast and Midwestern cities, metropolitan areas frequently feature a dis-

---

environment analysis, regional development, and social services. MAG is the designated Metropolitan Planning Organization for transportation planning in the Maricopa County region and has also been designated by the Governor's Office to serve as the principal planning agency for the region in a number of areas including air quality, water quality, and solid waste management. In addition, through an executive order from the governor, MAG develops population estimates and projections for the region. MAG has defined an urban planning area, which consists of 1,768 square miles, where development has already occurred or is expected to occur within the next twenty years. Because MAG has no implementing authority, it does not have enforcement power and many of its initiatives or recommendation have not been fully carried out.

tressed central city confined to its boundaries by fast-growing suburbs. In the center, the old downtown becomes a catch basin for the region's poor and minority residents, while middle-class families, corporations, and job growth migrate to the suburbs.[8]

Popular views of the Sunbelt, by contrast, assume that metropolitan Phoenix exemplifies the unpopular word *sprawl*. Phoenix in this view is denounced as a vast, auto-centered collection of retirement communities and a sea of red-tiled roofs. Or worse, it is portrayed as a low-density urban behemoth that lacks both a center and an "edge," as the architectural critic Michael Sorkin noted: "Phoenix has become the dreaded polycentric automotive metropolis."[9]

To be sure, aspects of both of these accounts of metropolitan Phoenix growth hold true. But for the most part the picture of the region's development that emerges is subtler than either the traditional or popular Sunbelt view and belies easy preconceptions.

Population

Metropolitan Phoenix grew faster than any other large metropolitan region between 1970 and 2000, more than tripling in size. About 35 percent of this growth occurred in the city of Phoenix. Another 47 percent went to cities close to the core—Tempe, Scottsdale, Mesa, Chandler, and Glendale—and the remainder of the region grew 18 percent. The city of Phoenix's share of the regional population dropped from 60 percent in 1970 to 45 percent in 2000 (see table 5-1 and figure 5-1). The growth rate in the southern and central portions of the city of Phoenix trailed the numbers recorded elsewhere in the region. The metropolitan area's largest pockets of population decline were also in these areas.

That the city of Phoenix and other inner-ring cities are still growing at a rate close to the regional average suggests that the region's center is not emptying out as it is in many other metropolitan areas. Between 1970 and 1999, for example, the city of Atlanta's population decreased 14 percent while the region's population increased 114 percent.[10] The city of Phoenix's growth rate was 114 percent between 1970 and 2000, while the region gained 220 percent.

The metropolitan Phoenix region has a much more fluid population than most other metropolitan areas. Approximately 70 percent of the

8. Rusk (1995); U.S. Congress, Office of Technology Assessment (1995); Orfield (1997).
9. Sorkin (1995).
10. Metropolitan Policy Program, Brookings (1999).

Table 5-1. Population Growth in Arizona by Jurisdiction, 1970–2000

Locality	1970	1980	1990	2000
Avondale	6,625	8,168	17,595	35,850
Buckeye	2,599	3,434	4,436	8,650
Carefree	...	964	1,660	2,790
Cave Creek	...	1,518	2,394	3,955
Chandler	13,763	29,673	89,862	176,970
El Mirage	3,258	4,307	5,001	9,910
Fountain Hills	...	...	10,030	19,105
Gila Bend	1,795	1,585	1,747	...
Gilbert	1,971	5,717	29,149	108,745
Glendale	36,228	97,172	147,070	211,555
Goodyear	2,140	2,747	6,258	19,645
Guadalupe	...	4,506	5,458	5,400
Litchfield Park	...	...	3,303	3,960
Mesa	63,049	152,404	289,199	388,185
Paradise Valley	6,637	11,085	11,903	13,395
Peoria	4,792	12,171	51,080	108,295
Phoenix	584,303	789,704	988,015	1,249,450
Queen Creek	...	...	2,667	3,955
Scottsdale	67,823	88,622	130,099	207,145
Surprise	2,427	3,723	7,122	32,815
Tempe	63,550	106,919	141,993	162,000
Tolleson	3,881	4,433	4,436	4,690
Wickenburg	2,698	3,535	4,515	5,175
Youngtown	1,886	2,254	2,542	2,800
Region	869,426	1,509,175	2,122,101	2,784,440

Source: Figures for 2000 are Arizona Department of Economic Security estimates. All other data are from the U.S. Census Bureau.

region's population increase is due to net in-migration. For the past several years, the metropolitan Phoenix area has had a net in-migration of approximately 60,000 persons per year, with some 170,000 persons moving into the region per year and 110,000 moving out. There is high mobility between Phoenix and California (with one out-migrant to California for every two in-migrants to Phoenix).

Contrary to popular perception, however, most in- and out-migrants are young adults, not the elderly. Although Maricopa County was the leading retirement destination in the nation for elderly migrants between 1985 and 1990, net migration of young adults (twenty to thirty-four years old) now exceeds that of the entire older population of those over

Figure 5-1. Population Growth in Metropolitan Phoenix, 1970–98

Popluation (millions)

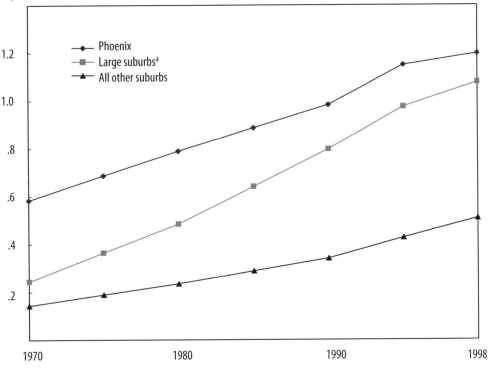

Source: Morrison Institute for Public Policy using data from U.S. Census Bureau.
a. Large suburbs refer to Chandler, Glendale, Mesa, Scottsdale, and Tempe.

fifty-five.[11] The younger in-migrants tend to be either recent college graduates beginning their careers or mid-career couples with young families who settle in the inner-suburb cities. Older migrants tend to settle in planned retirement communities located on the metropolitan fringe.

Metropolitan Density

The Phoenix region, contrary to its sprawling, low-density image, is actually growing fairly compactly. Very large population increases have driven the rapid expansion of the urbanized area in metropolitan Phoenix. Between 1960 and 1990 the urbanized land area grew 199 percent, while population increased 263 percent.[12] Albeit starting from a

11. Rex (2000b).
12. This is the latest date for which reliable data are available based on U.S. Census Bureau urbanized land measurements.

Figure 5-2. Land Consumption Relative to Population Growth in Metropolitan Phoenix, 1960–90

Percent change in density

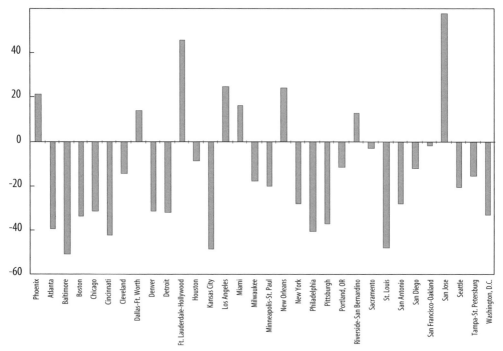

Source: Morrison Institute for Public Policy using data from U.S. Census Bureau.
Note: Urbanized areas with population over 1 million in 1990. Does not include Norfolk-Virginia Beach.

low base, density rose 22 percent to 2,707 people per square mile between 1960 and 1990; at that point it was only about 10 percent less than the national median for large urban areas (2,975 persons per square mile). Unlike metropolitan areas such as Atlanta, Denver, and San Diego, the Phoenix region is one of only a handful of large metropolitan areas (including Dallas and Los Angeles) that consumed land at a slower rate than population increased. By contrast, the Atlanta region consumed nearly twice as much land as the Phoenix region (almost 900 square miles compared with about 500) to accommodate approximately the same amount of population growth (see figure 5-2).

Density increases in metropolitan Phoenix appear to stem from increased construction of multi-family dwellings, decreases in average lot size, and considerable "in-fill" construction. At the simplest level, population density is a function of occupied housing density (units per square mile) and average household size. An analysis of housing types and sizes suggests that favorable tax rules in the 1980s led to the construction of an unusually high proportion of multi-family housing units. Also, high interest rates at that time limited residents' ability to purchase single-family houses. During the 1980s, much of the single-family and multi-family housing construction occurred on parcels that initially had been skipped over. At the same time, median lot size in metropolitan Phoenix dropped from 7,828 square feet in 1980 (about one-sixth of an acre) to 7,200 square feet in 2000.

The region is being built at quite even densities and lot sizes, even at the fringe. With few exceptions, most new neighborhoods in metropolitan Phoenix continue to be built at densities similar to the county average, rather than at the much lower densities common in some regions. This is true even in the prime new-home construction ring that now circles metropolitan Phoenix about eighteen to twenty-one miles from downtown Phoenix. The median lot size usually does not vary too much from city to city. Most of the cities have been within 10 percent of the county average, although each quadrant of the region has some areas with larger and smaller lot sizes.

Population density in central or downtown Phoenix has also increased. During the 1970s and 1980s population density decreased within a three-mile radius of central Phoenix. Between 1990 and 1995, however, density increased in the center even though there had been little residential construction in the area. The turnaround is due mostly to a sharp decline in housing vacancy rates and an increase in household size, largely related to the center's growing Hispanic population.

Recent research appears to support this finding and also shows that the region's density increased throughout the 1990s. For example, work by the Center for Business Research of Arizona State University suggests that population density in the region increased throughout the 1990s, with advances being somewhat greater during the first half of the decade. Population density increased by more than 1,000 persons per square mile in areas three to seven miles away from downtown Phoenix and areas nineteen to twenty-five miles out. Density increased by a little more than 500 persons per square mile in areas eight to eighteen miles away from downtown Phoenix.[13] A study by William Fulton and colleagues supports this assertion and notes that Phoenix was the eleventh most dense metropolitan area in 1997 and ranked third in density gains

13. Rex (2001, p. 5).

Table 5-2. Residential Movement Outward from Central Phoenix, 1990–98

| | Southeast | | Northeast | | Northwest | | Southwest | |
Year	Distance (miles)[a]	No. of housing units	Distance (miles)	No. of housing units	Distance (miles)	No. of housing units	Distance (miles)	No. of housing units
1990	16.4	3,930	17.1	2,249	18.1	2,483	19.2	197
1991	16.7	5,442	17.2	3,176	17.7	3,238	18.9	227
1992	16.5	7,205	17.4	4,806	17.1	4,455	19.6	284
1993	16.5	7,753	18.1	5,481	17.9	5,861	16.8	387
1994	17.1	10,314	18.4	6,612	18.1	7,644	16.8	431
1995	17.7	10,461	19.1	6,870	17.3	7,943	16.7	585
1996	18.8	11,883	19.0	8,245	17.3	9,696	18.8	729
1997	19.9	10,262	19.6	7,537	18.2	9,716	19.6	818
1998	20.6	10,498	19.4	8,142	18.5	10,432	20.1	904

Source: Gober and Burns (2000); data from the Maricopa Association of Governments.
a. Distance from the intersection of Washington Street and Central Avenue.

during the period.[14] Furthermore, a *USA Today* index released in June 2001 ranked Phoenix twenty-fifth among metropolitan areas according to the percentage of the population living in urbanized areas.[15]

Residential Construction

Metropolitan Phoenix's residential construction is moving outward swiftly. Homes are going up most quickly in a ring about eighteen to twenty-one miles from downtown Phoenix. From 1993 to 1998 the urban edge moved outward nearly one-half mile per year. But in the southeast quadrant the rate was faster, approaching three-fourths of a mile a year. With the exception of the southwest quadrant, which contains south-central Phoenix and absorbed only about 3 percent of new residential development, new construction has been quite evenly distributed geographically (see table 5-2 and figure 5-3).

A close look at the data suggests that development across the region during the 1990s followed a three-step pattern. Construction in the early 1990s took place within a zone approximately twelve to eighteen miles from downtown Phoenix that left a band of bypassed development between the initial urban fringe and the new edge. This was followed by in-fill construction along with further development of the outer zone. Finally, construction was expanded from the outer zone to the current

14. Fulton and others (2001).
15. Haya El Nassar and Paul Overberg, "A Comprehensive Look at Sprawl in America," *USA Today*, June 19, 2001.

Figure 5-3. New Residential Outward Movement in Metropolitan Phoenix, 1990–98

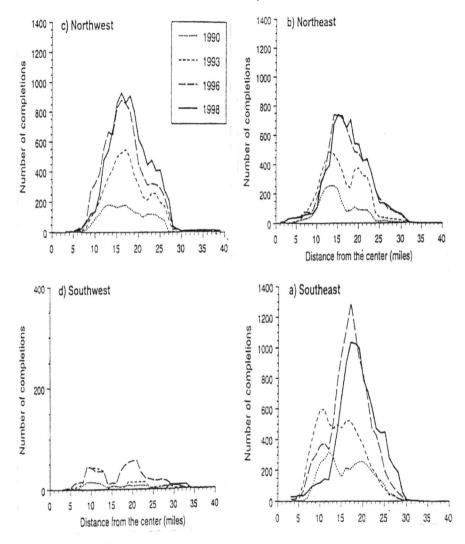

Source: Maricopa Association of Governments data.

twenty-one-mile distance.[16] This discontinuous development pattern appears to be due in large part to the real estate crash in the late 1980s. During its immediate aftermath, developers took fewer risks in site selection and turned their attention from the farthest "pioneer" fringe of development to safer, closer-in zones of in-fill activity and peak develop-

16. Gober and Burns (2000).

ment. During this time the average distance of new home construction from the core barely increased. Only after the local and national economies rebounded did developers turn back to the outer sector, which they pushed outward rapidly after the middle of the decade.

Migration on the Urban Fringe

People who have moved from one part of metropolitan Phoenix to another represent a solid majority of new residents on the urban edge, according to Morrison Institute survey data gathered in September 1999.[17] Almost 60 percent of new residents at the urban periphery (eighteen miles or more from downtown Phoenix) came from another metropolitan address, rather than from outside the region. New arrivals also chose homes at the fringe, but they constituted a smaller share of these residents.

For every local mover who came closer in, two moved farther out. Recent movers went outward an average of nearly five miles. In other words, they left a home about ten miles from downtown Phoenix for one fifteen miles out. The main destinations of outward movers were the north, northeast, and southeast edges. Meanwhile, one-third of metropolitan Phoenix movers moved inward an average of two-and-a-half miles. These relocations, however, cannot be construed as a "back-to-the-central-core" movement because their destinations were primarily suburban sections of northeast Phoenix and older areas of Scottsdale.

Persons over fifty-five years of age represent almost one-third of new urban fringe residents. These residents tend to congregate in the numerous age-segregated retirement communities located along the northwest and eastern edges of the urban area. These senior migrants are likely to arrive at the edge directly from outside the region.

Migrants to the fringe have higher incomes than their more centrally located counterparts. About two-thirds of recent edge migrants reported household incomes above $50,000, compared with one-half of movers to more central locations. This figure contradicts the notion that affordable housing is the primary motivation for moving outward.

Transportation Investments

Metropolitan Phoenix is one of the last major metropolitan areas in the United States to assemble a freeway system. In early 2000 it completed a freeway system that was begun in 1957 but expanded little

17. Morrison Institute for Public Policy (1999). The survey respondents overrepresented affluent homeowners and underrepresented low-income renters.

between 1970 and 1985. In 1985 voters approved a county sales tax increase for freeway construction, and over the next twelve years limited-access lane miles tripled from 290 to 870. Today as a result, metropolitan Phoenix makes do with a less-extensive limited-access road network than most regions its size. This belatedness also has made the region rely inordinately on arterial streets. In fact, in 2004, the region is only now building beltways around the urban area about ten to twenty miles from downtown Phoenix (see color plates, map 5-3).

The grid of arterial roads also increased substantially from 2,400 miles to 2,940 miles. As a result, while traffic is increasing, its negative impacts have not yet become unmanageable. The Texas Transportation Institute also found less congestion in the city of Phoenix than in comparable cities. Daily vehicle miles traveled per capita increased in the early 1990s, but have remained on par with the rate of population growth. While Phoenix violated the federal ozone standard on eleven days as recently as 1995, the Environmental Protection Agency recently recognized the region's achievement of going three years without violating the standard.

At the same time, public transit has been neglected. While investments were made in highways, a lack of local and state funding has constrained the Regional Public Transportation Authority. This disparity helps explain why the number of transit-service miles in metropolitan Phoenix (seven miles per capita) remains among the smallest for any large metropolitan area in the United States, and far below almost all other comparably sized metropolitan areas (eleven transit service miles per capita in San Diego, twenty-three in Seattle, and twenty in Denver). These patterns are a large part of the reason why transit is a limited option for most residents. Lower-income citizens are especially locked into a bus system that, despite improvements in routes and schedules, still limits their access to employment and other activities. These conditions may begin to change with the sales tax assessments authorized by voters in Mesa, Tempe, and Phoenix in the late 1990s. The new funds will pay for more bus service and the start of a thirty-four-mile light-rail project that will run through the central employment areas.

More Diversity, More Divisions

The Phoenix region's population is 72 percent white. Most of the nonwhite residents of the region are Hispanic, according to 2000 Census data. The Hispanic population has surged, increasing from approximately 13 percent of the region's population in 1980 to 25 percent in

2000. Most of the region's Hispanic and African American residents live in the city of Phoenix, where 44 percent of the city's population belongs to a minority group. In contrast, only 27 percent of the population of the five largest suburbs combined belongs to minority groups (see color plates, map 5-4).

But another racial divide exists within the city of Phoenix. A line along State Route 202/ I-10 separates a majority-white area from a majority-nonwhite area. And the north-south division is growing more dramatic. In 1980 minority residents accounted for 9 percent of north Phoenix and 47 percent of south Phoenix. By 1995, 28 percent of north Phoenix residents belonged to ethnic minority groups, and the percentage living in south Phoenix had grown to 77 percent.

As the region has grown, the geographic extent of poverty in metropolitan Phoenix has also expanded, but it has done so in line with the expansion of the urbanized area. Overall, 12.3 percent of the region's people lived in poverty in 1990.[18] At the same time, however, several high-poverty clusters have grown larger and more pronounced, notably in central and south Phoenix, covering a fifty-eight-square-mile area of distress. In the middle of this cluster are the region's highest poverty rates (in excess of 40 percent). In this struggling area the median income was $11,500 in 1989, whereas countywide the median income was $30,797 and $16,750 for the entire south and central Phoenix poverty zone. Other poverty clusters are evident in some portions of downtown Tempe and much of the west side of the region. Glendale, Tempe, and Phoenix experienced an increase in the poverty rate between 1979 and 1989. The 1989 rate in Phoenix and Tempe was higher than the metropolitan average, though university students inflate Tempe's rate. By contrast, poverty rates are low and income levels high in much of the northeast and southeast. In the most affluent part of the northeast quadrant, the 1989 median per capita income was $62,900.

Home values also show a divide similar to that for race and poverty. The north and northeast parts of the region have high home values, while lower-value housing and rental values are concentrated in the southern and central parts of the city of Phoenix. For example, in 1990 the median value of older south and central Phoenix homes hovered around $50,000, while homes in north Phoenix were valued around $98,000, with prices even higher to the northeast. The region's lowest-

18. The latest year for which poverty and housing estimates are available at this level of detail is 1990. The most recent U.S Census Bureau county estimates (1997) project that the poverty level in Maricopa County was 12.7 percent.

Table 5-3. Employment Cores in the Phoenix Metropolitan Area

Indicator	Downtown/Midtown Phoenix (primary, level 1)	Sky Harbor/Tempe/ Scottsdale/Metrocenter (secondary, level 2)	Level 3	Level 4
Employment density[a]	> 6,800	4,100–4,800	2,800–3,700	1,700–2,700
Employment to population ratio[b]	> 2	> 1.5	> 1	…
Number of industries with concentration	7 to 8	5 to 7	3 to 5	…
Total employment	…	…	…	> 15,000

Source: Calculated from Maricopa Association of Governments 1995 employment database.

a. Based in part on natural breaks. Employment density = employment per square mile.

b. Compared with county figure of 0.5.

priced housing and rental values—those affordable to families with $20,000 in yearly income (approximately equivalent to two minimum-wage earners)—were almost exclusively clustered in the south and central area. The core's low rents and valuations, however, are less than affordable to the central area's low-income residents. New high-density construction caters to more affluent citizens living some distance from the core. Most of the approximately 10,000 units constructed annually since 1996 are being built ten to fifteen miles from downtown Phoenix. Most of these units appear to be aimed at high-end markets, even though the core's lower-income residents are the ones most in need of rental housing.

Employment at the Core

Employment in the region is growing and is now 1.7 million, up from 1.2 million in 1990. The primary employment core is located in downtown-midtown Phoenix. This central area of the city of Phoenix has the highest employment density and the greatest number of industries (see table 5-3). The jobs are in high-paying industries such as finance, insurance, real estate, professional services, and government, and many of them require substantial education.

The second strong employment core includes some of the city of Phoenix, but also stretches into central and downtown Tempe and south and downtown Scottsdale. Arizona State University, Sky Harbor International Airport, public utilities, communication assets, and government are located in this employment core. Access to the region's first two freeways helped portions of Tempe become the largest employment center outside of the downtown-midtown Phoenix core (see color plates, map 5-5). Scottsdale's employment success can be traced to its proximity to affluent residential areas. Combined, the two employment cores contained 32 percent of the region's jobs, but cover only seventy-six square miles. Only 13 percent of the population lives within these two core areas.

Since 1994 the region's greatest job increases have occurred in outlying areas with 117,500 jobs (a 44 percent change), but this high growth rate was a product of increases from a small base. Areas with the fewest jobs and the least job growth are in south Phoenix, west of Central Avenue, and in the Ahwatukee Foothills south of South Mountain Park.

The employment core is so strong today that even with little growth in the next twenty years it would still be the primary employment area for the region. In 1997, MAG issued a set of employment projections in line with its population projections. The data forecast a 50 percent gain in regional employment by 2020. Employment in the primary core was expected to remain steady over the next twenty-five years. However, the core still would have the highest employment densities in 2020 at more than 7,000 employees per square mile. The secondary core would retain its status with employment densities between 5,000 and 6,200 employees per square mile.

This employment strength contrasts sharply with that in most other metropolitan areas. Between 1972 and 1995, core employment in Chicago, for example, declined 19 percent, while other areas in the region grew 97 percent.[19] Central Phoenix's strength bodes well for providing alternative transportation options and more close-in, middle-class residential areas. It also continues to give the central city the inherent advantages of plentiful face-to-face contact and access to infrastructure (such as airports) that have always fostered economic growth but which are critical for new economy firms and global businesses.

Metropolitan Phoenix ranks twelfth among metropolitan areas in the total number of high-tech jobs.[20] But, employment in industries such as aerospace, information, bioindustry, plastics, and software is limited in the primary core. As noted earlier, the industrial mix in central and downtown Phoenix is heavily weighted to the retail and tourist services, government, finance, insurance, and real estate industries. Software and information industries have a large presence in Tempe and Scottsdale, part of the secondary employment core. Large high-tech manufacturing companies, especially in aerospace and semiconductors, are generally

19. Great Cities Institute (2000).
20. American Electronics Association (2000).

Figure 5-4. Housing Value, Jobs, and Retail Sales for Phoenix and Its Five Large Suburbs

Percent of regional average

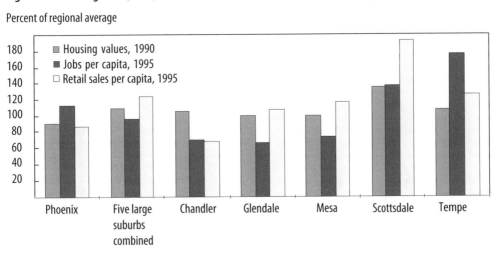

Source: Morrison Institute for Public Policy; data on housing units from U.S. Census Bureau; on jobs from Maricopa Association of Governments; on retail sales from League of Arizona Cities and Towns, Arizona Department of Revenue, Phoenix Department of Revenue, Tempe Department of Revenue.

Regional average = 100 percent.

located on large parcels outside the core areas in the northwest and the southeast portions of the region.

Jobs, Housing, and Retail Sales

Many urban regions in the United States suffer from gross disparities in the distribution of people, jobs, and economic and social resources between their core cities and their suburbs. Fortunately, metropolitan Phoenix does not. The region's central city and its major suburbs display relatively even distributions of housing, jobs, and retail sales. This balance likely results from the fact that the city of Phoenix contains a mix of established central areas, old and new suburbs, and recent fringe development. The city of Phoenix has more jobs than the per capita regional average. Retail sales and housing values are somewhat below the regional average. These figures suggest that the city of Phoenix, unlike many core cities of metropolitan areas, has maintained a broad revenue base to pay for services for residents.

Among the five populous suburbs, the measures of housing values, jobs, and retail sales vary widely. Tempe and Scottsdale are the region's leaders in all three measures (see figure 5-4). In 1995, Scottsdale's per capita retail sales figure was almost twice that in the region, and in 1990

Figure 5-5. Housing Value, Jobs, and Retail Sales for Eighteen Smaller Cities and Towns of Metropolitan Phoenix

Percent of regional average

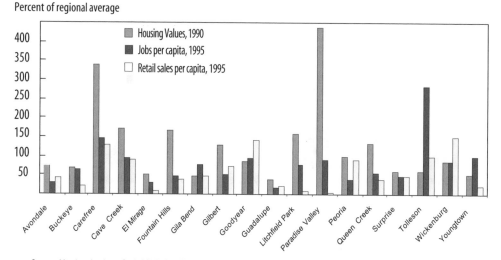

Source: Morrison Institute for Public Policy; data on housing units from U.S. Census Bureau; on jobs from Maricopa Association of Governments; on retail sales from League of Arizona Cities and Towns, Arizona Department of Revenue, Phoenix Department of Revenue, Tempe Department of Revenue.

Regional average = 100 percent.

its housing values were 37 percent higher.[21] Tempe has attracted almost 80 percent more jobs than the regional average. Tempe and Scottsdale are part of the region's secondary employment core. Smaller outlying communities tend to have lesser concentrations of jobs and retail. In nearly all of these municipalities, the per capita retail sales and jobs per capita figures are below the regional average. Conversely, the availability of housing in some communities on the east side of the region is well above the metropolitan average (see figure 5-5).

Unlike urban regions in the country's Northeast and Midwest, metropolitan Phoenix cities rely heavily on sales tax revenue and relatively little on property tax collections. Arizona law limits property tax. Conversely, sales tax collections can be set at the discretion of each city. In 1998 sales tax collections accounted for about 62 percent of local tax revenues in the region, compared with 27 percent nationwide. In contrast, the property tax is the primary source of local revenues nationally. Housing values (an indicator of property tax collections) account for 32

21. The bed and use tax was excluded from this study because varying definitions limited comparisons.

percent of local tax revenues in the region, compared with 53 percent nationally.

As the first part of this chapter suggests, Phoenix has evolved a distinctive urban form since the early 1970s. It is fairly compact yet still auto-oriented. Employment remains centralized in core parts of the region to a remarkable degree, though residential development is moving outward rapidly. A divide between affluent and poor areas exists, but it is not as extreme as in other regions. And in keeping with the vitality of the center, the region retains a measure of "balance" between its core city, Phoenix, and its largest suburbs, Scottsdale, Glendale, Mesa, Tempe, and Chandler.

Metropolitan Phoenix, in short, has grown at a phenomenal pace without succumbing to the center-city disinvestments and deep social and economic divides that often accompany metropolitan growth and development patterns. To that extent, the region confounds large parts of the traditional model of urban development and the Sunbelt stereotype.

Negative Impacts of Phoenix's Growth Patterns and Metropolitan Form

Taken together, the trends in population, density, employment, transportation, and land use tell a compelling story about metropolitan Phoenix. In some important ways, metropolitan Phoenix's growth is a success story. Yet the pattern of development in the region also has negative implications that need to be addressed.

Land Use

Metropolitan Phoenix is rapidly losing desert and agricultural areas to urban uses. Between 1975 and 1995 metropolitan Phoenix's urban area more than doubled. Many other regions have urbanized their land more quickly than Phoenix. Still, urban development now covers more than 40 percent of the MAG planning area, compared with 15 percent in 1975. Undeveloped desert in 1995 represented only 33 percent of the land in the planning area, compared with 49 percent in 1975. A 49 percent increase in recreational land mitigated the agricultural and desert losses somewhat (see color plates, map 5-6).

Local governments have moved to offset development with open-space protection and recreation areas. In 1995, Maricopa County had almost 2 million acres (or over 3,000 square miles) of dedicated open space, including federal lands, city and county parks, and mountain preserves. Much of this space is in unincorporated sections of Maricopa County. This figure represented an increase of nearly 2 percent since 1990.[22] Nevertheless, open-space acquisition lags behind population growth and development in most communities. Countywide, open space set aside declined on a per capita basis from .84 acres per person in 1990 to .71 in 1995. Furthermore, open-space acquisitions are fragmentary. This results partly from Phoenix's setting, which has dictated the location of the region's mountain parks. But "patchy" open-space provisions also follow from the divergent political orientations and financial conditions of metropolitan Phoenix's local governments.

In addition to the loss of open space, the development of almost 500 square miles of desert and fields in the MAG planning area has had several other environmental consequences. For example, the "urban heat island" effect of mass paving has pushed nighttime low temperatures in the urban area a full eight degrees higher than fifty years ago—a change with a significant impact on a desert climate's livability. And the movement of most building onto open desert from retired fields in recent years raises additional concerns. Home construction is now cutting remaining patches of natural vegetation into smaller and smaller fragments, while the channelization or blockage of riparian corridors is creating flood control problems and disrupting wildlife migration corridors and natural drainage patterns.

Divided Schools

Although metropolitan Phoenix is divided by race, income, and housing values, it is not as sharply divided as some other metropolitan areas. This regional divide places higher-than-average numbers of poor and minority students in the schools of central Phoenix and the southwestern portion of the region. Out of fifty elementary and unified school districts regionwide, the ten with the highest percentage of Hispanic students were predominantly in central and southwest Phoenix. In fact, central and southwest Phoenix districts respectively averaged only 20 percent and 41 percent white students. In contrast, the five northeastern school districts averaged 87 percent white students.

An achievement gap also exists. The region's lowest-achieving districts, based on percentile ranking of standardized test scores, are in central Phoenix and the southwest. The best-performing school districts were mostly in the fringe areas that are predominantly white (see color

22. The figure is based on land-use reports submitted by individual cities and towns to MAG between 1990 and 1995.

plates, map 5-7). In 1998 northeast elementary school districts had the highest test scores and the highest percentage of white students; and between 1990 and 1998, except for Scottsdale, those districts grew the most. In addition, lower rates of high school completion in the poor, nonwhite center add to the educational gap, since poverty can reduce the likelihood of finishing high school.

The education divide exacerbates growth at the edges and makes the region's center less economically viable. The weak schools of the center present a powerful impetus for decentralization. Schools with high proportions of low-income, minority, or underachieving students may influence where families with children choose to live. Specifically, such schools could drive middle-class families—and the businesses that employ them—away from central Phoenix toward better-performing, white-dominated schools farther out in the metropolitan area. Such a change could increase the viability of the fringe at the expense of the core.

Rapid Growth

In three years of surveying metropolitan Phoenix residents for its annual quality-of-life report, the Morrison Institute found urban growth to be the one issue that transcends most discussions about regional quality of life. For the fall 1999 edition of *What Matters in Greater Phoenix*, the institute added several questions to its regionwide random sample survey to better measure public sentiment on the issue of urban growth.[23]

In this survey, 80 percent of greater Phoenix residents said they were either concerned or very concerned about the region's growth. These responses support the nearly 75 percent who have said in each of the past three years that the region's population is growing "too fast." With rapid growth as the most common reason, nearly half of the residents in the 1999 survey indicated they would leave the region tomorrow if they had the ability to do so. This nearly even split runs across many subpopulations in the survey population, including a close to 40 percent "yes" response from those aged 18–34, those earning between $50,000 and $75,000 per year, and those who had lived in the region for ten to twenty years. Respondents cited climate (33 percent), environment (11 percent), and openness or wide-open spaces (5 percent) as attractions of living and working in the region.

23. Morrison Institute for Public Policy (1999).

Challenges to Municipalities

Eighteen less-populous cities on the urban fringe now control nearly as much land as the city of Phoenix and the five largest suburbs combined, although they are home to less than 20 percent of the region's population. These smaller jurisdictions have annexed land far in advance of urban development—sometimes decades ahead. With continued population growth and a strong preference for low-density development among the region's residents, the result could be endless plots of far-reaching planned communities.

Moreover, because the smaller communities tend to have larger amounts of housing relative to job and retail assets, they may lack the resources necessary to absorb rapid growth. Although many have impact-fee structures in place to fund some of the needed services, resources may not be readily available to fund other needs associated with growth, such as schools, community resources, or open-space protection.

Because the challenges of growth cross jurisdictional boundaries, the responses of these communities to rapid growth can either undermine or encourage compact development patterns and quality of life throughout the region. As new players who control so much of the region's undeveloped land, their involvement in regional cooperation and their access to tools and resources will become increasingly important.

Public Policy and Governance

The preceding pages have painted a picture of the Phoenix metropolitan region past, present, and future. Yet, to better understand the likely evolution of the region, it is important to explore further the ways in which metropolitan Phoenix's growth patterns have been shaped by inherent local factors, the region's governance patterns, and more important, a wide variety of public policy decisions. Policies that have affected the current state of the metropolitan region's growth include those that address land and water management, transportation, development patterns (including impact fees, strengthening downtown cores, and annexation), and conserving the region's quality of life. Some have been instrumental in helping the region avoid the negative consequences of its rapid growth; others appear to have been less successful.

Land Management

Federal land holdings and several Indian reservations create a de facto urban growth boundary for metropolitan Phoenix. The restrained pace of the state of Arizona's sales of its school trust land has also fostered compactness, at least thus far. As noted earlier, the state constitution requires that the trust lands be managed to maximize their benefit to the state's schools. This requirement has always raised the possibility that these lands could be sold or leased to developers. However, analysis of State Land Department records suggests that such transactions have had only a minor influence on the region's physical form. Many states sold off their trust lands for short-term gain decades ago. By contrast, Arizona retains more than 90 percent of its original grant. To date, the State Land Department has sold off just 7,446 acres of land near all of the state's cities.[24] The net effect is that the state now retains a reservoir of more than 200,000 acres of vacant land around metropolitan Phoenix.

The Urban Land Management Act of 1981 also has limited sales of state trust land for development. This law anticipated the approach of the urban edge to state lands and sought to supervise the state's participation in the real estate business. The act gave the State Land Department new authority to plan, zone, and merchandise lands within or near the metropolitan areas. It directed the Land Department to encourage "appropriate" development and "in-fill," and to discourage "urban sprawl" and "leapfrog" building.

A series of policy initiatives are likely to inhibit the Arizona Land Department's sale of land in the future. The Arizona Preserve Initiative, passed in 1996, encouraged the preservation of state lands near urban centers as open space and created the opportunity for cities and counties to buy some State Trust Lands for conservation purposes. Proposition 303, passed in November 1998 as part of Governor Jane Hull's "Growing Smarter" program, made up to $20 million a year in matching grants available to Maricopa County for the next eleven years to purchase or lease trust lands classified for conservation or to purchase development rights. Legislation called "Growing Smarter Plus," passed in November 2000, provides mechanisms to set aside, exchange, or donate trust lands. Similarly, the Development Rights Retirement Fund was established to grant monies for purchase, lease, or transfer of development rights of private lands, although it has yet to be funded.

Water Management

Early, bold federal and state efforts made water a facilitator of regional growth. Without a reliable water supply, Phoenix would never have developed into a large metropolitan region. In the early years of

---

24. Arizona State Land Department (2000).

the twentieth century, Phoenix-area government and business leaders persuaded the federal government to construct massive dams and water delivery systems. Among these projects was the Salt River Project (SRP), which had its beginnings with the building of Roosevelt Dam in 1911, and the Central Arizona Project (CAP), a 365-mile-long system of aqueducts, tunnels, pumping plants, and pipelines begun in 1986. Through the SRP and CAP, metropolitan Phoenix has access to as much as 1.7 million acre-feet per year of surface water. By some estimates, this is enough water to support a population at least double the region's current number.

The Groundwater Management Act (GMA) of 1980 further supported growth, but with an eye to conservation and careful management of its water resources. With the act, the state of Arizona moved aggressively to administer its substantial, but finite, water supplies and control groundwater pumping. Specifically, the GMA limits groundwater pumping in the Phoenix region and, until 1998, required developers to verify that projects had a 100-year water supply that would not further deplete the aquifer. These requirements responded to several negative environmental impacts of metropolitan Phoenix's expansion such as land subsidence due to groundwater pumping. Named as one of the Ford Foundation's ten most innovative programs in state and local government in 1986, the GMA likely has limited the region's spread somewhat as subdivisions were forced to refrain from unrestrained groundwater use and usually had to connect to existing water infrastructure. Also, the need to use existing water and sewer infrastructure provides developers and local governments with considerable incentive to use land efficiently.

However, the GMA does not prohibit "leapfrog" development, in which developers skip over properties to obtain land at a lower price further out despite the existence of utilities and infrastructure that could serve the bypassed parcels. It only makes developers financially responsible for securing long-term water supplies. Many developments approved since the GMA have fulfilled their obligations by joining a regional "groundwater replenishment district," securing groundwater rights and paying what amounts to a mitigation fee, even if replenishable water supplies are unavailable nearby.

Transportation

The initial decision not to build a comprehensive freeway system into the outer reaches of the region promoted more compact development, notwithstanding the inconvenience it caused. By blocking construction of beltway-like freeways and concentrating investments close to the core, freeway opponents delayed the types of highways that facilitated large-scale decentralization in many other metropolitan areas. Almost one-third of the $4.8 billion spent on highways between 1986 and 1998 (in 1998 dollars) funded freeways at the center of the region (see table 5-4 and color plates, map 5-8). An additional 28 percent of the expenditures went to roads that serve the southeast, the fastest-growing residential area, including the Loop 101 and State Route 60.

Delaying freeway construction also promoted reliance on the region's one-mile grid of arterial streets, which has tended to encourage relatively even development patterns. The streets provide the driver with multiple routes and detours around congestion and are easy to build as needed. As development attorney and urban observer Grady Gammage Jr. has pointed out, the arterial streets afforded the city a way to serve new areas of settlement in an "incremental" way that did not distort ongoing development patterns with sudden additions of capacity.[25]

How the future completion of the Loop 101 and 202 beltways will affect the urban form remains to be seen. The decision to expedite this construction may speed the dispersal of employment into affluent suburban areas. If so, the current round of freeway construction may leave a more ambiguous legacy than the last one did.

Growth Management Tools

Local government growth management programs are fairly widespread in the Phoenix region and more prevalent than conventional wisdom would predict. In 2000, the Morrison Institute surveyed the twenty-five cities and towns (including Apache Junction and Maricopa County) to better understand the nature and level of local growth management efforts. In developing the questionnaire, the institute used the Lincoln Institute of Land Policy's description of a systematic growth management framework.[26]

The Morrison Institute's survey revealed surprising activities in the county and the other eighteen responding jurisdictions. The region's diverse growth management policies constitute a surprisingly well-ordered system. Though levied independently, the array of approaches

25. Gammage (1999).

26. The framework included: strategies to discourage sprawl and encourage compact urban development, in-fill, and revitalization of blighted or troubled areas; provision of infrastructure (roads, schools, water service, parks) at the time of development; urban design requirements that aim for aesthetically pleasant urban areas, mixed uses, and environmentally friendly places; policies and programs that protect sensitive lands, rural areas,

Table 5-4. Federal and State Highway Spending in Metropolitan Phoenix, 1986–98

Region	Number of route segments	Federal and state highway spending[a]	Percentage of federal and state highway spending
Northwest	19	842,865,377	17.6
Northeast	11	868,081,289	18.1
Southeast	24	1,347,625,827	28.1
Southwest	9	289,068,344	6.0
Central	15	1,445,647,559	30.2
Total	78	4,793,288,396	100.0

Source: Dr. Elizabeth Burns, Department of Geography, Arizona State University; data from Arizona Department of Transportation.

a. Spending for projects over $1 million in 1998 dollars; does not include federal and state highway funds going directly to cities.

points to the emergence of a "Phoenix style" of growth management that focuses on requiring new development to "pay for itself" rather than on restricting it. However, the individual growth management practices adopted by each jurisdiction cannot be characterized as universal or uniform across the region (see table 5-5). The survey shows that several smaller towns have as many management tools in place as the larger cities. And fringe towns and cities on the eastern side of the region tend to wield more restrictive growth management tools than their western counterparts.

Impact fees constitute the region's leading growth management response. The survey shows that fifteen of the region's jurisdictions have established impact fees to recoup the costs of building infrastructure and providing public amenities. Cities vary widely in their use of the fees, although most often the assessments are used to fund water and sewer service. Moreover, the amount charged by the region's towns varies widely (see figure 5-6). The fees charged ranged from $1,800 per single-family house in Tempe to $13,000 in parts of Peoria. Also, the survey reveals a staged array of impact fees within the region that clearly responds to regional growth patterns. Impact fees often are higher at the fringe and much lower in the core of cities. Setting them in this way is both a way to pay for new growth and a de facto in-fill strategy because it is less expensive in such a scenario to develop a subdivision in a vacant area that already has sewer and water.

The cities and towns were asked to estimate what percentage of costs for streets, traffic lights, sewers, water, parks, public safety, and libraries

and open spaces; policies and programs to ensure that affordable housing is a major component of new development; and growth management boundaries.

Table 5-5. Growth Management Tools in Nineteen Arizona Cities, 2000

Location	Impact fees	In-fill incentives	Adequate public facilities ordinance	Downtown urban design guidelines	Revenue for open space	Urban line limit	Limits on population growth
Apache Junction	Yes	Yes	No	Yes	No	No	No
Carefree	No	No	Yes	Yes	Yes	Yes	No
Cave Creek	Yes	No	No	Yes	No	No	No
Chandler	Yes	Yes	Yes	Yes	Yes	No	No
Fountain Hills	No	No	No	Yes	No	No	No
Gilbert	Yes	No	Yes	Yes	No	No	No
Glendale	Yes	Yes	Yes	Yes	No	Yes	No
Goodyear	Yes	No	Yes	No	No	No	No
Litchfield Park	No	No	No	No	No	No	No
Mesa	Yes	No	Yes	Yes	Yes	Yes	No
Peoria	Yes	No	Yes	Yes	No	No	No
Phoenix	Yes	Yes	Yes	Yes	Yes	Yes	No
Queen Creek	Yes	Yes	Yes	Yes	Yes	Yes	No
Scottsdale	Yes	No	Yes	Yes	Yes	Yes	No
Surprise	Yes	No	No	No	No	No	No
Tempe	Yes	Yes	Yes	Yes	No	No	No
Tolleson	Yes	Yes	Yes	Yes	Yes	No	No
Youngtown	Yes	No	No	No	No	No	No
Maricopa County	No	No	No	No	Yes	No	No
Percentage using tool	79	37	63	74	42	32	0

Source: Morrison Institute for Public Policy (2000).

were covered by fees. Respondents replied that impact fees typically balance the majority of costs. Whether this array of fees promotes regional compactness, however, remains unclear. Recent national research concluded that metropolitan areas that rely on impact fees rather than tax revenue to finance new public infrastructure are more likely to develop in a compact manner.[27] However, the Morrison Institute analysis did not draw conclusions on this issue.

Annexation

As noted in the introduction, aggressive annexation by cities has been a distinctive feature of metropolitan Phoenix growth since 1970. Since then, the city of Phoenix has added 230 square miles to its territory. The

27. Pendal (1995, pp. 555–71).

Figure 5-6. Impact Fees by City in Metropolitan Phoenix

Impact fee for single-family homes (dollars)

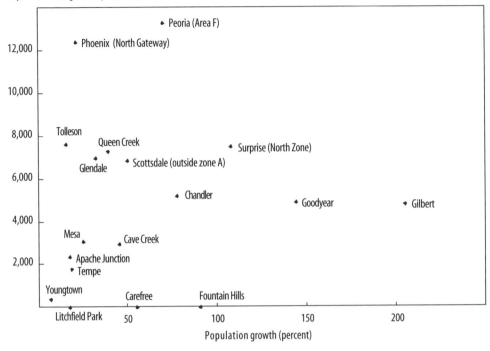

Source: Morrison Institute for Public Policy (2000).

annexation has helped prevent gross disparities from arising between the regional core and its largest suburbs. By extending its boundaries, the city of Phoenix has been able to compete with the surrounding cities for desirable populations, jobs, residential development, and retail activity. This has promoted "balance" in the region; the city of Phoenix contains not just old central core areas and old suburbs, but new suburban areas and recent fringe development as well.

The larger suburbs also have annexed heavily, with Scottsdale, Glendale, Mesa, and Chandler moving to the fore in the 1970s. Only Tempe, the only landlocked city among the five populous suburbs, did not annex large tracts of land during that time. Combined, the five suburbs added some 329 square miles. More recently, the movement to annex has shifted outward. Since 1980 each of the region's municipalities with populations of less than 100,000 has annexed land even more aggressively than their more established neighbors. By 1998 these cities and towns

Figure 5-7. Land Annexation Trends in Metropolitan Phoenix, 1919–2000

Square miles annexed

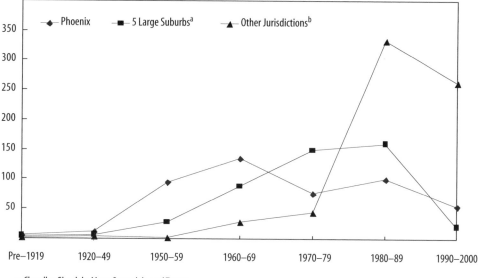

a. Chandler, Glendale, Mesa, Scottsdale, and Tempe.
b. The remaining incorporated cities in Maricopa County.
Source: Morrison Institute for Public Policy using data from Maricopa County Association of Governments.

encompassed some 667 square miles, compared with Phoenix's 470 square miles and the five large suburbs' 449 square miles (see figure 5-7).

Controlling the quality and cost impacts of growth in nearby unincorporated areas was rated the most important reason for annexations in the Morrison Institute's survey of cities' growth management techniques. The second most important reason cited was developers' threats to build in adjacent unincorporated areas of the county where there are fewer land-use and zoning regulations. Other important motivations included obtaining additional sales and property tax revenue and water resources.

One positive result of the annexation has been to keep the political map simple. Large-scale annexation has brought large amounts of unincorporated land under established government, which is potentially an advantage for more orderly development in the region. But it also has kept at a minimum the number of municipalities in the region. Although it is one of the largest metropolitan areas in the United States, the region consists of only twenty-four relatively large cities and towns: the city of Phoenix, with almost 45 percent of the region's population and nearly

30 percent of its land area, plus twenty-three other municipalities. This political map contrasts sharply with a metropolitan region such as Chicago (with 265 municipalities) or Los Angeles (with approximately 180). Moreover, annexation has brought large amounts of unincorporated land under established government, which is potentially an advantage for more orderly development in the region. For example, with one-third of the region's urbanized land area in the city of Phoenix, much of the region "lives by the same rules."

Both of these effects—annexing unincorporated land and a simple political map—may well have promoted more orderly development in the region by reducing the number of possibilities for excessive fragmentation that can lead to land-use mismanagement. However, as the region's less-populous, farther-out towns gain control of more land, the future of the region depends increasingly on some new players. Their responses to rapid growth can either undermine or encourage compact development patterns and quality of life in both cities and suburbs.

Open Space

Protecting open space and desert land has long been a concern among local residents and, as noted in earlier sections, the open-space response goes back a long way. These efforts have kept vacant land or parkland in key areas within the urban form of metropolitan Phoenix despite the effects of phenomenal population growth. For example, the city of Phoenix has doubled the size of its parks system since 1964 through the addition of 17,000 acres, more than any other city except San Diego. Together the city of Phoenix and Scottsdale—which has slated 40 percent of its area to be protected as open space—have been moving toward the creation of major greenbelts in the region. In addition, virtually all of the region's jurisdictions have set aside considerable amounts of open space. Including the lands added by the cities of Phoenix and Scottsdale, together the eight largest municipalities doubled the amount of open space within their jurisdiction from 14,720 acres in 1975 to more than 30,000 acres in 1995. These efforts were most often funded by municipal sales taxes, although some communities financed purchases with bond issues or impact fee revenues.

For all this activity, though, open-space acquisition does not appear to be keeping pace with population growth. As noted earlier in the chapter, the amount of dedicated open space available on a per capita basis countywide has declined, and much of the new open-space acquisition appears to be piecemeal.

Government Structure

A final contributor to the region's relatively balanced growth has been its government structure, dominated by strong local governments. As described earlier, the existing regional government structure consists of a voluntary regional association of governments, a weak county, and strong independent municipalities. While state and federal policy has often shaped the larger patterns of metropolitan growth through land-holding, transportation, and natural resource policies, historically the state government has not played a major role in determining the land-use or tax policies of regional and local governments.[28] The result is that the region's governance structure is one of strong cities, weak regional entities, polarized civic agendas, and spotty state leadership—each adding to and detracting from the region's success.

CITIES AND CITY-BASED LOCALISM PREDOMINATE. Phoenix, Mesa, Scottsdale, Glendale, Tempe, and Chandler are sizable cities with significant fiscal and managerial capacity. Moreover, metropolitan Phoenix cities possess "home-rule charters" that guarantee them unusually robust powers. This state of affairs has seen individual cities achieve much in terms of planning, tax collection, and downtown development. But it has also made it difficult for localities to align their agendas to solve problems that affect the whole region. Differing political orientations and financial conditions, for instance, delayed the now nascent framing of a light-rail system. At the same time, the relatively small number of cities in the region and the sheer size of the city of Phoenix have helped to reduce the fragmentation that can lead to gross land-use mismanagement.

MARICOPA COUNTY AND MAG LACK STRONG AUTHORITY. Only in 2000 did the "Growing Smarter Plus" legislative package give counties the same power as cities to impose impact fees and provide restrictions on further city annexations. Moreover, voters have consistently rejected expanding Maricopa County's powers, most recently in 1996 when they turned down a proposed home-rule charter for the county much like those of major cities in the region. Since the 1970s,

---

28. For example, the state government did not require local governments to adopt comprehensive land-use and zoning ordinances until recently. Even with this change, the state does little to ensure that locals implement such laws; no state agency exists to monitor compliance. Since 1998, cities, towns, and counties have had to adopt new land-use plans for ten-year periods, and amendments to the general plans need a two-thirds vote of the city council or county supervisors (rather than, as in the past, a majority of members). While the 1998 legislation mandates some important changes in traditional practices, there is still no state agency to monitor compliance.

MAG has helped to promote uniformity in planning and programming of various activities, especially as required for various federal transportation and other programs, but the association lacks the power to enforce decisions. Even MAG's ability to produce voluntary approaches to regional problems has been limited. Recent efforts to craft a vision for the year 2025 have not been successfully incorporated into the region's culture or governance.

Another conspicuously weak entity is the Regional Public Transportation Authority (RPTA). The authority is hobbled by funding constraints, which leaves it ill-equipped to adequately address the region's transportation needs, let alone manage growth as similar authorities in other cities do.

THE REGION'S CIVIC CULTURE REMAINS FRACTIOUS. The lack of a regional consensus on a number of growth-related issues has generated new polarization and litigation. Action on air-quality issues in the 1990s, for example, came only under the pressure of lawsuits brought by the Arizona Center for Law in the Public Interest. Dissatisfaction with legislative responses to growth pressures resulted in the placement of a Sierra Club–sponsored initiative on the November 2000 state ballot that would have required cities to create urban growth boundaries. The initiative did not pass. Meanwhile, a court challenge embroiled a rival legislative proposition to dedicate a portion of the state's land near cities to open space. In short, metropolitan Phoenix's political culture has hardly been conducive to the broad-based consensus building likely to drive effective responses to the regional impacts of rapid growth.

THE STATE PROVIDES INCONSISTENT LEADERSHIP. The Groundwater Management Act and the Urban Land Management Act of the early 1980s underscore the potential for creative regional problem solving by the governor and the legislature. However, for most of the 1990s the state was essentially a nonplayer on growth issues. More recently, responses have emerged under the threat of citizens' action, but these have been of mixed quality. Although the state has sponsored initiatives to address the emerging problems of growth (for example, requiring cleaner gasoline and requiring local governments to maintain comprehensive land-use and zoning ordinances), these efforts cannot be said to constitute a strong or comprehensive approach to the issues raised by fast growth across the region. Moreover, other comprehensive growth management initiatives placed on the ballot have failed to gain approval by voters; and the parts of the initiatives that have been acted on (for example, the Development Rights Retirement Fund) have not been funded and hence are not operational.

Recommendations

Metropolitan Phoenix has grown in ways both like and unlike other regions of its type. The region has arrived where it is today through a combination of special attributes, timing, and national trends and public policy. Considered together, these cross-currents challenge Phoenix to think carefully in the early twenty-first century for two reasons. First, the strong role timing has played in metropolitan Phoenix's rise raises the possibility that the region's relative health thus far is attributable mainly to its extreme youth. To be sure, a number of particular local twists of topography, land ownership, water policy, and massive annexation have made the Phoenix region different from many. Yet for all that, metropolitan Phoenix's resemblance to cities that have grown since 1970 suggest it may not be so much different as younger than other more troubled cities.

At the same time, the region faces the future at a moment when many "givens" about what matters in region building have been changed by the age of knowledge. Phoenix came into its own during the automobile era, but the region's next chapter will be written in a new era. The new economy is altering much about the way companies, people, cities, and governments operate. Metropolitan Phoenix's economic competitiveness depends on successfully managing its past and current growth trends so as to avoid becoming a region of haves and have-nots and to prevail as a lifestyle mecca for talent and cutting-edge companies. And yet the problems on display in Atlanta, Washington, D.C., and Denver may be inseparable from the maturity toward which Phoenix is moving. If that is so, the region should think hard about how to avoid the pitfalls of maturity while seeking its benefits. More than likely such planning will require important and controversial policy choices.

For example, Metropolitan Phoenix's leaders will soon need to deal with dilemmas or "Catch-22s" with both positive and negative potential.

—*Looming transportation and land-use conundrums.* In contrast to other regions, highway building in metropolitan Phoenix has supported the region's central area. The present round of suburb-to-suburb freeway extensions, however, could create problems. By making jobs and homes away from the center more accessible, the presence of freeways will intensify land consumption on the fringe. But should employment remain concentrated in the cores and home building continue to move outward, commute times could worsen. The challenge to unraveling this Catch-22 will be finding transportation and land-use initiatives that create dispersed mixed-use clusters of greater residential and employment density and that do not detract from the vitality of downtown Phoenix, the region's signature core.

—*State trust land questions.* Large tracts of state-owned trust land near the urban fringe constitute an irreplaceable asset for the region's quality of life. This land could serve as a growth boundary that provides a vast reservoir of open space. However, the state constitution requires that these lands be managed to maximize revenues for Arizona's educational needs. The mandate bars wholesale conservation of the lands and increases the likelihood of future land sales to developers. The challenge for the region will be to amend the Arizona constitution and state-enabling act to allow for trust land to be dedicated to open space while maintaining the ability to fund schools.

—*Growth agendas in the smaller cities.* Eighteen less-populous cities on the urban fringe now control nearly as much land as the city of Phoenix and the five largest suburbs combined. These areas also lag behind the region in open-space protection and use of growth management tools. This means that the municipalities in the region least equipped to deal with the effects of fast growth will soon be making decisions with enormous implications for the entire region. The challenge will be to bring a regional perspective to the planning efforts of all cities while respecting the region's tradition of local control.

—*Fixing the schools of the core.* The region has reason to worry about the education of children in central Phoenix and the southwest portion of the region. Individual economic success correlates particularly with educational attainment (the number of years of school completed). The weak schools of the center present a powerful impetus for decentralization. Schools with high proportions of low-income, minority, or underachieving students may influence people and businesses to locate elsewhere. This increases the viability of the fringe at the expense of the core. Ironically, though, the region and its cities possess limited authority to address the unique problems of schools. The challenge will be to encourage more effective collaboration between school districts and city leaders and to include education issues in both fringe growth management and core revitalization strategies.

—*Conflicting views on sprawl and density.* Residents of metropolitan Phoenix decry sprawl, but they also dislike density. Unfortunately, controlling one usually means encouraging the other. To confront this Catch-22, regional leaders and residents will need to find an acceptable way to promote greater density with "quality" development that fosters convenience, diversity, transit options, and access to open spaces. One approach will be to reevaluate traditional zoning ordinances with their rigid and segregated land uses and consider new rules that foster acceptable combinations of residential and commercial uses.

—*Regional authority dilemma.* City coordination, although valuable, especially as the eighteen less-populous communities become a stronger force in the regional dynamics, will only go so far. However, the creation of a binding regional authority has been rejected so often that implementation of such a concept appears unrealistic for metropolitan Phoenix. The challenge will be to reap the benefits of regional "governance" without having to adopt a formal "regional government" structure.

—*An on-and-off relationship with Washington.* The region historically has benefited from federal assistance with water and public works projects that have sustained a growing population. In recent years, state leadership—executive and legislative—has disdained federal help with similar projects, believing that the state should be more independent from Washington. This stance handicaps the region's ability to finance major growth management initiatives, such as light rail or open-space acquisition, which neither the state nor any single municipality can afford on its own. The challenge will be to get back to a long-term regional agenda so compelling that it would be unthinkable for any elected official not to support it.

—*Tensions that surround state support of metropolitan Phoenix.* In today's economy metropolitan regions are increasingly overtaking states as the drivers of growth. The situation in Arizona is no exception; the metropolitan Phoenix region currently accounts for 70 percent of the state's total personal income and is responsible for over 70 percent of new job growth. Thus, ensuring a viable metropolitan Phoenix should be a top priority of state government. However, other communities across Arizona have needs that also must be addressed at the state level. The challenge will be to support the Phoenix region in a way that does not neglect the needs of other localities, but accepts that prosperity brought forth by a strong regional driver benefits the state as a whole.

—*Water's changing role.* Although the region has ample water for its current population, water management will be more important given that there are no potential projects on the scale of the Central Arizona Project to increase the future supply of water. As such, water management will be increasingly related to growth management, as water becomes an invaluable regulator by influencing where homes and businesses may locate. However, discussions on water management and growth management currently take place in separate spheres. The challenge will be to bring together the water mavens and the urban planners to come to an understanding of how water policies could be used to manage growth.

These near Catch-22s will not succumb to old ideas. Bold, innovative policy decisions will be needed. This does not mean simply replicating the big ideas of a Seattle or a Denver. It requires the region's key stakeholders to think deeply and creatively about local causes, conditions, and future trends and to take action. It also requires that everyone understand the full range of issues that shape the region's growth and development patterns. The region's emerging divisions, transportation challenges, loss of desert lands, and the many other growth issues that threaten metropolitan Phoenix's quality of life are inextricably linked. The challenges cut across jurisdictional boundaries and must be addressed comprehensively, rather than piecemeal.

References

American Electronics Association. 2000. *Cyberstates 4.0*. Santa Clara, Calif.

Arizona State Land Department. 2000. *Annual Report 1998–1999*. Phoenix.

Burns, B., E. Matranga, and L. Valenzuela. 2000. *Transportation Trends, Urban Freeway Expenditures, and Spatial Disparities in Metropolitan Phoenix*. Working Paper. Tempe: Arizona State University, Morrison Institute for Public Policy.

Fulton, William, Rolf Pendal, Mai Ngyuen, and Alicia Harrison. 2001. "Who Sprawls Most? How Growth Patterns Differ across the U.S." Brookings Institution Center on Urban and Metropolitan Policy.

Gammage, Grady, Jr. 1999. *Phoenix in Perspective: Reflections on Developing the Desert*. Tempe, Ariz.: Herberger Center for Design Excellence, College of Architecture and Environmental Design, Arizona State University.

Gober, Patricia, and Elizabeth K. Burns. 2000. "The Size and Scope of Phoenix's Urban Fringe." *Journal of Planning Education and Research* 21, no. 4: 379–90.

Great Cities Institute. 2000. "Summary Findings of the Chicago Metropolitan Case Study" (draft). University of Illinois at Chicago, College of Urban Planning and Public Affairs.

Metropolitan Policy Program, Brookings. 1999. "Moving beyond Sprawl: The Challenge for Metropolitan Atlanta."

Morrison Institute for Public Policy. 1999. *What Matters in Greater Phoenix: Indicators of Our Quality of Life*. Morrison Institute for Public Policy, Arizona State University.

———. 2000. *Growth Management Survey*. Morrison Institute for Public Policy, Arizona State University.

Orfield, Myron. 1997. *Metropolitics: A Regional Agenda for Community and Stability*. Brookings and Cambridge, Mass.: Lincoln Institute of Land Policy.

Pendal, Rolf. 1995. "Do Land-Use Controls Cause Sprawl?" *Environment and Planning* B26, no. 4: 555–71.

Rex, Tom. 2000a. "Development of Metropolitan Phoenix: Historical, Current and Future Trends." Working Paper. Arizona State University, Morrison Institute for Public Policy.

———. 2000b. "Population Demographics in Metropolitan Phoenix." Working Paper. Arizona State University, Morrison Institute for Public Policy.

———. 2001. "Population Density Rose during the 1990s in Phoenix Area." *Arizona Business* 48, no. 6: 5.

Rusk, David. 1995. *Cities without Suburbs*. Washington: Woodrow Wilson Center Press.

Sorkin, Michael. 1995. "Can Williams and Tsien's Phoenix Art Museum Help This Sprawling Desert City Find Its Edge?" *Architectural Record* 185, no. 1: 84–97.

U.S. Congress, Office of Technology Assessment. 1995. *The Technological Reshaping of Metropolitan America*. OTA-ETI-634.

CHAPTER 6

Pittsburgh: Economic Restructuring and Regional Development Patterns, 1880–2000

Robert E. Gleeson and Jerry Paytas

The physical development pattern of most regions was transformed dramatically during the second half of the twentieth century as commercial, industrial, and residential development moved away from central cities and economic activity shifted from manufacturing to services. Over time, new highways, beltways, and other public infrastructure interconnected growing suburban places and created individual development corridors outside the boundaries of traditional center cities. The rise of suburban housing subdivisions, low-rise suburban office parks, beltway loops, enclosed malls, and eventually "edge cities" were all part of the shift of American society from city to suburb, factory to cubicle, and blue collar to white collar that characterized much of the twentieth century. These shifts forever transformed most urban areas into decentralized metropolitan regions. Today's debates about managing growth in the United States occur in the context of how to cope with new forms of development in a widely sprawled, multi-centered metropolis.

Not all cities followed the same development trajectory during the last half of the twentieth century. Consequently, the debate over growth management today, especially at the federal level, must accommodate the effects of different historical experiences. This chapter reviews the experience of the Pittsburgh metropolitan region. Pittsburgh is an example of a large U.S. region (approximately 2.2 million residents in six counties) that has not mirrored national trends. Local, state, and federal policy choices regarding new development in the Pittsburgh region are not rooted in the context of growth-induced sprawl creating a multi-centered dispersed metro region, but rather sprawl in the context of minimal or negative growth pressure. Growth in Pittsburgh after World War II did not transform the prewar pattern of development until the 1990s. Instead, growth was accommodated within an earlier decentralized pinwheel pattern, one that was established to accommodate the economic and social needs of heavy manufacturing between 1880 and 1920 and which established the basis of the growth coalition that directed Pittsburgh's attempts to manage fundamental economic restructuring. Ultimately, the coalition that defended the core of the region saw its power and agenda eroded by successive waves of economic restructuring.

This chapter begins with a review of the region's historical development patterns. Pittsburgh's modern development is rooted in this history, but it is also a story of competing forces for and against the preservation of the core. Some of the forces are internal state and local forces and some are external economic or federal forces. The chapter first explores the forces defending the core, then discusses those that weaken it. The chapter concludes with a summary of the forces that affect the region's development and policy recommendations for the future.

Spatial Development: A Historical Overview

Before 1880 the Pittsburgh region had a dense urban core inside the city of Pittsburgh and a series of small river towns spread out along the region's extensive network of rivers and creeks. The core was a chaotic mixture of industrial, commercial, and residential structures. Railroads ran down the middle of streets, and houses, factories, and small stores all shared the scarce amount of flat land where the Allegheny and Monongahela Rivers met to form the Ohio.

Between 1880 and 1920, however, the Second Industrial Revolution transformed the region into one of the nation's principal centers of manufacturing production. Sweeping technological advances in manufacturing and transportation altered the region's economy from one based on iron to one based on carbon steel. The merger wave of the 1890s and 1900s created unprecedented concentrations of corporate capital, which allowed steel companies to exploit new minimum efficiencies of scale in production by building new facilities that dwarfed the region's early iron mill sites.[1]

1. A history of the merger movement is provided by Lamoreaux (1985). For a specific discussion of the iron and steel industry's merger wave, see Mancke (1972, pp. 220–29). General histories of the iron and steel industry are found in Temin (1964) and Hogan

Because of the region's rugged, hilly terrain, the flood plains were the only available sources of flat land for these gargantuan mills. This topography contributed to the decentralization of production that pulled newly arrived immigrant workers out of the central city and into new industrial towns that sprang up outside the gates of the new mills. It also pulled workers from the region's heavily industrialized countryside.[2] These towns grew rapidly and soon overshadowed the relatively few river towns that had preceded them.[3] Some mills stretched for miles along the rivers and employed as many as 20,000 workers within a decade of their establishment.

The network of industrial towns, spread out along the region's rivers and principal creeks and encircling the central city, was a distinctive element of the Pittsburgh region's development. Tens of thousands of working-class families moved to these towns in order to be close to the mill gates. This pattern was decentralized, but it was not sprawled. Mill towns were overcrowded, polluted, unsanitary, highly centralized urban places. The mills themselves were interconnected extensively via railroads and waterways, but mill towns were isolated communities. There were few road or streetcar connections between them and many social divisions within them.

Neither World War I nor the Great Depression changed the region's underlying geographic patterns of work or residence. New mills were built in the river flood plains. Working-class families remained close to their jobs, and downtown owners and managers remained in their enclaves. Indeed by 1950, census data reveal that more than 70 percent of all of the region's upper-income families continued to live in Pittsburgh's East End, a series of suburban-style neighborhoods within the city limits.[4] A few middle-class suburbs had become established outside

---

(1971). The history of iron and steel making in the Pittsburgh area is presented in Ingram (1991).

2. The countryside in the Pittsburgh region was hardly bucolic. Before 1900 it housed tens of thousands of small beehive furnaces and coking operations. The entire region had been denuded of forests to fuel these operations. Coal mines and coal patch towns were pervasive, and the region's oil industry scarred the hillsides with thousands of oil drilling towers. When the advent of the large steel mills made many of these operations obsolete, the region's rural industrial workers began moving into mill towns.

3. Examples of older river towns include Sewickley and Beaver on the Ohio River, Oakmont on the Allegheny River, and Elizabeth on the Monongahela. The physical layout of these towns remains very different from that of mill towns. Most important, they have retained direct access to the riverfronts. Most mill towns have no such access, since factories and railroad rights-of-way dominated their riverfronts.

4. To be classified as "upper-income" in 1950, a family needed to have an income of approximately $53,500 in 1990 dollars.

the city limits, but most of the region surrounding Pittsburgh remained dominated by mill towns.

The Pittsburgh region began as a network of industrial towns and affiliated residential suburbs that has been struggling to develop into a metropolitan region. Pittsburgh provides a unique case for studying the development patterns in a metropolitan area because it was less centralized than many other urban areas before the long postwar national economic expansion set off waves of suburb building. By 1960 much of the initial "demand" for suburbanization was already supplied: 63 percent of the population resided outside the central city.

The network of mill towns and residential suburbs was connected by hilltop corridors that ran away from the rivers (primarily to the east, north, and south) and that evolved into downtown-oriented middle-class residential communities. Each had its own list of marginal road improvements that would improve downtown commuting. None of these groups were interested in building circumferential connections to each other. The alternating pinwheel pattern of middle-class, working-class, and mill town corridors radiating outward from the city reinforced the wide social gulf between blue-collar and white-collar workers and obscured the potential benefits of connecting their communities. Pittsburgh remains not a unified metropolitan area, but a collection of many smaller subregions that cannot decide whether to defend the core or abandon it.

Defending the Core

Local and state efforts played a critical role in shaping the development of metropolitan Pittsburgh. Pittsburgh's traditional settlement patterns and aggressive local efforts to defend them explain part of the region's deviance from the general model of metropolitan development. A coalition of influential East End business leaders and working-class Democratic politicians that showed its muscle in environmental politics before the war became the enduring foundation for Pittsburgh's postwar "Renaissance" and subsequent development efforts. The goal was to rebuild the Pittsburgh region as a model for how industrial strength could accommodate modern environmental and social progress, preserving the status quo as much as possible.

Popular accounts personified the coalition by focusing on the tie between Mellon Bank chairman Richard King Mellon and Pittsburgh's mayor, David Lawrence.[5] The power of the coalition was its depth on

---

5. There is no scholarly biography of Richard King Mellon. For the life of David Lawrence, see Weber (1988).

both sides. Hundreds of minor officials and staff members in city and county government agencies worked with hundreds of elite volunteers on boards and advisory panels. The division of labor during the Pittsburgh Renaissance was clear. Privately funded organizations did the planning. Public agencies and new public-private authorities did the implementation.

Chief among the private planning groups was the Allegheny Conference on Community Development (ACCD). The ACCD was an umbrella group whose design recognized that national politics during the New Deal and wartime had forever changed the distribution of political and economic power in Pittsburgh. Unions and the Democratic politicians whose political base rested on working-class voters had become a permanent part of the region's political landscape. Consequently, the ACCD's original members included selected working-class politicians such as the mayors of Pittsburgh, McKeesport, Duquesne, and Clairton, as well as the Allegheny County commissioners. Even token union leaders were asked to join.

Through the ACCD coalition, the East End Republican elite and the Democratic politicians elected by their working-class employees found ways to accommodate each other in a period of rapid social change. The central goal of the ACCD coalition's civic agenda was to modernize selected components of the region in order to retain its ability to function as a major center for traditional manufacturing production. The agenda selectively sought reform, not revolution, and accommodation, not transformation. The impact of the ACCD coalition on the region can be understood by examining what it did do, and what it did not do. The first wave of ACCD-inspired initiatives between 1945 and 1960 sought to clean up the environment, redevelop the downtown, and support the status quo, efforts that mostly took the form of opposition to comprehensive transportation planning and development.

The environmental clean-up efforts were a clear success. Smoke control was the most visible result. The new ACCD coalition brought its full power to bear in lobbying Harrisburg to expand smoke control beyond the city to all of Allegheny County. The measure was controversial, and it imposed real costs on every business and homeowner in the county. Yet its success cemented the public's willingness to accept the ACCD's leading role in regional policymaking. The visible difference was extraordinary. One estimate at the time concluded that within a year city residents saw 39 percent more sunshine.[6] The environmental

6. Weber (1988, p. 247).

clean-up efforts provided benefits to the entire region. The efforts to preserve downtown and the opposition to highways had more direct spatial impacts and are addressed in the following sections.

Office Construction

Downtown redevelopment succeeded in preserving office space and service employment. Between 1949 and 1959 the amount of office space in downtown grew almost 25 percent with the construction of 2.2 million square feet of new buildings.[7] By the mid-1960s almost 25 percent of the 330-acre downtown district had been rebuilt.[8] The new buildings attracted national and international attention. They were modern glass and steel structures. They stood in sharp visual contrast to the city's inventory of soot-blackened masonry skyscrapers. They ensured downtown's primacy as the region's principal office address (see figure 6-1).

Before 1960 only one small suburban office park had been established (Parkway Center, inside the city's limits at the first exit on the Parkway West), and it had only two small buildings. The relocation of downtown corporations into their new Renaissance headquarters buildings continually flooded the region's office market with older space in the downtown. The steady availability of such space effectively killed the market for suburban office buildings since the region was not experiencing much net growth.

This pattern continued throughout the 1960s and 1970s. When corporations outgrew their original Renaissance buildings, they built new ones downtown. None chose to move their headquarters to a suburb. Only two suburban corridors added more than 1 million square feet of office space during the entire decade of the 1960s. One was Monroeville to the east, where downtown corporations that chose to make Monroeville their center for R&D facilities constructed the majority of new office buildings. The first independent office park in Monroeville did not begin construction until 1964 (Penn Center), and the second did not start until 1968 (Parkway Center East). As late as 1970 these two parks together had only five small buildings. The second was the Route 28

7. Among the new buildings were the U.S. Steel–Mellon Bank Building (1950), which also came with a $4 million one-square-block public park with underground parking known as Mellon Square; Gateway Center One, Two, and Three (1952); and the Alcoa Building (also 1952). The Manor Building, a state office building in Gateway Center, and the H. K. Porter Building all followed in 1957. Another Gateway Center office building (for Bell Telephone) and downtown's first major new hotel in a generation (the Hilton), complete with a nearby underground parking garage for 750 cars, were all added in 1958 and 1959.

8. Lubove (1996, p. 127).

Figure 6-1. Pittsburgh Area Office Space, by Corridor and Decade

Millions of square feet

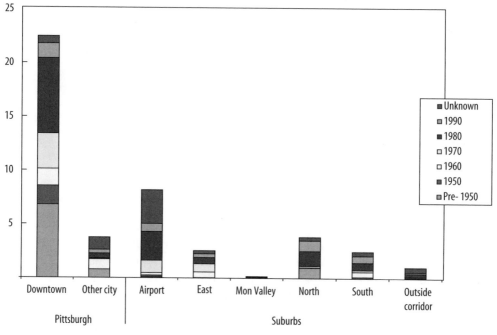

Source: Data compiled by authors.

corridor along the Allegheny River. All new building in this corridor was located in a small, experimental office and industrial park built by a nonprofit agency created by the ACCD. No substantial development occurred independently.

Pittsburgh's mayor in the late 1970s, Richard Caliguiri, focused on redeveloping downtown Pittsburgh. Between 1977 and 1982, Caliguiri's "Renaissance Two" used Urban Development Action Grants (UDAGs) and other funds to persuade six large companies to build or anchor new office towers, adding almost 7 million square feet of new office space downtown. In addition, Caliguiri worked with Allegheny County and federal officials to invest $500 million in a new light-rail system between downtown and the South Hills as well as new busways between downtown, the East End, and nearby eastern suburbs.

Opposition to Highway Construction

Federal and state highway planners in the 1950s proposed systematic highway improvements in the Pittsburgh region. New highways were envisioned to cut through the region on the north-south and east-west axes. They would be interconnected by a continuous beltway, almost all of which would lie inside Allegheny County. Traffic within the beltway would be eased by yet another series of highways crisscrossing in downtown and the East End.

Indeed, the consequences of building such a network ran directly counter to the established pattern of development and the collective civic vision for Pittsburgh's future. A new beltway would be an expensive disruption to the development pattern that supported manufacturing without providing any tangible benefit to the mills. (Trucks were not a major factor in moving steel in the early 1950s.) Regional leaders maintained a unified front against the highways that were proposed by state and federal planners.

Corporate and city leaders were not alone in their failure to embrace new highways and a beltway in the 1950s. Even suburban leaders failed to embrace regional highway planning. Rather, they sought to improve the small, winding roads that connected the mill towns up and down the long river valleys. Too much highway infrastructure, argued civic leaders, would encourage people and commerce to leave the city. While the utopian highway plans of state and federal road planners were left to gather dust, the efforts to preserve the existing pattern by developing smaller arterial roads in lieu of a beltway ultimately failed to stem the outward shift of population along these corridors. Despite the lack of an interconnected highway network, population spread out along the arterial corridors (see color plates, map 6-1).

Opposition to highway development buttressed the region's stable, centralized geography of office space and provided the most powerful constraint on the pattern of development. The civic agenda of the ACCD supported market forces that concentrated work sites downtown and in the industrial river valleys. This civic agenda maintained the basic pattern of work that had been put in place before World War I, but it would not be able to withstand external economic forces.

Discarding the Core

As the region's large mills closed forever, some of its greatest corporations evaporated, and others downsized their downtown presence. The tie between the region's economic functions and its entrenched spatial development pattern loosened considerably. Isolated mill towns in the industrial valleys suffered most. While plant closings were robbing the industrial valleys of their economic infrastructure, city leaders tried to spare downtown Pittsburgh from a similar fate. Unfortunately, the downtown preservation agenda was undone by external forces and by its own shortcomings as a *regional* strategy.

State and local efforts to retain the region's manufacturing base accelerated in the 1960s and 1970s in order to counterbalance the growing trend to relocate manufacturing away from older urban regions such as Pittsburgh. Low interest financing was the principal retention tool. After a lethargic start in the 1950s, the Regional Industrial Development Corporation (RIDC) emerged in the 1960s as an aggressive local agent for the statewide Pennsylvania Industrial Development Authority's (PIDA's) lending programs. Between 1963 and 1979, PIDA loaned $106.8 million to ninety-six projects in the six counties of Allegheny, Beaver, Butler, Fayette, Washington, and Westmoreland. RIDC was the most active local packager of PIDA loans.

For its part, the Allegheny County government created its own development financing capability through the Allegheny County Industrial Development Authority (ACIDA). The county's IDA began operations in 1970. In its first ten years the ACIDA became the region's most aggressive source of development capital by packaging $647 million in low-interest loans. Seven other smaller IDAs were established in Allegheny County alone.

More than half of all financing was used by steel-related companies to defray the costs of meeting Environmental Protection Agency (EPA) standards for air quality in order to help retain their mills in the region. Of the $353.3 million in pollution control equipment financed by ACIDA, $327 million went into U.S. Steel's various Monongahela (Mon) Valley mills. The remaining $129.4 million in loans to industrial projects helped finance the construction of new light industrial buildings and warehouses in the RIDC parks and in scattered sites in traditional mill valleys. These programs were essential in maintaining the viability of many industrial plants.

The ACCD-led strategy of limited reforms designed to buttress the status quo in changing times worked until the early 1970s. During those decades Pittsburgh was a world-famous model of industrial strength, upward mobility for working-class families, civic progress, and environmental improvements. Success required constant vigilance as powerful external forces of globalization continually worked to erode the status quo. These forces eventually became too strong to resist by the early 1970s. Between 1975 and 1995 the economy of the six-county Pitts-

Figure 6-2. Change in Service and Manufacturing Jobs, 84 MSAs in the U.S. Industrial Heartland, 1970–96[a]

Percent change in manufacturing

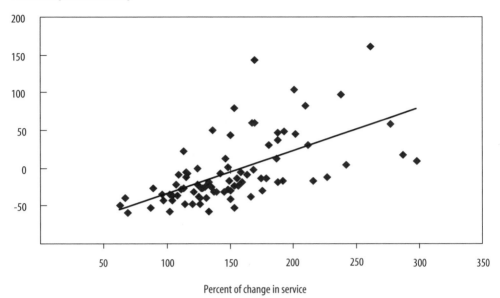

Percent of change in service

Source: U.S. Census Bureau.

a. For Pittsburgh, the change in manufacturing is –57 percent and in service jobs 102 percent.

burgh region underwent fundamental restructuring.[9] The pattern of economic restructuring in the six-county Pittsburgh region had two principal components (see figure 6-2). Between 1970 and 1996 Pittsburgh suffered the third greatest percentage loss in manufacturing jobs (–56.85 percent) among all eighty-four MSAs in the industrial heartland west of the Appalachians, north of the Ohio River, and east of the Mississippi.[10] At the same time, Pittsburgh had one of the heartland's slowest-growing service sectors.[11] The average rate of job growth between 1970 and

9. See Clark (1989, pp. 41–67); Mehrabian, Florida, and Gleeson (1995); Hoerr (1988). A host of social and economic indicators of change in the region can also be found in a series of reports issued by the University Center for Social and Urban Research at the University of Pittsburgh. Several of these reports, which are titled *State of the Region*, were produced during the years discussed here.

10. Only Springfield, Illinois, and Wheeling, West Virginia, lost a larger percentage of their manufacturing jobs.

11. The only large metropolitan area that had slower service growth than Pittsburgh was Cleveland. The other MSAs with slower service growth than Pittsburgh were

1996 among heartland urban areas was 50.6 percent, compared with the U.S. national average of 63.9 percent. Pittsburgh's job growth was a meager 15.6 percent, from 1,108,150 to 1,280,704. Buffalo was the only large urban area with less growth.[12]

The scale and scope of restructuring exceeded even the most dire predictions of those who had warned about the possibility.[13] The suddenness of Pittsburgh's economic restructuring was unexpected by most local actors, both public and private. Pittsburgh's showplace industrial valleys collapsed into the despair of America's Rust Belt following the back-to-back recessions in the late 1970s and early 1980s. More than 157,000 manufacturing jobs were lost permanently in the six-county Pittsburgh region between 1970 and 1990.[14] More than half of all these losses occurred between 1979 and 1984. The percentage of the region's workforce employed in manufacturing dropped from 27.6 percent in 1970 to 10.3 percent in 1996, compared with U.S. national averages of 21.6 percent and 12.9 percent.[15]

Soon after the wave of plant closings peaked, and while the downtown spending spree was in full force, an unexpected second wave of corporate restructuring hit Pittsburgh hard in the mid-to-late 1980s. This time the brunt was borne by white-collar workers. Company reorganizations, downsizing, outsourcing, bankruptcies, and corporate raiding all eliminated tens of thousands of jobs for middle managers, engineers, clerical staff, and secretaries. In spite of the spending spree, downtown Pittsburgh lost its status as one of the nation's largest concentrations of Fortune 500 corporate headquarters.[16]

Steubenville, Ohio; Wheeling, W.Va.; Youngstown, Ohio; Mansfield, Ohio; Cumberland, Md.; Decatur, Ill.; and Duluth, Minn. There is a positive relationship between the change in manufacturing and service employment, which runs counter to the notion that these economies were shifting from manufacturing to services.

12. The MSAs in the industrial heartland that had lower overall growth rates included: Wheeling, W.V; Youngstown, Ohio; Buffalo, N.Y.; Cumberland, Md.; Decatur, Ill.; Elmira, N.Y.; Mansfield, Ohio; Steubenville, Ohio; and Utica, N.Y.

13. See Hoover (1963).

14. See table CA25 of the Bureau of Economic Analysis Regional Economic Information System (www.bea.doc.gov/bea/regional/reis/ [June 13, 2000]).

15. See note 14.

16. Among the most visible victims of dramatic office downsizing and closure were Rockwell International, Gulf Oil (Pittsburgh's largest corporation), USX, Jones & Laughlin, National Steel, Joy Industries, H. K. Porter Company, Dravo Corporation, Duquesne Light Company, Westinghouse, Koppers, and Alcoa.

The Coalition Weakens

The glut of downtown space caused by corporate restructuring and new building soured Pittsburgh's image among national real estate developers, such as Lincoln Properties and Trammel Crow. These companies emerged as major players in the fast-growing national market for office space in the 1980s. They exploited opportunities in the growing U.S. service sector by creating diverse portfolios of suburban office parks outside many large U.S. cities. The dynamics of Pittsburgh's unusual real estate market made their strategy difficult to exploit. Consequently, none entered the Pittsburgh market.

Caliguiri's downtown strategy rekindled some of the unified action of the old ACCD coalition, but the old romance was short-lived. The disarray became apparent when the ACCD commissioned a new round of civic planning in 1981. Large committees were created and asked to devise plans for coping with the region's transformation. The irony of the ACCD's claiming authority for economic development planning when its own chair (U.S. Steel's CEO) was the chief proponent of closing local mills was not lost on the community.

After three years of frustrating effort, the best the ACCD could do formally was to recommend a series of road improvements around Three Rivers Stadium and to suggest creating a new set of nonprofit organizations to boost the fortunes of small high-tech companies.[17] In the continuing wake of corporate restructuring and downsizing, the ACCD's CEOs urged the region to look instead to small entrepreneurial companies as the region's best hope for creating new jobs.

By 1984 the coalition supporting the core had weakened considerably. The first partner to leave the fold was the Allegheny County government. The most powerful figure in county government throughout the 1980s and 1990s was Tom Foerster, a lifelong city resident who rose through the ranks of city and state politics during the Renaissance. Under Foerster's guidance the county participated in Caliguiri's downtown strategy by providing low-interest ACIDA loans for renovating older downtown buildings. However, the scale of potential tax growth in the downtown paled in comparison with the tax base the county was losing as companies continued to close massive steel mills in the river valleys.

The Allegheny County commissioners moved Pittsburgh's airport in 1952 from its location on a landlocked plateau in the Mon Valley (in

17. ACCD (1984).

West Mifflin) to a very large site (over 10,000 acres) sixteen miles west of downtown in undeveloped Findlay Township. Moving the airport to the western edge of Allegheny County allowed major airlines to keep Pittsburgh on their routes since the new runways could accommodate newer, larger planes. It also ensured future growth capacity since there was plenty of available land.

Led by Foerster, Allegheny County broke from tradition and tried to convert the undeveloped suburban corridor between downtown and the airport into a new employment center, thereby hoping to attract both real estate developers and service-based companies. The centerpiece of the strategy was a billion-dollar plan to double the gate capacity of the airport by constructing new terminal buildings between the existing runways. After complex negotiations, U.S. Air agreed to anchor the plan if it could control most of the gates, and if the county promised to prevent the old terminal buildings from being used by any other airline.

Foerster justified the deal by arguing that tax revenues from airport-area growth would allow the county to pay for the human services that were needed by poor and working-class families who were caught in the throes of economic and social change. He appeased his critics in the river valleys by negotiating a complex set of agreements with U.S. Steel to transfer ownership of its huge abandoned mill sites in the Mon Valley to the county, using the RIDC as an intermediary. Ownership would transfer gradually over time, tied to hazardous waste clean-up and the pace of redevelopment. The deal gave the county a crucial say in the future of these key properties. He also lobbied the state and federal government to build a new radial highway from downtown to the Mon Valley in order to open it up to downtown commuting.

While Foerster packaged the new airport terminal project, he directed the ACIDA to shift gears away from its earlier focus on financing improvements for big mills and factories. Funding for industrial modernization was cut in half and retargeted to smaller companies that were struggling to stay in business. Although the ACIDA preferred its nonindustrial projects to be located in the airport corridor, it worked with virtually any kind of project. Between 1980 and 1986, when new federal legislation sharply curtailed the activities of local IDAs nationwide, the ACIDA lent another $697 million to a wide range of projects. The agency also coordinated with the RIDC and other state-authorized lending agencies to package an additional $127 million of PIDA financing. The airport area received the bulk of the largess, largely facilitated by the increasingly independent nonprofit RIDC's decision to join the airport strategy by opening its own office park at the corridor's most strategic road intersection.

Moving the airport to the western edge of the county created a problem for automobile access because it meant going through or around the steep Mt. Washington ridge. The solution was a new highway and a new set of automobile tunnels to connect the airport directly to downtown. State and federal funds were used to help pay for the new road. The road went directly from downtown to the airport and stopped there with only four exits in between. It was not integrated into any larger highway network. Even though the airport relocation contributed to the development of the suburban airport corridor, its impact was muted by continuing opposition to highway development.

By the end of the 1980s the separate efforts of the city, Allegheny County, and the RIDC resulted in simultaneous building booms downtown and in the suburban airport corridor. More than 7 million square feet of new office space was added downtown, and another 2.7 million square feet was built along the airport corridor. More than 13 million square feet of new office space was added in Allegheny County during the 1980s, exceeding the entire amount of office space that existed at the start of the Pittsburgh Renaissance in 1945. It was an ambitious attempt to use public dollars to build the region's way out of economic collapse.

The office construction projects did not by themselves constitute a strategy for economic transformation. They were publicly financed efforts to cope with the consequences of a collapsing older order, but there was no capital for growing new companies that could occupy all of the space. The principal sources of capital for new job creation were a handful of new agencies created by state and philanthropic grants. Philanthropies helped finance the new Pittsburgh High-Technology Council with the hope of creating a junior cousin for the old ACCD coalition. In addition, they collaborated with the state to create a local outlet for the state's new Ben Franklin Partnership, designed to help transfer new technologies from universities to the marketplace, and they created a new agency to provide direct assistance to technology entrepreneurs.

With so much excess space, the region's real estate market stumbled in the early 1990s. Between 1990 and 1996, less than 4.6 million square feet of new space was constructed in all of Allegheny County, approximately one-third the rate of the previous decade. Vacancy rates rose as corporate downsizing continued dumping space on the market. Many new office buildings, especially in the airport corridor, were lost to creditors, and ambitious plans for new office parks were put on hold. Even the opening of the new Midfield terminal at the airport in 1992 did not pump life back into the airport corridor. The county's grand gambit to undermine the region's existing development pattern by establishing a suburban job corridor near the airport, and then using the tax revenue from that growth to finance human services to ease the transition from traditional manufacturing industries, did not pay dividends.

Shifting Residential Location

The continued importance of the downtown central business district, known as the Golden Triangle, provided a measure of stability in the geography of work. No single location in the metropolitan area rivals the Golden Triangle in the concentration of office space and employment, but this dominance did not stabilize the geography of residence. The decentralization of employment and rapid expansion of family incomes provided the principal engine for suburb building. In 1950 approximately 36.3 percent of all families in Allegheny County lived on an annual income of less than $17,100 as measured in 2000 dollars. Only 8.6 percent of all families had incomes over the 2000 equivalent of $47,800. Between 1950 and 1970 an unprecedented wave of upward mobility swept the region (and the country). By 1970 fewer than 11.2 percent of all families in Allegheny County still earned less than the 2000 equivalent of $17,100, and the proportion earning more than the 2000 level of $47,800 had almost quintupled, to 42.4 percent.

New labor contracts between steel companies and the United Steel Workers, as well as similar fruits of collective bargaining in other industries, paid off handsomely by raising wages and benefits throughout the period. Working-class families rose from near-poverty to relative prosperity. In addition, favorable global trade policies allowed Pittsburgh-based companies to expand their operations worldwide, thus fueling rapid growth in local headquarters operations as well as research and development (R&D) facilities. Only Manhattan and Chicago's "Loop" housed more Fortune 500 companies than downtown Pittsburgh during these years. Global business growth and the rise of federal funding for defense-related R&D also allowed Pittsburgh to become one of the nation's largest centers of corporate-managed R&D.

Working-class families suburbanized in the 1950s and 1960s in a pattern different from the middle-class suburbs that were already well established. Middle-class settlements were located with access to downtown in mind. But working-class jobs remained in the industrial river valleys. The absence of circumferential roads, and indeed the lack of any public planning for such roads, made the hilltop townships directly above the river valleys the most attractive locations for working-class families. Smoke control had improved conditions in the hilltops, allowing builders to create new subdivisions of modest homes. The social gap between white collar and blue collar also discouraged blue-collar families from moving into established, pre-war, middle-class suburbs.

The combination of a growing managerial and professional middle class with a newly emerging middle-income working class presented the first challenge to the established development pattern, simply overwhelming the region's pre–World War II middle-income housing base and spilling development into a wide range of new suburban communities. The rapid rise in income, however, was not matched by a rapid rise in population. Between 1950 and 1970 the population of the six-county Pittsburgh region grew by only 7.3 percent, from 2.5 million to 2.68 million. The largest population shift occurred in Allegheny County as the city of Pittsburgh lost 23 percent of its population (157,000 residents) and suburban communities added 247,000 residents, for a net gain for Allegheny County of 90,000 (a 6 percent growth rate).

Despite the constrained dispersion of jobs and homes, the growth of suburban residential areas inside Allegheny County still put considerable pressure on the city's working-class and middle-class neighborhoods. Middle-class erosion was of special concern to the city's powerful East End elite, who worried that, if left unchecked, the city's fiscal stability could be threatened. The principal response was a series of three large-scale urban renewal projects made possible by new sources of federal money and the expanded power of the Urban Redevelopment Authority (URA).[18]

The results of the URA projects, however, were mixed. Bulldozers led to increasing citizen protest and racial tensions. In addition, the distinctively modern high-rise architecture of each new development clashed with the preferences of most middle-class city residents, who preferred the leafy style of older single-family neighborhoods that had been built in the city since the late nineteenth century. The URA's product held little appeal among its intended customers. These efforts at urban renewal did not stem the outflow of city residents that began in 1950s.

18. For more detail on these projects, see Lubove (1986, pp. 130–37, 142–76).

By the mid-1970s, most of Allegheny County had filled in the pin-wheel pattern of middle-class and working-class residential corridors radiating outward from downtown and following the contours of the industrial river valleys. Social barriers and the lack of circumferential road connections kept the borders between different corridors rather distinct, even as working- and middle-class suburbs began bumping into each other in the hilltops. Stable, highly concentrated locations for work (downtown and the big mills) kept decentralization almost entirely within the boundaries of Allegheny County.

The momentum of decentralization also subsided as the region's population began to stabilize. Overall, the total number of new housing units constructed in Allegheny County fell from 105,700 during the period 1950–59 to 73,300 between 1960 and 1969, and to 65,562 between 1970 and 1979. The city maintained a steady share of new housing construction throughout the 1950s and 1960s, not succumbing to losses until the 1970s. From 1950 to 1980, new housing construction, much like the population trend, dropped precipitously. Fewer than half as many units were constructed in the 1980s as in the 1950s. In the 1980s, when Pittsburgh captured nearly 22 percent of the new housing construction, the number of units built was still far fewer than were built in the city in the 1970s. By the 1990s, housing construction had rebounded, but new housing was not being built in the city or the eastern and Mon Valley corridors. The airport and northern corridors captured more new housing than the other corridors (see table 6-1).

By 1980 the largest portion of the county's population resided in the suburbs within fifteen miles of downtown (see table 6-2). The inner and middle rings have been fairly stable since the 1980s. There has been a small decline in the city and the growth of the outer ring, especially in the northern corridor (see color plates, map 6-2). Even though these are small shifts, they are occurring in a no-growth region, which increases the challenge for revitalizing the core.[19]

THE INFLUENCE OF HIGHWAYS. In Pittsburgh, the lack of a beltway system may have delayed or even limited the city's population losses, but it did not stop them. It also appears that sprawl was delayed because the region suffered from severe losses of population and

19. In map 6-2 (see color plates), the percentage changes on a small base can be misleading. In this case, the map demonstrates the dramatic changes happening in the region and is representative of the areas that are growing and not growing. Maps of the population change per acre or other normalization show that there is very little growth in the region and that what has occurred is generally outside the city.

Table 6-1. Market Share of New Housing Units in Allegheny County, by Corridor, 1950s to 1990s

Percent

Corridor	1950s	1960s	1970s	1980s	1990s
Pittsburgh	19.2	19.0	13.1	21.9	11.6
Airport	4.4	7.3	7.2	14.1	18.9
Eastern	14.7	14.4	12.1	12.1	5.8
Mon Valley	14.0	9.0	10.7	8.9	6.0
Northern	7.9	10.7	13.6	19.0	16.5
Southern	11.3	13.1	12.3	12.6	12.2
All other municipalities	28.6	26.4	31.0	33.4	28.9
Total	100	100	100	100	100.0

Source: U.S. Census Bureau.

Table 6-2. Decentralization of Allegheny County's Population, 1940–2000

Year	City	County population (percent)		
		Within 10 miles of downtown Pittsburgh	10–15 miles from downtown	Over 15 miles from downtown
1940	48	24	22	6
1950	45	25	23	7
1960	37	29	27	8
1970	32	31	28	9
1980	29	31	30	10
1990	27	31	31	11
2000	26	31	31	12

Source: U.S. Census Bureau.

employment after the periods of greatest suburban road building. Furthermore, the lack of a beltway and the continued importance of downtown Pittsburgh as a job center helped to contain population within the inner- and middle-ring suburbs until the 1990s. When growth returned, however, it did not fill in the gaps created by previous population loss. It occurred instead on the fringes, farther not just from the city, but also from most established and older communities.[20] It is important to remember, however, that in 1960 metropolitan Pittsburgh was already more decentralized than the average American metropolis (37 percent vs. 51 percent, respectively). From a smaller initial base, the share of population in the city declined by 11 percentage points; for the average

20. For additional and more recent evidence and analysis on this issue, see Katz and others (2003).

Table 6-3. Pittsburgh Region's Share of Population and Federal Roads, 1940–1996
Percent

	No federal roads		Federal roads		
Year	Industrial suburbs	Residential suburbs	City of Pittsburgh	Industrial suburbs	Residential suburbs
1940	24	17	48	3	8
1950	22	20	45	3	10
1960	19	27	37	3	13
1970	17	32	32	3	16
1980	16	35	29	3	17
1987	15	36	28	3	17
1990	15	37	27	3	18
1992	15	37	28	3	18
1996	15	37	27	3	18

Source: Authors' analysis of road segment data from Southwestern Pennsylvania Commission.

U.S. city the decline was 13 percentage points. Pittsburgh remains a smaller-than-average central city relative to its metropolitan population, with 26 percent of the total population compared with 38 percent for all U.S. cities.

Most of the federal roads were added between 1950 and 1969, when the regional population was growing. Road building slowed after 1970, when the population began a steep decline. Within this context of decline, new roads provided greater mobility that dispersed people and jobs in the region. Because the residential suburbs without federal roads gained both population and jobs, it is not clear that these places directly benefited from federal roads.[21] However it also seems clear that the greater mobility created by new roads facilitated the drain of people and jobs from the city and the industrial suburbs without federal roads. The roads diverted growth to the fringes, draining residents and jobs from the communities through which they passed (see table 6-3).

The federal roads were developed as part of a larger network of state and local roads. As a whole, this network has been often criticized for its lack of efficiency in design and extremely poor signage. These qualitative factors could not be modeled in the analysis, but they may help to explain why the effect of roads on development patterns is so mud-

21. Road projects are planned long before they are built. A road may not be completed until decades after the initial conception and planning. On the one hand, this means that road planning and hence speculation precede road construction; on the other hand, roads appear to follow population changes, even though people may move in anticipation of a new road.

dled.[22] Another critical element affecting the impact of federal road construction is how well the federal system is integrated with state and local roads. The lack of coordination between these three road networks also provides some insight into the results of this analysis. Political pressure from city and downtown interests prevented the development of a metropolitan beltway, the lack of which is unique among major urban areas.

The intensity of development of the three road networks provides an example of the lack of coordination among them (see table 6-4). Each unit of government built roads according to its own agenda. In absolute terms the federal roads were concentrated in the residential suburbs, but if one accounts for the size of the municipalities, the city captured more of the federal roads and the industrial suburbs had greater concentrations of state and local roads. Pittsburgh's unusual pattern of metropolitan development is not solely the outcome of federal policy. Local and state actors prevented construction of a beltway and directed their road development in other parts of the metropolitan area. These efforts have been critical in shaping the region's pattern of development since 1945. This pattern of road building and development may have helped to reduce commute times and traffic congestion on the freeways, but it has done so by pushing more traffic and more congestion onto arterial roads (see table 6-5).[23] Traffic congestion increased more rapidly in Pittsburgh between 1982 and 1990 both on arterials (33 percent) and on freeways (20 percent) than it did in comparably sized regions (25 percent and 12 percent, respectively).

OTHER FEDERAL FUNDING. The federal government provides a wide variety of funding to municipalities, individuals, and corporations. Direct federal spatial funding is in the form of loans, grants, and procurement contracts.[24] An even larger amount of money is provided to individuals in the form of salaries, pensions, disability payments, and

22. This analysis does not fully resolve the causal link between road development and population changes, primarily because of uncertain lag times between road planning and construction. For example, the Mon Fayette Expressway, under construction at this writing in 2004, was conceived approximately thirty years ago.

23. Slower economic growth would also account for some portion of the lower levels of traffic congestion.

24. For this analysis the federal funds that were awarded directly to municipalities are determined to have been spatial funds. If any of those funds were not directly allocated to a municipality in the Consolidated Federal Funds Report, then those amounts were left "undistributed." Essentially, this means that those funds were left to allocation formulas or the discretion of county or local officials for final distribution. Therefore the analysis does not attribute any effect these funds might have had to the federal government. Any allocation formulas devised for the purposes of this analysis would bias the conclusions.

Table 6-4. Road Networks in the Pittsburgh Region

Lane miles per square mile

Network	City of Pittsburgh	Industrial suburbs	Residential suburbs
Federal roads	959	576	861
State roads	2,352	6,101	1,257
Local roads	583	4,097	3,179
All roads	3,894	10,773	5,297

Source: Authors' analysis of road segment data from Southwestern Pennsylvania Commission.

Table 6-5. Traffic Congestion in Pittsburgh and Comparable MSAs, 1982 and 1990

Vehicle kilometer of travel per lane kilometer, unless otherwise noted

Data	Pittsburgh	Comparable regions	All regions
1982			
Freeway	7,123	10,615	10,485
Principal arterial	5,807	5,239	5,108
Peak-period freeway travel congested (percent)	15.0	32.7	32.0
Peak-period principal arterial travel congested (percent)	50.0	41.4	42.9
1990			
Freeway	8,195	13,258	12,707
Principal arterial	5,995	5,760	5,742
Peak-period freeway travel congested (percent)	20.0	40.9	39.6
Peak-period principal arterial travel congested (percent)	60.0	46.4	48.6

Source: State of the Nation's Cities Database, Center for Urban Policy Research, Rutgers University (http://policy.rutgers.edu/cupr/sonc/sonc.htm). Comparable regions are defined by the size of the region.

welfare transfers. Another large and often uncounted form of federal spending is tax credits and other subsidies.

There was no direct federal intervention to alleviate the external forces buffeting Pittsburgh. For the most part, federal policy and funding were not independent factors in the region's development. Federal resources shaped some of the local development agenda, but local interests were able to influence the flow of funds and in the case of highways, prevent the construction of a beltway (see table 6-6).

In per capita terms the city of Pittsburgh has received the bulk of the federal spatial funding. The Industrial suburbs have received by far the least—only 6 percent of the spatial funds that were awarded to Pittsburgh and 16 percent of the spatial funding spent in residential suburbs. The residential suburbs received 38 percent of the federal funds per capita spent in the city. Pittsburgh also received a significantly higher

Table 6-6. Annual Federal Funds per Capita in Allegheny County, 1986–96
Dollars

Funding type	Undistributed	Industrial suburb	Residential suburb	Pittsburgh	Total
Spatial					
Direct loans	9	14	2	7	15
Other direct payments	26	(0)	0	0	26
Grants	720	19	1	925	985
Guaranteed or insured loans	312	20	12	42	334
Procurement contracts	388	71	764	1,056	1,106
Insurance	224	0	0	0	224
Individual					
Salaries and wages	721	0	0	0	721
Payments to individuals	1,580	41	8	296	1,675
Retirement and disability	3,766	0	0	0	3,766
Total spatial	1,678	124	779	2,030	2,689
Total individual	6,067	41	8	296	6,162
Grand total	7,745	165	787	2,326	8,852

Source: Consolidated Federal Funds Report (1987–96).

Note: The rows do not sum to the total because the amounts are divided by the population for that category and the results are rounded off. The undistributed funds and total funds are divided by the population for Allegheny County.

level of federal payments to individuals, reflecting the different demographics of the city and suburbs.

There are significant differences in the types of direct federal funding that municipalities receive. Residential suburbs get the bulk of the procurement contracts, while the industrial suburbs receive the largest portion of the direct loans, followed by direct loans to the city. However, 63 percent of the direct loans are not distributed to municipalities. The city also receives a sizable portion of the federal grants, but 73 percent of those funds are also undistributed. Ultimately, the amount of federal money that is not directly distributed by the federal government—for example, the amount left to the discretion of county or other local officials or allocated via need-based or other formulas—outweighs the direct federal spending. While the federal government may place controls on the local expenditure of these funds, these funds will achieve goals more in line with local priorities than with federal ones.

The mortgage interest deduction is a large annual subsidy for homeowners. On average the deduction per homeowner in Allegheny County in 1990 was $4,500 per year and reduced each federal tax bill by several hundred dollars. Compare this deduction with direct federal spending of

Table 6-7. Total Annual Mortgage Interest Deduction, 1990s
Dollars

	City of Pittsburgh	Industrial suburbs	Residential suburbs
Total mortgage interest deduction	271,931,608	126,138,416	1,272,064,330

$124 to $2,030 per capita annually. Furthermore, the mortgage interest deduction is automatic: it does not require annual applications or costly reporting on the part of the municipality or the taxpayer. The mortgage interest deduction is one of the largest forms of indirect federal spending that counters the flows of direct federal spending (see table 6-7).

The direct spatial spending from the federal government, however, is vastly outweighed by indirect spending, such as the mortgage interest deduction (see appendix at the end of this chapter). While these funds are not directed to specific locales by local, state, or federal agents, they do have a significant spatial impact. The residential suburbs benefited the most from the mortgage interest deduction, although the city on the whole fared better than the industrial suburbs. The average homeowner in the city received only 57 percent of the subsidy of the average home-owner in the residential suburbs, while the homeowners in the industrial suburbs received less than 34 percent of that subsidy. The age of housing and homeowners affects the value and number of homes under mortgage. The city and industrial suburbs contained older housing and older residents, thus limiting their benefit from the mortgage interest deduction. Furthermore, the benefit from the mortgage deduction is contingent on the level of homeownership: municipalities with a large proportion of renters receive less benefit than municipalities with a large proportion of owners.[25] In fact, the residential suburbs receive a benefit of about $1.2 billion, which is more than 4.5 times that received by the city of Pittsburgh (just under $272 million) and ten times that for the industrial suburbs (just over $126 million).

Shifting Employment Location

Many suburban communities were affected as much as or more than the central city by the collapse of traditional manufacturing. Between 1982 and 1987 the inner-ring industrial suburbs lost 56 percent of employment, the city of Pittsburgh 55 percent, and the middle-ring

25. The analysis did not attempt to calculate any rent subsidies or subsidies for the construction of rental units. It is most likely, however, that the city and the industrial suburbs would have received the bulk of this benefit, but it may not have countered the benefit of the mortgage interest deduction.

Table 6-8. Jobs in Major Industries in Allegheny County, 1982–97

Year	Pittsburgh	Inner suburbs (within 10 miles)	Middle suburbs (10–15 miles out)	Outer suburbs (more than 15 miles out)
Residential communities				
1982	...	52,843	54,556	8,694
1987	...	38,821	39,038	8,997
1992	...	54,072	57,755	9,314
1997	...	51,402	53,353	18,220
Industrial communities				
1982	320,252	37,444	85,734	2,435
1987	142,787	16,467	22,811	4,100
1992	137,651	17,778	22,781	4,917
1997	134,974	17,821	43,042	3,315

Source: U.S. Census Bureau, *Economic Census, 1982–97* (manufacturing, retail, services, and wholesale only).

industrial suburbs nearly 75 percent. The outer-ring suburbs, both residential and industrial, were able to maintain their job bases during this period of transition (see table 6-8). The city of Pittsburgh continues to be the dominant location for jobs in the county, despite enormous job losses after 1982. The transition to service industries in the late 1980s, combined with the emergence of technology-based industries in the late 1990s created a more decentralized geography of employment with a weak core (see color plates, map 6-3). Since 1992 job growth has occurred primarily in suburbs at least ten miles from the city.

THE INFLUENCE OF HIGHWAYS. Did federal roads reshuffle jobs from the city to the suburbs and from industrial towns to undeveloped and residential areas? The roads were built primarily in or near the job centers, but we do not know how they changed traffic flows. The evidence is mixed, and there is much variability across sectors and over time. The dominant trend is a shift toward the residential suburbs in general, particularly those without federal roads (see table 6-9).

The construction of federal roads in the Pittsburgh region has interacted with the dynamics of industrial restructuring and alternating industry trends. The pattern is muddled by a tendency for jobs and people to concentrate in municipalities with access to roads, but not necessarily when the roads pass through the community. When we see all industries together, there has been a shift away from industrial towns, whether or not they have federal roads. The absolute number and percentage of total jobs in the industrial suburbs and the city declined. The city of Pittsburgh, however, remained the top employment location in

Table 6-9. Share of Jobs, by Type of Community in Allegheny County, 1982 and 1997
Percent

Year	Pittsburgh	Federal roads		No federal roads	
		Industrial suburbs	Residential suburbs	Industrial suburbs	Residential suburbs
1982	57	2	8	20	13
1997	40	1	14	19	26

Source: U.S. Census Bureau, *Economic Census, 1982–97* (employment in manufacturing, retail, services and wholesale only).

1997, whereas all six of the top industrial suburbs were replaced by residential suburbs (see table 6-10). Meanwhile, jobs grew more concentrated in the residential suburbs, primarily those without federal roads. Residential suburbs with federal roads also increased their employment, but these communities still accounted for fewer than 47,000 jobs compared with nearly 86,000 in the residential suburbs without the federal roads. Residential suburbs without federal roads added more than 12,000 net jobs between 1982 and 1997, while those with federal roads added slightly more than 4,000.

SPATIAL IMPACT OF STATE AND LOCAL SPENDING. Whereas federal government spending had significant spatial impacts even though it did not directly distribute the bulk of its funds, state and local funds were consciously spent to direct development in specific locations. Between the end of World War II and the mid-1970s the ACCD coalition in Pittsburgh implemented a remarkable strategy to maintain the region's status as a major manufacturing center through an era of pervasive social and economic change. By cleaning the environment, redeveloping the downtown, modernizing the industrial base, improving air service, selectively implementing downtown-oriented road improvements, avoiding the construction of a beltway, and fighting a rear-guard action to counterbalance the growing appeal of suburban living among the city's middle class, the Pittsburgh Renaissance achieved relative regional stability in an era of widespread upward mobility and profound change in social and business affairs.

Absolute and per capita investment by the state clearly favored the residential suburbs, although in the 1980s and 1990s the city captured more Pennsylvania Industrial Development Authority (PIDA) money than in previous decades (see table 6-11). PIDA funding focused most intensely on the residential suburbs in the period from 1960 to 1980, and then shifted to the city and industrial suburbs in the 1980s and

Table 6-10. Top Employers by Municipality, 1982 and 1997

1982	Area type	1997	Area type
Pittsburgh	City	Pittsburgh	City
McKeesport city	Industrial	Monroeville	Residential
Monroeville	Residential	West Mifflin	Residential
Clairton city	Industrial	Green Tree	Residential
West Mifflin	Residential	Moon	Residential
Ross	Residential	Ross	Residential
Duquesne	Industrial	Penn Hills	Residential
North Braddock	Industrial	Upper St. Clair	Residential
McKees Rocks	Industrial	Bethel Park	Residential
Swissvale	Industrial	Plum	Residential

Source: U.S. Census Bureau, *Economic Census, 1982, 1997* (employment in manufacturing, retail, services, and wholesale only).

Table 6-11. Distribution of PIDA Funds, 1960s–90s
Dollars

Decade	City	Residential suburbs	Industrial suburbs	Suburbs total
Total PIDA funds				
1960s	2,224,060	8,971,457	1,203,040	10,174,497
1970s	1,394,160	18,644,047	4,243,300	22,887,347
1980s	13,831,609	31,912,983	6,458,068	38,371,051
1990s	8,492,367	8,598,247	6,734,527	15,332,774
PIDA funds per capita				
1960s	3.70	13.60	3.3	9.90
1970s	2.70	24.40	13.3	21.10
1980s	32.60	42.40	23.6	37.40
1990s	23.70	8.10	28.0	11.70

Source: Authors' calculations based on PIDA reports.

1990s. PIDA funding has gone where local development activity has not. PIDA funds were invested most heavily in the residential suburbs during periods when very few jobs were located in those communities. It appears that these investments, combined with state road development, have helped to shift jobs toward the residential communities.

State and local development activities have flowed in opposite directions. In the 1960s and 1970s, per capita PIDA investment in the residential suburbs was six times the investment in the city of Pittsburgh. During that time, however, all of the suburbs accounted for only 30 percent of the office space. In the 1980s and 1990s, these intense levels of investment pushed more than half of the office space developed in those

Table 6-12. Distribution of Office Development in Allegheny County, 1940–96

Years	Suburbs (percent)	Pittsburgh (percent)	Total space (million sq. ft.)
New office space, 1940–79	30	70	25.3
New office space, 1980–96	53	47	20.1
Total office space, 1940–96	40	60	45.4

Source: Compiled by the authors.

decades to the suburbs (see table 6-12). With the region's decentralized structure, many communities outside the city itself suffered from the loss of major employers, especially the industrial towns. The downtown preservation agenda pushed for Pittsburgh held little benefit for these places and thus never provided a *regional* agenda. Each community therefore pursued its own revitalization efforts, often at the expense of others. Without clear federal or state policy, these conflicting strategies were able to find elements to support their cause and to disperse more jobs and housing into less developed areas.

Summary

The picture of local development factors that emerges from this analysis is one of conflicting alignments of forces (see table 6-13). City interests were supported by several elements of federal policy, while suburban interests were supported by state policy and other elements of federal policy. Both alignments have achieved victories, but the advantage has gone to the residential suburbs. The federal policies that supported the suburbs tended to be those that supported market mechanisms. In conjunction with state policies favoring suburban development, a significant amount of population and large numbers of jobs shifted to the suburbs. There was no monolithic suburban bias, as many of the established industrial suburbs suffered more and received lower levels of investment. The city, with support from direct federal spatial funding and in later years from state funding, has managed to maintain the city as the primary office market and employment center.

The tools that the federal government used to affect spatial development are mostly indirect or difficult to trace historically. Direct federal spatial investment favored the city, but far greater investment and subsidies were provided through allocation formulas or passed through local or county officials for disbursement. Most of these expenditures discriminated against older communities. In combination with road development that increased the mobility of the population, the federal

Table 6-13. Summary of Development Factors in Allegheny County

Expenditure type	Impact
Federal	
Direct federal spending	City, with residential suburbs second
Indirect federal spending	Left to local discretion
Mortgage deduction	Favored residential suburbs and white-collar workers
Federal roads	Mixed impacts for suburbs, negative impact on the city
State	
PIDA investments	Primarily favored residential suburbs
State roads	Concentrated in industrial suburbs, which they drained
Local	
Office development	City has dominated but residential suburbs are catching up
New housing	Favored the residential suburbs

intervention in housing, through the mortgage interest deduction, created more choices for some people that ultimately drained people and jobs from the city. It is wrong, however, to assume that federal policy affected all suburbs equally. Many of the industrial suburbs also suffered from the increased mobility and flexibility of business and residents. Residents in these communities might find it hard to perceive a federal suburban bias in favor of their communities.

The city has managed to capture a significant proportion of direct federal spatial funding to assist its development efforts. City interests were able to maintain a downtown that, despite some erosion, continues to dominate the regional office market. The dominance of downtown, combined with the region's lack of a well-developed road network, had the effect of limiting much of the population to within a ten- to fifteen-mile radius of downtown during a time when other regions expanded rapidly. Local efforts to maintain downtown and to limit residential development to the inner and middle suburbs may have delayed or limited suburbanization, but it did not stop it. The region's continued economic malaise, which depressed economic and population growth, most likely also limited sprawl. The combination of negative growth, concentrated office development in downtown, and a constrained road network is a recipe that few others would or could imitate.

Furthermore, the city has been less successful in retaining parts of its job base; although it maintains the bulk of the jobs in manufacturing and wholesale, it has slipped significantly in retail and services. The city continues to encourage office development and retail activity in downtown and several of the closest neighborhoods. One key problem that the city has not addressed in maintaining the viability of the downtown is how to get people there given the changing geography of residence. There is no plan for transit solutions or for increasing the availability and affordability of parking. In fact, cuts in transit service, coupled with increased parking taxes, have only compounded the threat to the city's future as a regional employment hub.

Elements of state policy have been at odds with efforts to defend the core, including the downtown, and have worked in favor of diversifying jobs and population into the suburbs. State investment has focused on both the industrial and the residential suburbs. State road development concentrated in the industrial suburbs and state development funds have predominantly favored the residential suburbs. These state funds are usually awarded to local development agencies, especially county development agencies. In Allegheny County, state aid largely supported suburban rather than city interests. Only in later years was the city more successful in capturing a larger portion of the state's development funding.

Policy Recommendations

As Pittsburgh moves forward, it must address two interrelated challenges. The first is the need for a regional development strategy that balances efforts to preserve and revitalize older communities, as well as accommodates new growth. Second, the region must implement growth management policies that reflect the regional strategy. A key component of managing growth is targeting development incentives. The region has more areas of need than it has capacity to invest. Only through a regional strategy and effective growth management can the region make the political and economic choices required by limited resources. Finally, the strategy and growth management processes must explicitly link efforts across functional boundaries, especially those between economic development and workforce development. Linking workforce and economic development will enable the development of a strategy that serves the region, rather than requiring the region to serve the strategy.

The region remains deeply split regarding its social and economic condition and future. Some argue that candid assertions of weaknesses are self-defeating and that confidence-building measures could help restore growth. Others argue that the goal of reigniting growth is itself flawed. Perhaps Pittsburgh would be better off accepting its position as a much smaller place, thereby avoiding many of the problems that growth has caused in more dynamic regions. Still others view Pittsburgh's problems as the natural result of integrating the U.S. economy into the world. Interference, they argue, would simply harm the process of globalization. Too much local interference in the past, it has been argued, sheltered the region for too long and led to its abrupt restructuring in the first place.

A Regional Strategy

Successive waves of economic restructuring crippled many communities throughout the region and destroyed the economic logic that linked those communities. The supply chains of the industrial production network no longer defined them. This economic logic was also the backbone of the political networks that served the region. As the ACCD coalition has attempted to expand its civic vision to encompass the region, it has had no underlying economic logic to fall back on. Furthermore, the decentralized pattern of development that has prevailed throughout the region's history, and the governmental structure that supported it, does not easily accommodate a truly regional vision. In place of regional visioning and planning, the *regional development strategy* is merely the accretion of individual plans and strategies.

The coalition has reached out to a broader set of actors, such as "new economy" firms and outlying communities. Unfortunately this has taken the form of slicing a piece of the pie for everyone because there is no common agenda that unifies disparate interests. The state of fragmentation in the region is such that there is great distrust of activities originating in Pittsburgh or Allegheny County. For example, efforts to support new economy firms are viewed as a Pittsburgh-centric strategy that must be balanced by support for the projects of outlying communities and counties.

Regional strategies need to build on the core, but great care must be taken to avoid strategies that focus inward. A revitalization based solely on the downtown or city interests offers only a promise of trickle-down for other communities, and in the past this has not been sufficient to rally their support. Regional interests must rebuild some common ground to rediscover an economic logic for organizing development. For decades, the region has experimented with numerous strategies, and each community has pursued disparate and often conflicting interests. Political logrolling has led to scattershot development projects that compete with rather than complement each other. Few of these investments have had sufficient scale to achieve sustainability. Whose turn it is at the funding trough has mattered more than whether the investment provided a true regional opportunity.

Without a unifying regional strategy, the pinwheel development pattern will continue to dissolve as growth spills over the fringes. The urban core already faces the prospect of bankruptcy. In December 2003 the city of Pittsburgh was declared a fiscally distressed municipality under the state's Act 47 law, and a recovery coordinator was selected to oversee and advise city finances. In typical duplicative fashion, in 2004 the legislature appointed a separate Fiscal Oversight Board with different powers to operate concurrently and independently of the Act 47 coordinator. While these groups tangle over the solutions to Pittsburgh's fiscal woes, other communities in the metropolitan area face similar crises.

Growth Management

A new wave of airport corridor office construction began in 1995, posing yet another threat to the established supremacy of downtown. Coping with this trend will be more difficult, however, since it is a product of Allegheny County's continued strategy of emphasizing airport corridor job growth. The old ACCD coalition itself needs to resolve the contradictions between the goal of airport corridor growth and the goal of reinforcing downtown. This is complicated by the fact that the city has not chosen to stress downtown office tower construction in recent years, with the exception of two projects to provide back-office space for locally headquartered banks. Most of the city's efforts have gone into building new stadiums for the Steelers and the Pirates, as well as reinforcing the East End by establishing an entirely new upscale residential neighborhood. New office towers in the downtown have not been a priority.

Real estate developers and some new economy companies are feeding sprawl at the outer edges of the region's old middle-class residential corridors (Cranberry to the north, Peters to the south, Murrysville to the east, and the airport corridor). Because these groups are only loosely integrated into the region's long-standing ACCD-related organizations, they operate outside of the older tradition of reinforcing downtown and the close-in residential areas. More explicit growth management policies will need to be developed if the older system of less formal growth management is not revived.

The economic collapse of the industrial river valleys has made large amounts of flat land along the rivers and close to the center of Pittsburgh available for redevelopment. New jobs in these former mill sites would help to revitalize the housing stock and commercial areas that still exist in mill towns and in nearby hilltop working-class townships. These blue-collar areas face considerable fiscal stress as the changing nature of work in the region has converted many former one-income blue-collar households into two-income service sector households. In addition, the many small, winding roads that were built over the years to help mill workers get to their jobs throughout the region's river valleys would facilitate short commutes to work without the need for new highway infrastructure. Some redevelopment has begun on sites that give the region a considerable capacity to accommodate large-scale service sector job growth within its old development pattern without the need to sprawl.

Unlike the scattershot approach, this will require more focused and strategic investment. Market forces are one of the principal strategic considerations that have been overlooked in the region's development efforts. Retail and office development has competed for a shrinking pool of consumers and workers. The city of Pittsburgh has tried to strike back at the suburbs with the development of new upscale residential enclaves within the city limits, and with now defunct plans to restore downtown retail. Development that grows the market, rather than shifting it, should receive priority.

At this writing in 2004, the Pittsburgh region has more municipalities that require revitalization than there are funds available. In order to make the tough choices about who does and who does not get funding, there must be a true regional strategy that leverages new and existing investments and includes the rest of the region. This can be achieved by targeting development in regional hubs, with phased investment strategies radiating from each nucleus. Combined with tax increment financing (TIF) and tax base sharing (TBS), this nuclear pattern of development can provide the revenues for later stages of development while making the best use of limited resources. The Allegheny County Department of Development is working on just such a strategy for the Mon Valley (see color plates, map 6-4). This is a strategy that can build the necessary scale to achieve sustainability. If investment is spread too thin, then it is more likely to be washed away by external forces.

In transportation planning in particular, federal legislation has broadened the input of interests from outside Allegheny County, thereby stimulating more interest in decentralized transportation infrastructure. The voting structure of the Metropolitan Planning Organization (MPO), which also serves the Economic Development District, ensures that each county receives equal votes regardless of population.[26] Outlying counties

26. The Southwestern Pennsylvania Regional Planning Commission (SPRPC) is the original regional MPO, which formed the Southwestern Pennsylvania Regional Develop-

are eager to appropriate "their share" of federal funding, but in a no-growth environment that occurs at a cost to the region's core. The ACCD coalition that once embraced downtown revitalization is aggressively pursuing a strategy to increase industrial parks: "The development of new industrial sites and buildings was recommended for every county in the region, with priority consideration given to "Brownfield" (former industrial) sites and to sites and facilities that could be used by expanding technology firms."[27] Southwestern Pennsylvania is competing to host a major demonstration project for a high-speed maglev system. This nodal system could fit well into the region's centralized structure and help reinforce it against decentralizing forces. Regional highway projects, however, are currently the major priority for investment.

The federal government can have greater influence on coordinating regional development planning through the MPOs. The power and authority of MPOs has waxed and waned with different administrations and federal programs, but their role should be strengthened and expanded. Currently, MPO activities are focused on transportation planning, with the assumption that these plans can be coordinated with other planning and development activity. Unfortunately, it can be very difficult to coordinate natural resource planning with housing, workforce, and economic development with the MPOs. Each of these domains either has no coordinating body or is an independent body with geographic boundaries that do not align. Housing is organized primarily at the municipal level, but not above the county level. The city of Pittsburgh and Allegheny County have separate housing authorities that operate semi-autonomously from their respective governments. Workforce activity is coordinated through Workforce Investment Boards whose territory often does not align with other regional actors and whose functional responsibility may divide K–12 from adult education, making it more difficult to provide a continuum of service. The Economic Development Administration requires the development of Comprehensive Economic Development Plans, and the inclusion of housing and workforce interests in the strategic planning committee, but there are no methods for "fixing" unsatisfactory plans and no effective mechanisms for compliance. The current structure of multiple interacting domains does little more than provide opportunities to shift the blame.

---

ment Commission (SPRDC) to perform the development function. They are now merged in the Southwestern Pennsylvania Commission (SPC).

27. See www.accdpel.org/05_02_case_04.html.

Rationalizing these boundaries would be a good first step toward coordinating development policy across domains.

Conclusion

Since 1996 the region has continued to lag state and national averages for job and population growth. Data from the 2000 Census reveal that the Pittsburgh region remains one of only a handful of urban areas that is losing population, and its rate of job growth hovers at about one-third of the national average. While most U.S. regions cope with the problems of rapid immigration, job growth, uncoordinated suburban sprawl caused by ineffective growth management policies, and unexpected opportunities to redevelop ghettoized urban cores, Pittsburgh struggles to cope with population loss, sluggish job growth, and a fragile tax base. The uncoordinated series of development efforts that followed in the wake of economic restructuring have not yet coalesced into a new regime that is capable of reestablishing the ties between the sources of regional economic growth and the spatial distribution of new development. The disconnection between the social and economic needs of growing sectors in the regional economy and the legacy of Pittsburgh's past social and economic development pattern has not yet been resolved. In the meantime the region continues to drift. In the face of these many challenges, desperation to do something should not outweigh the need to do the right thing.

As the region moves into the future, it must avoid the introverted attitudes that separate us from the rest of the world. An undeniable achievement during Pittsburgh's golden Renaissance years was the building of regional "walls" to stave off powerful external forces. These walls kept assets inside the core and provided some benefits, but many of the assets from those years are gone. Today any walls simply prevent new assets from coming into the region. Consequently, any regional strategies that are pursued by the city and Allegheny County must emphasize the importance of integrating the region with broader flows of national and global investment. The solution to Pittsburgh's prolonged stagnation lies in building a local and regional coalition that supports growth by welcoming new investors, and perhaps most important, new immigrants. Indeed, the twin legacies of Pittsburgh's unique development pattern and its recent decades of stagnation create an unusual opportunity for the region to accommodate substantial new investment and population growth without automatically triggering explosive sprawl. The challenge remains for its civic and governmental structure to restore discipline and rationality to its development pattern by reforming it to accommodate the spatial needs of externally focused, market-oriented, globally competitive growth in the twenty-first century.

Appendix: Methodology for Calculating the Mortgage Interest Deduction

For each decade, the number of owner-occupied housing units was multiplied by the percentage of the population over sixty-five years old. This was done to estimate the number of homes that would no longer be under mortgage. Then the value of the housing was reduced by 80 percent to reflect the estimated value of the mortgage. The estimated value was multiplied by the estimated number of mortgages to derive a total value for all mortgages in the municipality. This amount was then divided by the number of owner-occupied housing units to determine an average amount per homeowner per year.

The deficiency of this methodology is that it does not account for the differences in taxable income rates that ultimately determine the value of the mortgage interest deduction. Furthermore, the estimate does not truly capture the number of homes under mortgage: some of those assumed to be paid off may have been refinanced. It also does not accurately set a value for how much the deduction is worth in a particular year. The value of the deduction for each homeowner will decline as the principal is paid off and the amount of interest paid decreases. The goal of this analysis was not to develop the best methodology for estimating the federal mortgage interest deduction, but instead to estimate which places may benefit more or less from this subsidy. The method developed here does provide a benchmark for comparing the value of this subsidy between municipalities and thus was useful for this analysis.

Comparison with Other Methods

This method focuses on owner-occupiers and does not consider differences between benefits to owner-occupiers and those to landlords. Furthermore it does not compare the value of the subsidy with other investment returns or tax-subsidy vehicles. For this analysis we have estimated only the value of the mortgage interest deduction, not the value of any property tax deductions. This estimate also does not consider income levels of the owners, which can influence the estimate: lower-income property owners may not get the benefit because they are less likely to itemize deductions. This estimation therefore overestimates the benefits to communities with lower-income property owners and may produce a conservative estimate for those communities. For a more complete methodology of estimating housing subsidies that addresses these issues, see Sinai and Gyourko (2004).

References

Allegheny Conference on Community Development (ACCD). 1984. "Economic Development Plan." Pittsburgh.

Clark, Gordon L. 1989. "Pittsburgh in Transition: Consolidation of Prosperity in an Era of Economic Restructuring." In *Economic Restructuring and Political Response*, edited by Robert A. Beauregard. New York: Sage.

Consolidated Federal Funds Report. 1987–1996. U.S. Census Bureau database.

Hoerr, John P. 1988. *And the Wolf Finally Came: The Decline of the American Steel Industry*. University of Pittsburgh Press.

Hogan, William J. 1971. *Economic History of the Iron and Steel Industry in the United States*. Lexington, Mass.: D. C. Heath.

Hoover, Edgar M., ed. 1963. "Report of the Economic Study on the Pittsburgh Region." Pittsburgh Regional Planning Association. University of Pittsburgh Press.

Ingram, John N. 1991. *Making Iron and Steel: Independent Mills in Pittsburgh*. Ohio State University Press.

Katz, Bruce, and others. 2003. "Back to Prosperity: A Competitive Agenda for Renewing Pennsylvania." Metropolitan Policy Center, Brookings.

Lamoreaux, Naomi. 1985. *The Great Merger Movement in American Business, 1895–1904*. Cambridge University Press.

Lubove, Roy. 1996. *Twentieth Century Pittsburgh*. University of Pittsburgh Press.

Mancke, Richard B. 1972. "Iron and Steel: A Case Study of the Economic Causes and Effects of Vertical Integration." *Journal of Industrial Economics* 20 (July): 220–29.

Mehrabian, Robert, Richard Florida, and Robert E. Gleeson. 1995. "Toward a Shared Vision for Southwestern Pennsylvania: A Report of the White Paper Committee of the Allegheny Conference on Community Development." Carnegie Mellon University.

Sinai, Todd, and Joseph Gyourko. 2004. "The (Un)Changing Geographical Distribution of Housing Tax Benefits: 1980–2000." Working Paper 10322. Cambridge, Mass.: National Bureau of Economic Research (February).

Temin, Peter. 1964. *Iron and Steel in Nineteenth-Century America: An Economic Inquiry*. MIT Press.

Weber, Michael P. 1988. *Don't Call Me Boss: David L. Lawrence, Pittsburgh's Renaissance Mayor*. University of Pittsburgh Press.

Contributors

ARIZONA STATE UNIVERSITY RESEARCH TEAM

Mary Jo Waits, associate director, Morrison Institute for Public Policy

Tina Valdecanas, senior research analyst, Morrison Institute for Public Policy

Mark Muro, senior research analyst, Morrison Institute for Public Policy

Len Bower, economist

Elizabeth Burns, professor, Department of Geography

William Fulton, president, Solimar Research Group

Rebecca Gau, senior research analyst, Morrison Institute for Public Policy

Patricia Gober, professor, Department of Geography

John Hall, professor, School of Public Affairs

Alicia Harrison, research associate, Solimar Research Group

Kent Hill, assistant research professional, Department of Economics

Glen Krutz, assistant professor, Department of Political Science

Tom Rex, research manager, Center for Business Research

Scott Smith, support systems analyst, Department of Information Technology

Christina Kinnear, graduate assistant, Morrison Institute for Public Policy

Laura Valenzuela, graduate assistant, Morrison Institute for Public Policy

Jamie Goodwin-White, graduate assistant, Morrison Institute for Public Policy

PETER DREIER, Dr. E. P. Clapp Distinguished Professor of Politics, Occidental College

ROBERT E. GLEESON, director, Regional Development Institute, Northern Illinois University

JOSEPH GYOURKO, Martin Bucksbaum Professor of Real Estate and Finance, and director, Zell-Lurie Real Estate Center at Wharton, University of Pennsylvania

JANET ROTHENBERG PACK, professor of Business and Public Policy, and of Real Estate, Wharton School, University of Pennsylvania; nonresident senior fellow, Brookings Institution

PASCALE JOASSART-MARCELLI, assistant professor of economics, University of Massachusetts–Boston

MANUEL PASTOR JR., professor of Latin American and Latino Studies, and director, Center for Justice, Tolerance and Community, University of California–Santa Cruz

JERRY R. PAYTAS, director, Center for Economic Development, H. John Heinz III School of Public Policy and Management, Carnegie Mellon University

JOSEPH PERSKY, professor of economics, University of Illinois–Chicago

KIMBERLY SCHAFFER, College of Urban Planning and Public Affairs, University of Illinois–Chicago

ANITA A. SUMMERS, professor emeritus, Department of Business and Public Policy and Department of Real Estate, and director of research, Zell-Lurie Real Estate Center at Wharton, University of Pennsylvania

WIM WIEWEL, provost and senior vice president for academic affairs and professor of public affairs, University of Baltimore

JENNIFER WOLCH, professor of geography and urban planning and director, Center for Sustainable Cities, University of Southern California

Index